Law, Liberty and Livelihood

The Editors :

Parth J Shah is founder president of Centre for Civil Society, New Delhi, a think tank for public policy solutions within the framework of rule of law, limited government, and competitive markets.

Parth's research and advocacy work centres on the themes of economic freedom (law, liberty, and livelihood campaign), choice and competition in education(fund students, not schools), property right approach for the environment (terracotta vision of stewardship), good governance (new public management), and rule of law (tort reforms for consumer health and safety).

The Livelihood Freedom Test, education vouchers, food stamps, community ownership of natural resources, ward-based urban management, Duty to Publish Act are some of the radical ideas he has introduced into public policy debate. He has conceptualised and organised pioneering liberal educational programmes for the Indian youth : Liberty and Society Seminar, Liberty, Art and Culture Seminar, Researching Reality Internship and Fellowship.

He has edited *The Morality of Markets, Profiles in Courage: Dissent on Indian Socialism, Friedman on India, Do Corporations have Social Responsibility?* and co-edited *Terracotta Reader, BR Shenoy: Economic Prophecies, BR Shenoy: Theoretical Vision, and Agenda for Change*. He has addressed a number of local, national and international workshops and conferences, and writes for newspapers and magazines. He is the youngest Indian member of the Mont Pelerin Society, the premier international association of classical liberals. He is in the vanguard of India's Second Freedom Movement.

Naveen Mandava is a Research Associate with the Centre for Civil Society and is also the Coordinator of the Research Internship Programme Researching Reality. He shifted from electronics to applied microeconomic research when he saw the ability of public policy solutions to influence the lives of the poor. His varied experience includes the research coordination of *State of Governance: Delhi Citizen Handbook 2003,* conducting Researching Reality workshop for students of economics, journalism and documentary making, and designing education voucher programmes.

Law, Liberty and Livelihood

Making A Living On The Street

Editors

PARTH J SHAH
NAVEEN MANDAVA

PUBLISHED BY ACADEMIC FOUNDATION IN ASSOCIATION WITH
CENTRE FOR CIVIL SOCIETY, NEW DELHI

Centre for Civil Society
New Delhi

Academic Foundation
New Delhi

First published in 2005 by

Academic Foundation
4772-73 / 23 Bharat Ram Road, (23 Ansari Road), Darya Ganj, New Delhi - 110 002 (India).
Phones : 23245001 / 02 / 03 / 04. Fax : +91-11-23245005. E-mail : academic@vsnl.com
www : academicfoundation.com

Published in association with :

Centre for Civil Society, New Delhi
www.ccsindia.org

Law, Liberty and Livelihood : Making a Living on the Street
edited by Parth J Shah and Naveen Mandava.

ISBN 81-7188-448-2

Designed and typeset by Italics India, New Delhi.
Printed and bound in India.

Contents

...Contd. ...

...CONTD. ...

List of Photographs

Contributors

Chapter 1: **Introduction: Making a Living on the Street**

Parth J. Shah and Naveen Mandava

Chapter 2: **Street Hawking: Spend to Vend**

Naveen Mandava with support from Gaurav Tiwari, Devhuti Bakshi, Neha Sharma, Rathi Ravi, Anupriya Singhal, Bhaskar Roy and Shalini Singh from Delhi; Kakali Bhattacharya from Kolkata with support from Sandeep Chatterjee; Tushar Chaudhari from Mumbai with support from Meenal B Bhosale; Nimisha Srivastava from Vadodara; Ranjit Koshi, Karthikeyan TC, Sherin J Angela, Theepa, Rahul Cherian, Shobha Rajan, Nitya M S, Priyadarshini G, Perciveal Brooks, Jyotis Sreekumar and Sakthivel from Chennai; Rupangunta Indu, Pheroze Lawrence Vincent and Rudra Pratap Shah from Vijaywada; Dhanuraj D, Sween Varghese and Jaison P Varghese from Cochin. The Chennai, Vijaywada and Cochin teams were coordinated by Sujatha Muthayya. Mukesh Anand has been very helpful with regard to lending legal insight into the key issues.

Chapter 3: **Setting up Shop: Shopping for Legality**

Neha Sharma with support from Shalini Singh, Ravi Garg, Devhuti Bakshi, Prashansa Poddar, Shivani Daga, Rathi Ravi, Neha Swetambari, Eva Maria Weidrich, Anupriya Singhal, Bhaskar Roy, Kumar Gaurav and Gaurav Tiwari

Chapter 4: **Urban Land Management Plans: Master Plan for Disaster**

Naveen Mandava and Neha Sharma with support from Shalini Singh and Saurabh Goel

Chapter 5: **The Meat Market: Meeting Market Demand**

Jacob Xavier with support from Ashish Kumar Jha and Neha Sharma

Chapter 6: **Auto Rickshaw Permits: Limited Permits, Unpermitted Licences**

Jacob Xavier with support from Neha Sharma and Prashansa Poddar

Chapter 7: **Cycle Rickshaw Licensing: Cycles of Poverty**

Prashansa Poddar with support from Bhaskar Roy, Neha Sharma and Sapna Bajaj

Chapter 8: **Licensing of the Railway Porters: Burden of the Badge**

Mayank Singhal

Chapter 9: **Opening a School in Delhi: A Learning Experience**

Bhaskar Roy with support from Saurabh Goel

Chapter 10: **Household Based Industry: Is Big Brother Watching?**

Saurabh Goel with support from Bhaskar Roy, Gaurav Tiwari, Prashansa Poddar and Jacob Xavier

Preface

May I preface this preface with a confession. Despite more than 25 years as a journalist in India I remained unmindful of the plight of street vendors until Madhu Kishwar of *Manushi* started her passionate crusade for their rights. She invited me to one of her public hearings in Delhi where she showed us a series of documentaries she had made on the manner in which these most marginal of India's entrepreneurs lived under constant dread of being crushed under the jackboot of what, at their level, is truly a police state. Hundreds of hawkers had come to talk to us about their problems and grievances, and by the time they finished I was convinced that if you wanted to understand fully the most evil aspects of the Indian state then you needed to see it through the eyes of a street vendor. What can be worse than being treated as a criminal simply for trying to earn a living?

As someone who believes that liberalisation and the abolition of the licence-quota-permit *raj* was the best thing that happened to the Indian economy it also struck me as absurd that the poorest Indians were the only people who are still ground down by licenses and quotas. Was it not in the name of the poor that our 'socialist' economic policies were formulated? Was it not to curb the wealth of the rich that licences and permits first came into being? Madhu's public hearing inspired me to write in my column about the terrible injustice that hawkers faced in our cities and it pleased me that Atal Behari Vajpayee himself took notice of this piece and an article Madhu wrote and ordered the Delhi government to take a more compassionate view of the problem. In a detailed note to the Lieutenant Governor of Delhi the Prime Minister's office drew up a full policy and ordered it implemented. Madhu said it was a very workable policy and actively took up the manner with municipal and state authorities while I watched closely from a distance.

What happened? Nothing. The Prime Minister's order was treated with total disdain by the Lieutenant Governor and the Delhi police, and cycle rickshaws and street vendors continued to be routinely swept off the streets as if they were vermin. When they crept back because it was the only thing they could do if they and their families were not to starve they were allowed to stay only if they paid higher and higher bribes to the police and municipal officials.

By this point I had become personally involved in helping street vendors and street children in Mumbai. As a frequent traveler to that city I came to know many of them during my morning walks on Marine Drive. What attracted me was their indomitable spirit and their extraordinary capacity for hard work. Ali the *idliwallah*'s daily routine was to wake at 3 a.m and help his mother cook vast amounts of food which he then brought to Marine Drive by train so he could run his breakfast stall between 7 and 9.30 a.m. Mahipal who sold coconut water slept in the street even at the height of the monsoon because he could not afford to rent even a hovel in the city. He went home to Bhopal once a year for two weeks and, after years of working night and day, his only possession was a radio on which he listened endlessly to Vividh Bharati. There were *chaiwallahs* from Uttar Pradesh and cigarette and *paanwallahs* from Uttar Pradesh. And, in the evenings it would be another lot of hawkers who would arrive to sell hot, roasted corn, Chinese food and cold drinks. They worked with relative cleanliness and provided a service that was clearly needed. Many had earned a living this way for more than thirty years.

Then, one day they were gone. The municipality decided it was time to 'beautify' Marine Drive and that hawkers were an eyesore. So they were swept away and police vans patrolled to ensure that nobody tried to come back. Inquiries with the police revealed that there was really nothing anyone could do because the Supreme Court had given municipal authorities the right to decide in these matters. When I protested that these were people too poor to survive without their little stalls the police assured me that they would be relocated. Of course this never happened and of course it never will because only those with licences have some chance of being compensated and licences are harder to come by than the gold that supposedly lines the streets of Mumbai.

Licences and quotas are an enduring legacy from our socialist days which officialdom has no wish to abolish because it is through them that controls are exercised and small fortunes made. Of the hundreds of thousands of hawkers in Indian cities only a miniscule number manage to get licences, the rest survive by paying daily bribes to policemen and officials. Those who refuse to pay are locked up and their goods confiscated. Ironically, this kind of unfettered, brute state power comes from socialism. Equally ironic is the fact that while rich entrepreneurs are now free of the shackles of the state - thanks to liberalisation - the poorest still remain prisoners of a system that can only be described as evil. The Indian state has failed so far to create an economy capable of providing enough jobs for the poor not to be forced to depend entirely on their own entrepreneurship, and yet it believes it has the right to prevent the unemployed from exercising the right to livelihood. If this is not evil, it is hard to think what is.

Street vendors suffer not just because their poverty deprives them of a strong enough voice but also because they are seen as symbols of degradation in an India that seeks increasingly to be middle class and shining. What Indian babudom appears not to have noticed is that the richest cities in the world still have street vendors. They are an integral part of the city's landscape as they should be here. Any number of studies prove that a cluster of hawkers every half kilometer or so can be easily accommodated without being a hazard to either pedestrians or traffic. What is required is not licencing but simple registration and proper management of littering and hygiene. The only reason why no Indian city has so far done anything about it is probably because too many people would lose too much easy money if our street shops were taken out of the licence-quota-permit regime. Sadly, it has to be said in conclusion that the lot of street vendors does not look as if it will improve in the near future because if the Prime Minister could do nothing it's hard to think who can. At the same time something must be done if we are serious about poverty alleviation and providing comfort to the 'poorest of the poor'.

— Tavleen Singh

Acknowledgements

Researching reality amidst the ambiguity of information, ignorance or mistrust of government authorities and hours of painstaking fieldwork is never an easy task. That it has been so sincerely carried out by the interns and volunteers is evidence of their enthusiasm and grit from which this book has immensely benefited. Their names have been mentioned at the begining of the book. Of them, Neha Sharma deserves special mention for her research assistance through persistent visits to government offices and consistent documentation for the book. The research from the cities of Chennai, Vijaywada and Cochin was coordinated by Sujatha Muthayya, a no mean feat. Gaurav Tiwari, Jacob 'Jack' Xavier, Mayank Singhal, Kakali Bhattacharya and Tushar Chaudhari deserve special appreciation for their diligence at fieldwork.

We are indebted to the National Alliance of Street Vendors of India (NASVI) and Dr. Sharit K. Bhowmik for their permission to print sections from the *Hawkers in the Urban Informal Sector: A Study of Street Vendors in Seven Cities* for the chapter on Street Hawking. We are also thankful to the many insights provided by our association thorugh the course of the study with Anil Bakshi and Satish Chandra Gupta of *Pawan Putra Rehri Khomcha Sangh*, Delhi and Shaktiman Ghosh of *Hawkers Sangram Committee*, Kolkata. Mukesh Anand, practising advocate in the Delhi High Court and also a visiting lecturer at the Indraprastha University's School of Law and Legal Studies, has been very helpful with regard to lending legal insight into key issues.

The photographs, a definite value addition to the book have been provided by Abhishek Agrawal, Deepender Goyal and Rathi Ravi with help from Jacob Xavier, Ashish Kumar Jha, Bhaskar Roy, Saurabh Goel and Neha Sharma from Delhi, Sana Siddiqui and Tushar Chaudhari from Mumbai and Rahul Cherian from Chennai.

All the groundwork would not have been realised without the back office support from Manali Shah and P.V. Joshy. Seema Kumar helped to sharpen the contents of the book and make it worthy of a layman's reading through her deft editing skills.

Tavleen Singh enthusiastically penned the fiery preface despite other urgent deadlines. We hope that this book addresses her concerns.

Literature resource help for the book had been provided in various measures by Fred Foldvary, Randall G. Holcombe, Natarajan Ramachandran, Nicola Pratt, Dr. Amitabh Kundu, Daniel B. Klein, Adrian T. Moore, Binyam Reja and B.L. Bajaj.

The germinated reform ideas gained strength in light of the reviews of Mohit Satyanand, Dilip Rangachari, Dunu Roy, E.F.N. Ribeiro, Kiran Wadhwa, Amir Ullah Khan, A.G.K. Menon, Banashree Banerjee, K.C. Sivaramakrishnan, Raj Cherubal and Vidisha Maitra. Their comments helped us avoid a number of errors of interpretation or presentation.

The John Templeton Foundation provided financial support and Rituraj and Sanu Kapila of the Academic Foundation took a personal interest in the production of this attractive volume.

None of the above can be held responsible for mistakes, errors of judgement, or at other failings of this work, for which we accept responsibility, and hope that the rest of the material will be enough to stimulate insights and new trains of thought into urban livelihoods and public governance. The opinions expressed in this publication are those of the author(s) and do not necessarily reflect the views of the John Templeton Foundation or the Centre for Civil Society.

— PARTH J. SHAH
NAVEEN MANDAVA

1

Introduction: Making a Living on the Street

Why Liberalisation Has Failed the Poor?

After the 1991 liberalisation, the poor do not seem to have gained as much as the rich. How can you carry out liberalisation only for the rich and expect the poor to benefit? Trickle down can go only so far. The truth is there has been hardly any liberalisation for the working poor. For them it has been all LPQ (Licences, Permits and Quotas) and little LPG (Liberalisation, Privatisation and Globalisation). The poor still suffer under the weight of regulations, restrictions and harassment by government and lack basic economic freedom in the areas of their livelihood.

The *Law, Liberty and Livelihood: Making a Living on the Street* goes beyond mere macro-statistics and statistical controversies regarding the impact of liberalisation on the poor and endeavours to further the understanding of the processes and dynamics involved in various urban livelihoods. It documents through primary research the 'official' as well as the 'actual' regulatory and licensing processes by direct interactions with varied stakeholders. The case studies of railway porters, street vendors, small shop keepers, cycle and auto rickshaw drivers, household-based industries, as well as small school operators provide graphic details of what ails India's entry-level professionals—the bottom rung of the economic ladder through which the poor can hope to climb to economic prosperity while providing some of the most essential services to the people. These micro-studies also suggest a very direct and distinct set of reforms that would enable people to utilise their skills and realise their full potential.

The reasons for the plight of the poor are often depicted as exploitation by the rich or callous neglect by government authorities more interested in promoting pro-rich policies. But our path-breaking study that offers snapshots of the ground realities of urban livelihoods shows that the first purported cause is more of a mythology or folklore. The second cause of government neglect is true only in the sense that government has given more freedom to the richer sections of the society to make themselves wealthier. The government machinery, created in the name of protecting the poor against exploitation by the rich, itself has become the exploiter. It is the regulatory burden of government that is the real cause of the general plight of the working poor.

Contrary to the general perception that the rich, empowered by exploitative pro-liberalisation policies, squeeze the poor, the findings in the book adduce the fact that the poor remain poor because there has been no LPG in the areas that affect their livelihood. Their world is still dominated by the forces of extortion, arbitrariness and uncertainty brought about by restrictions on their economic life—the ubiquitous licence-permit-quota *raj*. It is the abolition of LPQ that has opened up the world for the richer sections of the country. The poor deserve no less.

Economic freedom is more valuable for those at the bottom rung of the economic ladder. Nobody appreciates free enterprise—absence of government regulations and controls—more than the poor unlicensed hawker. The rich can always find a way around government controls, the poor have no way out. Empower the poor with economic freedom.

The World Bank study *Doing Business* documents the problems in opening a simple business in various countries. The challenges of launching a business in India are captured through three measures: the number of procedures required to establish a business, the associated time and cost that each procedure commands. Entrepreneurs can expect to go through 11 steps to launch a business over 89 days on average, at a cost equal to 49.5 per cent of gross national income (GNI) per capita.

The data on our immediate SAARC neighbours reveal instructive facts. The number of procedures is lower in Sri Lanka, Nepal and Bangladesh and it takes less than one third of the duration in India to start a business in Pakistan. Compare these parameters with the more prosperous Hong Kong, Singapore and Australia to get an idea of the contribution of economic freedom towards economic prosperity or economic unfreedom towards economic poverty.

Starting a Business in India

Nature of Procedure (2004)	*Proc #*	*Duration (days)*	*US$ Cost*
Obtain pre-approval of name, have documents vetted	1	7	10.41
Stamp the Memorandum and Articles of Association	2	2	25.4
File for registration	3	9	193.6
Make a seal	4	7	10.41
Obtain PAN	5	60	1.35
Obtain TAN	6	45*	0
File for sales tax	7	15*	2.6
Register for Profession Tax	8	2*	0
Register with Mumbai Shops and Establishment Act	9	2*	20.82
File for EPF	10	2*	0
File for ESIC	11	1*	0
Totals	**11**	**89**	**264.59**

*: This procedure runs simultaneously with previous procedures.

Source: http://rru.worldbank.org/DoingBusiness/ExploreEconomies/BusinessClimateSnapshot.aspx?economyid=89

Country Comparisons of Starting a Business

	India	*Sri Lanka*	*Pakistan*	*Nepal*	*Bangladesh*	*Hong Kong*	*Singapore*	*Australia*
Number of Procedures	11	8	11	7	8	5	7	2
Duration (days)	89	50	24	21	35	11	8	2
Cost (% GNI per capita)	49.5	10.7	36.0	74.1	91.0	3.4	1.2	2.1

Source: http://rru.worldbank.org/DoingBusiness/ExploreEconomies/EconomyCharacteristics.aspx

Surely many other problems afflict the self-employed: access to credit, security of property, status in the society, social norms and customs. These too need to be addressed in order to open up economic opportunities. However government regulations are an institutional hindrance; they are simply self-inflicted. We should rationalise them so that they do not become the first barrier to earning an honest living.

Urbanisation and Development

The process of economic development has historically involved reduction in the proportion of population earning a living in agriculture and thereby expansion in the areas of manufacturing and services. This transition from agriculture to industry has typically resulted in increased urbanisation—migration of people from villages to cities and towns. This phenomenon of urbanisation is so common that development is equated with the degree of urbanisation in the country. Majority of people in developed countries live in urban areas, at times as much as 80 per cent of the population. Less than 10, and often less than 2, per cent of population lives on agriculture in developed countries. Urbanisation has been an integral part of economic development.

Is it necessary to urbanise to develop? History suggests so. Prosperous areas have been urban areas. Mohenjodaro and Harrapa were urban areas of their time. The root of the word civilisation is city. There has never been a rural civilisation!

Urbanisation in the sense of higher concentration of people and larger common market is integral to economic and social development. Of course this process has its own problems. But it would be suicidal to stop or retard urbanisation, instead of addressing the problems.

Intentions and Outcomes: The Law of Unintended Consequences

Many urban migrants find employment in factories, offices, and homes. But many do not. They need to create their own employment to join the urban economy through entry-level professions that require little capital and few skills. The government regulatory machinery, albeit well-meaning and well-intentioned, actually destroys livelihood opportunities for these poor entrepreneurs. Consider the regulations for cycle rickshaw pullers, street hawkers, and small shop keepers in the cities and towns of India.

Cycle Rickshaw Licencing: Cycles of Poverty

Delhi has more than half a million cycle rickshaws providing an affordable and accessible transportation service to the poor and the

Delhi Municipal Corporation

Cycle-Rickshaw Bye-Laws, 1960, Section 3

(1) No person shall keep or ply for hire a cycle rickshaw in Delhi unless he himself is the owner thereof and holds a licence granted in that behalf by the Commissioner on payment of the fee that may, from time to time, be fixed under sub-section (2) of Section 430. Provided that no person will be granted more than one such licence [Provided further that Commissioner may grant more than one licences to a widow or a handicapped subject to the maximum of five licences.]

lower middle class. The Municipal Corporation of Delhi has mandated that cycle rickshaws have to be licensed and fixed a limit of 99,000 licences. They claim to have fixed the number of 99,000 by taking into account the demand for rickshaw services, road space, and traffic congestion problems. Less than 75,000 licenses have actually been given out.[1] This makes more than 80 per cent of Delhi's cycle rickshaws illegal. This government created illegality exposes the pullers to constant harassment and extortion. One study suggests that on an average a bribe of Rs. 200 per month is paid by each cycle rickshaw puller. That makes the total amount stolen by the municipal and police officers at Rs. 80 million a month! This is the burden of the license-permit *raj*—of economic unfreedom—on the poorest of the poor in Delhi.

Article 3(1) of the Cycle Rickshaw Bye-Laws of 1960 under Section 481 of the Delhi Municipal Corporation Act of 1957 requires that the owner and the driver of the cycle rickshaw must be the same person. The intention behind this rule is ostensibly noble—to reduce exploitation of rickshaw pullers by the middlemen, the contractors or *thekedaars*. However, the actual effect of the rule is rather perverse. The law basically says one person can own only one cycle rickshaw: there is no room for growth for individual owners in the cycle-rickshaw business. The only business that the poor rickshaw puller knows well cannot be expanded. He is condemned forever to live at the subsistence level on the revenue from one cycle rickshaw. As a business, you can own multiple taxies or buses but not so for cycle rickshaws of the poor. Is this the way to help the poor emerge from poverty?

---

1. Parashar, Vikas. 2004. "Spoke in the Wheel". *Down to Earth*, 15 April, Volume 12, Number 22: 16.

Moreover, if the owner is unable to ply the rickshaw, falls sick or goes to his native place for a visit, no one in his family can ply it. His rickshaw must lie unutilised. Does the law requiring the owner and the driver to be the same person really help the poor?

The licensing system has turned most rickshaw pullers illegal and they have to pay bribes to ply the rickshaws. But even that payment does not preclude impounding of rickshaws by the authorities at regular intervals. Once the rickshaw is seized, it takes 5-15 days and more bribes to get it released. During this period, the puller loses his only means of livelihood.

Because of all these problems and uncertainties created by the licensing system, the pullers prefer to rent than own the rickshaw. More than 90 per cent of rickshaws in Delhi are rented and not owned! The law was supposed to outlaw the middleman, but it is only the middleman who thrives in the rickshaw market. The actual outcome is contrary to what was intended by the law. This mismatch between intentions and outcomes is so common for regulations controlling normal economic activities that it has been given the status of a law: the law of unintended consequences.

Delhi Municipal Corporation

Cycle-Rickshaw Bye-Laws, 1960, Section 17A

Any cycle rickshaw found plying for hire without a licence or found driven by a person not having proper licence as provided under bye-law 3(1) and (2) shall be liable to be seized by the Commissioner or a person duly authorised by him in his behalf. The cycle rickshaw, so seized shall be disposed off by public auction after dismantling, deformation of such process including smashing it into a scrap after a reasonable time as may be decided by the Commissioner from time to time.

Confiscated rickshaws at the MCD storage

The license regime does not really control the number of rickshaws in the city; it does not serve any purpose in traffic or public space management. It does serve one purpose, probably the only purpose: it

Delhi Municipal Corporation Act, 1957, Section 420

Street Hawkers: Technical Conditions

Sale of Ice-Cream by Hawking (Rule 6)

The icecream salesman will not shout to attract customers nor will he sit or lie on the trolley at any time.

makes most rickshaw business illegal and therefore open to extortion and harassment. Once a law is created, even a bad one, vested interests get formed who prevail despite attempts by higher authorities to revoke them.

Street Hawking: Spend to Vend

The heavy hand of government regulation is also present in other very common entry-level profession of street hawking. Delhi has more than 600,000 street hawkers, of whom only about five per cent have the *tehbazari* permit to hawk their goods on public space. The rest are subjected to continuous harassment through extortion and/or eviction. As documented in the chapter on street hawking, it is not true that hawkers free ride on public space. There are substantial payments to the authorities involved and losses due to frequent evictions despite street hawking being one of the easiest entry level professions for the poor.

Mumbai Municipal Corporation Act, 1888

Prohibition of deposit, etc., of things in streets

Section 313, Technical condition (iii)

They [hawkers] should not hawk within 100 metres from any place of worship, holy shrine, educational institution and general hospital and within the periphery of 150 metres from any Municipal or other market.

MCD truck with hawkers' confiscated wares after a raid at the Lajpat Nagar Market in Delhi

In a survey carried out on the hawkers at the Safdarjung Hospital, Delhi, payments to the authorities were in the range of Rs 800-1000 per month for a 6ft×4ft *patri*. Despite the payments, the raids were frequent to the extent of once a day, unless there was local election. Not surprisingly, the survey showed that street hawkers are ready to pay sizable rent for the security that legality would bring them.

> *Delhi Municipal Corporation Act, 1957*
>
> **Guidelines for grant of *Tehbazari* Rule (iv)**
>
> No tehbazari will be allowed on road which are visited by VIPs., like Bahadur Shah Zafar Marg, Subhash Marg, Indraprastha Marg, etc.

Opening a School in Delhi: A Learning Experience

India has a unique problem of 'educated unemployed.' Since they are educated, that is, have a college degree, they shun typical entry-level professions involving physical labour. On the other hand, there is severe paucity of primary schools, which limit access of the urban poor to basic education. What could be better and nobler than teaching other children or opening a school? It would solve both problems simultaneously. Not surprisingly, even education has its licence-permit *raj* in the form of Essentiality Certificate, which limits the number of schools that can be opened in a particular zone. The West A zone in Delhi has a pre-fixed maximum cap of six schools that can be opened in a year from 2004 to 2008. These controls are generally gotten around by the well-connected, but the poor 'educated unemployed' has little chance.

> *Delhi School Education Act, 1973*
>
> The school must obtain "Essential Certificate" by establishing that its existence serves the public interest. The Administrator decides by taking into account "the number and categories of recognised schools already functioning in that locality, and general desirability of the school with reference to the suitability and sufficiency of the existing schools in the locality and the probable effect on them."

Auto Rickshaw Drivers and Railway Porters: Limited Permits

The same cap on permits for enterprise finds an echo in the running of auto rickshaws where the permits are limited and give rise to illegality for most and limit livelihood opportunities for others. In the case of railway porters in Delhi, the limit on the number of licenced porters takes a dramatic turn with a porter's badge commanding a price upto Rs. 3,00,000.

Delhi Municipal Corporation Act, 1957, Section 420

Street Hawkers: Technical Conditions

Refrigerated Water Trolleys (Rule 5)

It has been decided by the Commissioner that distance of 50 metres between 2 water trolleys in congested areas of City, Sadr Pahar Ganj, Civil Line and K.B. Zones and 100 metres in less congested areas of Shahdra, New Delhi, South, West and Rural Zones be observed. However, this shall not hold good in case of parking of water trolleys near cinemas, markets and other places of recreation etc. Even at such places a distance of about 10 metres shall have to be maintained.

Delhi Municipal Corporation Act, 1957, Section 417 and 421

Shops: Technical Instructions

Barber's Shop/Hair Dressing Saloon (Rules 3 & 17)

- All implements in the barber's shop shall be kept clean and sharp. Razors, scissors and clippers shall be kept in 22% Cresol, Dettol, or Chlorosol lotion when not in use during working hours. Shaving brushes, after each shave, shall be washed in 1% soda solution and then washed in water.
- The floor area of a barber's shop shall be a minimum of six square meters for one chair, and two square metres for every additional chair. Sufficient number of fans shall be provided to keep the premises cool and comfortable.

Setting up Shop: Shopping for Legality

The opening and running of a small shop is also not without its share of woes. Government regulatory controls either make the shop illegal by virtue of its location (due to land use/zoning regulations)[2] or give ample leeway to the authorities for harassment and extortion by putting on the book detailed rules that are open to arbitrary interpretation. Several examples are given the accompanying boxes. These regulations neither help wealth creation nor address consumer concerns for quality and safety.[3]

The Meat Market: Meeting Market Demand

The Municipal Corporation of Delhi runs a monopoly slaughterhouse with a ban on private entry in that business. The capacity of the municipal slaughterhouse is limited to about 2000 goats & sheeps and 500 buffaloes a day. The quantity of meat demanded is far higher than the capacity of

2. Zoning regulates the location and uses of land. For example, industrial uses and activities might be barred in residential areas. Local governments usually pass planning and zoning ordinances to restrict land uses.
3. A sweetmeat shop in Delhi would have inspections from the municipal body, MCD trade license, health department, the Prevention of Food Adulteration Department, the Labour and Labour Welfare Department, the Department of Weights and Measures and others.

> *Delhi Municipal Corporation Act, 1957*
>
> **Private Markets and slaughter houses Section 407**
>
> Where a municipal slaughterhouse exists, it is illegal for animals to be killed anywhere else.

the slaughterhouse. Since private killing of animals is illegal, the goat and cattle owners have to go to the municipal house if they want to sell the meat legally.[4] The smaller capacity of the slaughterhouse meant that the owners had to stand in queue for long hours to be ahead in line. The long queue led to the practice of slaughterhouse workers taking animals through a back door for a fee and presence of widespread illegal and unhygenic slaughter in the Idgah area.

The Idgah buffalo slaughter house

To stop this corrupt practice, the government decided to allocate coupons to animal owners. Each coupon signifying the right to get one animal slaughtered on a given day. One owner can get a maximum of two coupons per day. We hope that you will agree that it doesn't require a degree in economics to figure out what happened in giving out the coupons. We should be grateful for the well thought out and minutely planned efforts of the government to serve the meat needs of the citizens of Delhi. As you would have easily guessed, despite all these, there is no word on private slaughterhouses, a reform that should have been rather obvious. Or may be management of a large capacity, clean, hygienic slaughterhouse is too complex a task for the Indian private sector.

In each case of licensing and regulation, the reality is vastly different from the objectives. Despite allegedly good intentions, the results are:

- Restrict the number of poor who can earn an honest living with their limited capital and skills in these entry-level professions.

4. The licensed meat is stamped with a blue ink sign for clear identification by the municipal authorities.

- Those who enter undeterred by these controls are rendered informal or 'outside the law' and hence subject to harassment and extortion by the regulatory officials. The informal status imposes severe costs on these entrepreneurs.
- A sizable part of the income is lost in the form of extortion/ corruption, thus leading to even lower quality of life and economic security for the poor entrepreneurs.
- Hernando de Soto has coined the phrase 'dead capital' to capture the capital locked in slum dwellings which have no legal title. The slum dwellings in any large city represent several billion dollar worth of capital but that capital cannot be leveraged (used as collateral to borrow against the dwelling) since no legal property titles exist for those dwellings. A similar situation for informal enterprises can be described as 'diverted capital.' It is the capital that is spent simply to maintain the existence of the enterprise, instead of being used to expand the business.
- The informality itself limits the expansion of business: a hawker on a side walk can spread his wares only upto the reach of his hands, as he has to be able to gather them and run as soon as the siren of the police vehicle is heard, else the wares would be confiscated. His business is limited by the extent of his hands! This cost of informality condemns the hawker to a lifetime of subsistence living. Even if he has savings or has the capacity to borrow to expand his business, he is unable to take advantage. The uncertainty created by informality takes away any capacity to plan the future of his enterprise. This impact can be termed as 'unrealised capital.'

Proposed Regulatory Solutions

Myriad approaches have been tried to solve or at least minimise the problems attendant to the modes of livelihood of the poor through various entry-level professions.

- An upper cap on numbers fearing their proliferation.
- Severe penalties for violations of the law, including complete eviction/ confiscation.
- Removal and rehabilitation of the affected at alternate locations, at times, in a multi-story shopping complex.

- Separation of zones for cycle rickshaw plying or street hawking. In case of shop licensing, it is more implicit and takes the form of zoning of urban land on the basis of usage.
- Attempts to 'regularise' the present offenders and then seek to stop any further encroachments.

These attempts have not really solved the problems. The particular chapters dealing with the various modes of livelihood go into details of why these attempts have failed. As a summary however consider these points: Market ultimately decides the number of cycle rickshaws or street hawkers. No matter what the number government decides, the consumer demand rules. Delhi fixed the number of cycle rickshaws at 99,000, but there more than five times as many on the roads. The consumer is sovereign, not the *sarkar* (government). Increased penalties simply mean more harassment and extortion because where there is a demand, there will be a supplier. Resettlement of street vendors in more 'appropriate' areas overlooks the fact that vendors chose the other areas because they are 'natural markets.' Bus stops, hospitals, formal markets and shopping malls – any place with large pedestrian traffic—are all 'natural markets' for hawkers. Urban planners cannot arbitrarily decide where the hawkers should be allowed to operate.

Moreover it would be wrong to presume that this book deals only with the pursuit of livelihood opportunities of the poor. We indeed address concerns of the other stakeholders in the use and management of urban public space. Pursuit of urban livelihoods by the poor need not be viewed as a trade-off *vis-à-vis* the quality of life of urban residents. It is not a zero-sum game. In fact, the same policy measures that have generated misery for the poor have unequivocally lowered the quality of life for all residents. With more informed and unbiased policies, a win-win situation can be created. Our objective is to provide a contextual space for discussions regarding costs and benefits of alternative institutional structures and policy frameworks.

Assumptions of Centralised Urban Planning

Urban planning is at the centre of the issues of urban space management. A critical component of urban space management is urban land use planning. As the Chapter 4 shows, livelihoods are invariably shaped by the urban land management plans which provide the framework for the economic development of the city. The ideas for most of these policy measures follow certain general assumptions which usually do not stand up on closer examination.

Government plans for resource allocations and regulations are good but it is in execution and implementation that they fail. Would we be better off if the upper cap on the number of cycle rickshaws in the city or the rule that the owner and the driver of the cycle rickshaw must be the same person were effectively implemented without any violations? If the law of unintended consequences is fully understood, then it is very evident that these regulations themselves are wrong. The regulators mean well, but they fail in analysing and understanding the actual impact of the rules on real people. The weak enforcement of these erroneous regulations actually provides a little relief—it is like a safety valve that has kept the poor entrepreneurs from full explosion. Think of the poor who would lose their livelihoods if these rules very honestly enforced, and how much more the government would have to spend to compensate for the loss of jobs in terms of welfare measures or employment programmes.

A group of intelligent men sitting in a chamber can take perfect and equitable decisions based on information collected through government channels and can frame general rules that can deal with all the different categories of problems and with the trade-offs necessary to address concerns of multiple stakeholders. The experience of socialist countries has demonstrated that central economic planning for the country as a whole is suicidal. A large urban economy and ecology is as complex and its centralised planning is equally suicidal. As Nobel Laureate F A Hayek has argued there are definite epistemological limitations to individual human mind or minds of a group of individuals and therefore to how effectively they can utilise the knowledge of the circumstances. For this reason, complex systems rely on spontaneous order—the type of order that is the result of human action but not of human design. The knowledge about resources and solutions is scattered among millions of residents of the city and the most effective way to utilise that dispersed knowledge is to let each resident participate in the decision making. Dispersed knowledge is efficiently gathered and utilised through decentralised decision making.

The choice is not between government master plan or no plan at all, but of whose plans and for what. It is not the case that if government does not design a master plan, no one would do any planning at all. Individuals, businesses, and communities would do the planning. Communities, businesses, and individuals through the competitive processes of exchange will discover knowledge that will help them to better utilise their resources. The best way to make the plans work is to allow them to rest in the hands of those for whom they are meant. The focus of urban management should not be on creating one right grand plan. It will never be. The focus should be on institutions and processes through which the plans of individuals and communities would emerge and get implemented.

People fear that without a master plan and zoning regulations, the city would become a disastrous mixture of houses, offices, factories and farms. Some of the most beautiful cities of the world were developed long before we knew of urban planning and zoning laws. In modern times, cities like Houston in Texas, USA have grown without any land use regulations. A network of private land use covenants assures residents of Houston that the neighbouring house would not turn into a primary school or a dry cleaner or a slaughterhouse. Restrictive covenants and the common law of trespass, nuisance, and torts perform the task far more efficiently than any master plan ever would.

The government's spending of tax payers' money or utilisation of resources truly reflects the best interests of the citizens. Consider the following matrix of spending decisions:

- If you spend your own money on yourself, you are very concerned about how much is spent and how it is spent.
- If you spend your own money on someone else, you are still concerned about how much is spent, but somewhat less concerned about how it is spent.
- If you spend someone else's money on yourself, you are not too concerned about how much is spent, but you are very concerned about how it is spent.
- If you spend someone else's money on someone else, you are not very concerned about how much is spent, or how it is spent.

Most government spending falls into the fourth category; politicians and bureaucrats are spending someone else's money on somebody else. Hence, there is no or little incentive for effective planning and implementation. We call this Friedman's Law of Spending, after the Nobel Laureate Milton Friedman.

Officials working in the government machinery always act in the public interest and put their self-interest on the back-burner. As any experience in dealing with the government and the Public Choice theory informs us, this is not the reality. The Public Choice theory challenges the dichotomy of human motivation in economics and in political science. Economics assumes that all humans are self-interested. Political science on the other hand assumes that they are all public-spirited, altruistic. The Public Choice theory points out the same self-interested human beings act in the economy as in the government. The self-interest of a businessman is singular profit maximisation but that of a politician may include maximisation of wealth, power, prestige, fame, and of course public good. The critical insight of Public Choice theory is that under the apparent multiple goals of a politician lay a single objective—that of re-election. The politician cannot maximise wealth, power or the public good without getting re-elected. With the maximand of re-election, it is easy to understand the real life political behaviour. Similarly the maximand of a bureaucrat is the size of his bureau's budget.

The Public Choice theory throws searing light on the how, what, and why of government spending and regulations. Many of the rules that seem to be passed for the benefit of the public may really have the intention of giving more power and money to *netas* and *babus*. This also explains why they generally oppose removal of certain rules and regulations. Despite a directive, for example, from the Prime Minister's Office to the Delhi government to abolish the licensing system for cycle rickshaws and street hawkers, no change really occurred. To view politicians and bureaucrats as self-interested is not being cynical but realistic. And realism should inform and drive the discussion and formulation of policy alternatives.

We should not leave the poor to market forces, but opt for a middle of the road approach. This is mostly a debating tactic to corner the opponent since no one would argue against helping the poor and the needy. The issue is not of intention but of outcome. All intend to help the poor; the question is which approach or policy actually helps the poor. All subsidies are given in the name of the poor but hardly any really reach the poor. The primary beneficiaries of most subsidies are the middle and upper class people. In most cities, people with municipal piped water connection pay pittance for the water they use. Under the argument that water is a necessity and everyone should have access to affordable water, municipalities give heavy subsidies. However the houses with piped water supply are not of the poor. The poor purchase their water from government intermediaries at market prices. They pay far more for a litre of water, as much as hundred times more, than what the other classes fortunate enough to have official water connection pay. The water subsidy nonetheless continues—in the name of the poor. The Indian Left—the alleged saviour of the poor—argues not just for continuation but expansion of these subsidies. With friends like these, the poor surely don't need enemies! There are more direct and well-targeted methods of providing help—food stamps, education vouchers, health insurance vouchers.

Moreover state interventions in the market system (such as regulatory controls) will unintentionally create distortions in other parts of the system (such as shortages or surpluses) which, in turn, will create more demands for intervention in order to solve those problems. Partial interventions into the economy beget more controls, which further choke the system, generating further lack of coordination and inefficiencies which only promote louder cries for systemic and all-encompassing intervention. This morass of controls is what the 'potato chip theory of regulation' predicts. Once a bag of potato chips is opened, it is hard to stop at one or a few chips. With the benefit of hindsight, we know that neither have those interventions worked (if they have not exacerbated the problem), nor do the underlying assumptions hold true. The poor without an effective voice to protest have slowly but surely been burdened by regulatory controls that hinder their economic freedom to earn a living in the vocation of their choice.

A Civil Society Approach: Delicence, Deregulate, Decentralise

So what could be the solution? In a nation preoccupied with arguing about the ideal decision to be made for a sweeping range of problems, this book argues that the most fundamental question is not *what* decision to make but *who* is to make it—through what processes and under what incentives and constraints, and most importantly, with what feedback measures to correct the decision. The incentives in a government structure typically insulate it from effective feedback and start off a vicious cycle of negative impact.

In a world of scattered knowledge, with different problems and differing priorities, systems which capture the essence of these complexities bode well for the individual and society as they give them the freedom to put scarce resources to their most appropriate economic use and to swiftly correct errors in decisions. The market-based mechanisms seem best suited: they offer maximum opportunities for wealth creation and simultaneously provide incentives to look for solutions in case of conflicts.

Ironically, the dismal conditions of the present reality are often viewed as an outcome of a market at work. Many people see the exchange of money between officers and hawkers as simply a form of market transaction. They claim that this awful situation is just as much the result of demand for hawking space by the hawker met by the supply of public space from the regulatory authority. They overlook a critical difference. A legal enterprise entitles the owner to the protection of the law and gives confidence in planning long term investments and expansions. The 'rent' paid by the hawker buys him at best a moment's reprieve, for the very next moment of paying the 'rent' his goods can be confiscated. Not even the Supreme Court would come to his rescue or entertain any Public Interest Litigation. Not to forget that market transactions are characterised by voluntary exchanges between private property right holders.

Reforms engendering economic freedom within the urban space would entail the following measures. These measures hold for all urban areas across India, even though they are discussed and outlined in the context of Delhi, the city of our primary focus of research.

Exit LPQ; Enter LPG

Remove all licences, permits and quotas across the board for entry-level professions. City managers would do well to stick to the main rule of doctors: First, do no harm. To open a school in a slum or a barber shop or a *dhaba,* to sell ice cream, or water, or fruits and vegetables, licences are made necessary, which limit livelihood opportunities immensely. Since the licenses are not easily obtained or in some cases are limited in number, people trade without them. This puts them beyond the purview of law and results in regular harassment and extortions at the hands of officials. On the one hand the government pours money into *rozgar yojnas* and subsidy schemes for the urban poor, and on the other hand, it prevents people from earning an honest living. The money for such schemes ironically comes also from the poor since indirect taxes contribute more to the exchequer than the direct taxes. Instead of taking money from a section of the poor in the name of helping the other section of the poor for their employment and welfare, the government should first let the poor earn their living themselves.

Should we do away with the license *raj* for rickshaws as we did for the industry in 1991? Despite the severe harm to the rickshaw pullers, many won't allow its removal for fear that the poor from the neighbouring states would clog the roads of the city with their cycle rickshaws. But, why are there 5,00,000 (five lakh) rickshaws in Delhi? And not four or six lakh? Because the market demand is for five lakh rickshaws. It is simple demand and supply. The licensed capacity is 99,000, but what impact did it have on the actual number of rickshaws? If the capacity was 50,000 or 1.5 lakh, how many rickshaws would actually be on the road? About five lakh! Irrespective of whatever the *sarkar* decides, the people get what they demand—five lakh rickshaws. If we abolish the license system, there will be about 5 lakh rickshaws in Delhi. Any additional rickshaw puller would not make enough to stay in that vocation. The licensing system does not control the number of rickshaws; it only empowers government officials against the poor—to harass and to extort.

If the government desires to know how many people are employed in a profession, it can put in place a registration system. Everyone practising a trade in the city will fill up a registration form. It should be obvious that the registration system is very different from the licensing system – registration system does not require any prior permission, it simply provides information to government.

Apply the Livelihood Freedom Test

Test all existing and new rules and regulations for their impact on the freedom to earn an honest living. Does any law of the city restrict opportunities of any person to earn an honest living, particularly the one that requires little capital or skills? If so, then Review, Revise, or Remove. Occupational delicensing and deregulation should take priority in the agenda of the government, before embarking on massive employment generation schemes.

Decentralise Governance to Ward Committees

The conditions are never uniform in any city, and more so for mega cities of India. Centralised decision-making can never accommodate the priorities of all the residents. So change the locus of decision-making from the single municipal body to multiple wards.[5] Any decentralisation in this direction would not only benefit the poor, but also enhance public governance.

This entails transfer of powers, ownership, and management to wards. The Ward Committee would manage all the public space of the ward except for major thoroughfares. Only the decentralised Ward Committees have access to the local knowledge, have the incentive to seek solutions for the problems that affect them more directly, and have the kind of accountability necessary to correct errors in decisions.

Upcoming urban areas/townships may choose to have their governance entirely privatised,[6] a process that we examine in the chapter on urban land management. Allow private entrepreneurs to purchase and develop any size of land plots that they and their customers deem economically viable. The resultant choice to citizens and competition between governance providers will have a dramatic impact on the quality of life for all. A hundred privately planned communities in a city competing to provide good governance for customers along with livelihood opportunities would be a welcome change from monopolistic mega municipalities. They would have the

---

5. The Virendra Prakash Committee has recommended breaking up the Municipal Corporation of Delhi, incidentally one of the world's largest civic bodies, into five separate bodies in order to ensure better accountability and availability of services to the citizens of the Capital. Our suggestion of ward-based urban management goes several steps further.

6. The idea is not so radical considering 30 million Americans already live in private cities and they are not necessarily the affluent ones. See 'America's new Utopias: The growth of private communities.' 30 August 2001. Accessed at http://www.economist.com/world/na/displayStory.cfm?Story_ID=760545 on 18 February 2004.

incentives to provide space for hawkers and cycle rickshaws if there is demand for them. They would do this not as charity but simply as profit maximisation. In the Sector 18, *Atta* market in Noida, the land adjacent to a major road is privately owned. The owner has divided the land into small plots, as small as four by four square feet, and given them on rent to hawkers. Some hawkers do sit on the public road, but as the police encroachment clearance van is heard, they jump over to the private land. And pay one time rescue charge to the owner![7]

Reliance on Market Institutions

Property rights and the rule of law provide opportunities for the pursuit of economic prosperity. The incorporation of the right to property as a Fundamental Right in the Constitution will be a right step in this direction. Right to Property is a Right to Prosperity! Look no further than the recent events in China where a minor shift from collective property to *de facto* private holdings of land engendered huge advances in agricultural production.[8] And contrary to widespread belief, the economic importance of property rights is not that they provide assets which benefit their holders, but that they give their owners sufficient incentive to add value to their resources by investing, innovating, or pooling them productively for the prosperity and progress of the entire community.

A government works best when it concentrates on it core competencies—the indispensable functions like the judiciary, police and defence—and performs them well. Hence resources should be devoted to building an effective and efficient judiciary and police for contract enforcement, dispute resolutions and protection of property rights. The government then becomes a facilitator for wealth creation and not a central planner for wealth destruction.

The Master Plan of every city of India should be rolled up into a glass bottle, corked, and thrown into the Indian Ocean. Corked, so that years later when the bottle is found, the absurdities of the Master Plan will become glaringly obvious when compared to the actual

7. Saha, Pravesh and Purnima Gandhi. 2005. "Street Hawking in Noida", *Researching Reality*. Delhi: Centre for Civil Society, forthcoming.

8. Douglas Wu. "China's quiet property rights revolution". *Cato Policy Report*. November/ December 2000. Accessed at http://www.cato.org/pubs/policy_report/ v22n6/china.pdf on 18 February 2004.

development of the city. It will be recognised that only after government mandated centralised plans for urban development were abandoned and decentralised ward level management was adopted that urban governance improved radically in the country.

The next steps entail a curb on all land acquisition by government; return of all undeveloped land to the original owners; permission to develop land by the private sector and adjudication of disputes related to property rights through the common law approach. This also implies adoption of legal instruments like restrictive covenants and deed restrictions.[9]

Land-use/zoning regulations encumber economic development. What the proponents of zoning do not seem to recognise is that separation of land use would occur without zoning. Houston, USA has no zoning laws, yet it has hardly turned into a massive municipal slum. In fact, it has developed upper-income, low-income and mixed income neighbourhoods which have created one of the most vibrant cities.

In conclusion, it must be said that civilisation and progress have been engendered by the economic prosperity of cities. Urbanisation is an inescapable trend and holds huge promise to generate economic growth and employment. No wonder the city attracts migrants for its sheer opportunities for wealth creation. It is economic freedom in urban areas that offers upward mobility for the poor. Until and unless the steps are taken to enhance livelihood freedom, the 1991 liberalisation will continue to be myopically blamed for short changing the working poor, making the rich richer on the backs of the poor and leading to greater income inequality. Champion livelihood freedom—for the sake of the poor.

— **Parth J. Shah**
Naveen Mandava

---

9. A restrictive covenant is a traditional provision in a deed limiting the use of property and prohibiting certain uses. For example, a landowner may promise or "covenant" not to develop residential housing on their piece of property and to use it only for industrial purposes. Restrictive covenants are a form of private controls.

Deed restrictions are written agreements that restrict, or limit, the use or activities that may take place on property in a sub-division. These restrictions appear in the real property records of the county in which the property is located. They are private agreements and are binding upon every owner in a sub-division. All future owners become a party to these agreements when they purchase property in deed restricted areas.

Bibliography

Anderson, Robert E. 2004. *Just Get Out of The Way: How Government Can Help Business in Poor Countries.* Washington, DC: Cato Institute.

Bastiat, Frederic. 1964. "What is Seen and What is Not Seen," *Selected Essays on Political Economy,* Irvington-on-Hudson, New York: Foundation for Economic Education.

Buchanan, James M. and Gordon Tullock. 1962. *The Calculus of Consent; Logical Foundations of Constitutional Democracy.* Ann Arbor: University of Michigan Press.

Block, Walter. "A Primer on Jobs and the Jobless." Accessed online on 18 February 2004 at http://www.mises.org/ fullstory.asp?control=1466

Bharat, A., and C. Chawla. *Urban Governance for Sustainable Development.* Accessed online on 18 February 2004 at http://www.commonwealth-planners.org/papers/governance.pdf

Centre for Civil Society. 2003. *State of Governance: Delhi Citizen Handbook 2003*. Delhi.

Beito, David T., Deborah Gordon, and Alexander Tabarrok, eds. 2002. *The Voluntary City: Choice, Community and Civil Society.* Oakland, CA: Independent Institute.

De Soto, Hernando and John Searle. April 12 to 15, 2003. "The Mystery of Capital and the Construction of Social Reality" multi-disciplinary workshop hosted by the University at Buffalo, Buffalo New York.

De Soto, Hernando. 2000. *The Mystery of Capital: Why Capitalism Triumphs in the West and Fails Everywhere Else*. New York: Basic Books.

————. 1989. *The Other Path: The Invisible Revolution in the Third World.* Translated by June Abott. New York: Harper & Row.

Debroy, B., S. Gangopadhyay, and L. Bhandari. 2004. "An Economic Freedom Index for India's States" In *Agenda for Improving Governance,* edited by Bibek Debroy. New Delhi: Academic Foundation.

Djankov, S., R. La Porta,, F. Lopez de Silanes, and A. Shleifer. September 2000. "The Regulation of Entry," National Bureau of Economic Research Working Paper No. w7892. Accessed online on 18 February 2004 at http://www.nber.org/papers/w7892

Dossier of Background Documents on the 74th Constitution Amendment Act. 2002. Bangalore: CIVIC Bangalore.

Dollar, David and Aart Kraay. April 2001. *Growth Is Good for the Poor.* Washington, DC: Development Research Group, World Bank.

Gwartney, J., and Robert Lawson. 2004. *Economic Freedom of the World.* Delhi: Centre for Civil Society and Academic Foundation.

Frank, Andrew U. *A Case for Simple Laws.* Paper read at the multi-disciplinary workshop "The Mystery of Capital and the Construction of Social Reality," April 12 to 15, 2003, hosted by the University at Buffalo, Buffalo New York.

Foldvary, Fred. 1995. *Public Goods and Private Communities: The Market Provision of Social Services.* Aldershot: Edward Elgar, 1994. Reprint, Aldershot: Edward Elgar.

Government of NCT of Delhi. 2002. *Informal Sector in Delhi (Non-Agriculture)*. Department of Economics and Statistics.

Gangopadhyay, S. and W. Wadhwa, eds. 2000. *Economic Reforms for the Poor.* Delhi: Konark Publishers Private Limited.

Hayek, Friedrich A. 1945. "The Use of Knowledge in Society," *American Economic Review,* 35: 519-30.

Holcombe, Randall G. 1995. *Public Policy and the Quality of Life: Market Incentives versus Government Planning*. Westport, Connecticut: Greenwood Press.

India's Invisible & Footloose Labour: An Analysis of the Situation of Children and Woman in the Informal Sector. 2003. New Delhi: Butterflies.

Kuchta-Helbling, C. "Barriers to Participation: The Informal Sector in Emerging Democracies." Accessed online on 18 February 2004 at http://www.cipe.org/pdf/informalsector/informalEnglish.pdf.

———. "Tapping Hidden Fortunes." Accessed online on 13 February 2004 at http://www.cipe.org/programs/informalsector/tapping.htm.

Milbert, I. "Decentralisation in India: Bringing Democracy Back to the Cities." Accessed online on 18 February 2004 at http://www.gruppo-cerfe.org/pdf/milbert.pdf

Schneider, Friedrich. 2002. "Size and measurement of the informal economy in 110 countries around the world." Accessed online on 12 February 2004 at http://rru.worldbank.org/documents/informal_economy.pdf

Shearmur, J. 2003. *The Construction of Social Reality: The Case of Land.* Paper read at the multi-disciplinary workshop "The Mystery of Capital and the Construction of Social Reality," April 12 to 15, 2003, hosted by the University at Buffalo, Buffalo New York.

Unruh, Jon D. *Poverty and Property Rights in the Developing World: Not as Simple as We Would Like.* Paper read at the multi-disciplinary workshop "The Mystery of Capital and the Construction of Social Reality," April 12 to 15, 2003, hosted by the University at Buffalo, Buffalo New York.

Asiaweek. "What Makes Good Governance?" Accessed online on 12 February 2004 at http://www.asiaweek.com/asiaweek/asiacities/governance.html

World Bank. 2004. *Doing Business in 2004: Understanding Regulation.* Washington DC: World Bank and Oxford University Press.

2

Street Hawking: Spend to Vend

Introduction

Street hawkers the world over have been a subject primarily of human interest stories. There have been very few studies done on the dynamics of their profession, more so in India. In this chapter we seek to explore the questions that have the greatest relevance to street vendors, public governance and you.

The chapter is divided into three parts. The first part looks at hawkers through surveys carried out at two well-identified markets in Delhi: one market which is illegal to a large extent the SDA market (majority of the hawkers are seated on the pavement – a public space) and the other which exists in conjunction with a market consisting of Lajpat Nagar Market licensed shops (here the hawkers are primarily on the street).

The second part looks at hawkers from different parts of India, drawing on surveys carried out by CCS researchers and available in contemporary literature: National Association of Street Vendors of India's (NASVI) 7-city study[1] between April 1999 and March 2000 and Small Business Service Institute's (SBSI) survey of Guwahati.

The third part builds on the findings of the studies and suggests why the usual proposed government policies have failed and will continue to fail, and then suggests reforms within the framework of property rights and ward-level management.

---

1. Bhowmik, Sharit. "Hawkers and the Urban Informal Sector: A study of street vendors in seven cities". National Alliance of Street Vendors of India. Accessed online at http.nasvi.net on 12 February 2004.

SECTION I

Case Studies from Delhi

Street hawking in Delhi is regulated by the urban local bodies – the Municipal Corporation of Delhi, the New Delhi Municipal Council and the Delhi Cantonment Board. However, for ostensible purposes of removing obstruction, even the police can exercise their jurisdiction over them.

Street Hawkers outside Safdarjung Hospital

There are 161 hawkers on this 500 m stretch. About 44 per cent of them sell eatables (*chole-bhature wallahs, paanwallahs*, tea-sellers, fruit and vegetable sellers) and the rest sell articles (clothes, books, cassettes and others) or services (barbers, cobblers, even ear-wax cleaners!). Of them, only 17 hold the *tehbazari* permit (The *tehbazari* denotes that in lieu of a fee of Rs. 120 for 4ft×3ft and Rs. 240 for 6ft×4ft the hawker is granted license by the municipal authorities—New Delhi Municipal Council in this case—to hawk goods). That makes the remaining 90 per cent of the hawkers illegal and unlicensed.

A little description of the area will help understand the situation better. The stretch is immediately adjacent to two of the most prominent hospitals in Delhi – the Safdarjung hospital and the All India Institute of Medical Sciences. The stretch also has two bus-stands and is at the corner of a prominent junction of wide roads. Apart from the hundreds of visitors to the hospitals, many office-goers and people change buses here en route. Given the size of "captive" customer base here, hawkers do try to avail of its benefit. It is very evident from the difference in the goods sold at different points. While eatables are available at both the hospital gates and the bus stands, fast food set-ups like *chole-bhature* or tea stalls are more prominent at the hospital gates, and lighter snacks like peanuts or fruits are available more at the bus-stands, for commuters. In fact, this stretch has 13 peanut-sellers in all. The other articles are more for the convenience of visitors to hospitals – booklets on pregnancy, ceramic pot-pans, etc. Moreover, being government hospitals, most of the customers to these stalls are from the poor and the lower middle classes.

In the course of our survey, we realised that the respondents were understandably paranoid about divulging information, especially the payments made to the various authorities for continuance of their hawking activity. In fact, after much persuasion, most of them mentioned amounts that others paid and denied that they too paid their own. The reasons given by them were: 'I am an upright citizen' or 'because of my long tenure in the market, the police don't force me'. We initially believed in their stories till we realised the explanations were being repeated time and again. Nevertheless, the following issues emerged in the course of our survey of about 35 hawkers.

The players: There are three principal players in the "hawk-osystem" here, apart from the hawkers, the municipal authorities, the police, and the *pradhan* who acts as an interface between the hawkers and the authorities. Each hawker pays about Rs. 200-500 monthly to the *pradhan,* who then forwards the amount collected, to the police and the municipal authorities.

The payments: The amount to be paid depends on various factors like space occupied, profitability of enterprise, "good" relations with the authorities and time period in the market. A "successful" hawker (in this case, usually the fast-food hawkers) on a 6 ft×4 ft *rehri* pays between Rs. 800-1000 per month which may go upto Rs. 1500 for the most profitable ones. A new entrant would pay about Rs. 1000 for a 3ft×2ft space.

The raids: The frequency of the raids varies. The municipal authorities usually carry out raids 2-3 times a day! But then, in a stretch of three days, a raid might happen only once. However, the raids dramatically lessen during election time as was the case when we carried out the survey. Raids may result in either eviction or *challaning* (levying a penalty). Eviction involves physical dislocation, where the hawkers' items are seized and taken away in the municipal authority's van. Hawkers have to retrieve the goods from the municipal godown later, after payment of requisite fine. Though physical eviction is the norm, sometimes *challans* are issued to the hawkers without confiscating their goods. Interestingly, the hawkers look forward to *challans* because they later serve as a proof of their existence and tenure in the market. Often, in the past, in Delhi, legality has been extended to the hawkers on submission of these *challans.*

The nexus: What troubled us most was why raids, especially physical evictions, take place when the authorities are paid their due payments. We found that since the municipal authorities have to do their "duty", the only concession they give the hawkers is enough time to pack their goods and flee. Thus, when on orders from above, the municipal officials prepare to raid the place, the *pradhan* is informed beforehand. Immediately thereafter, the hawkers pack their goods and hide. If caught, the officials do not spare them. Usually, when the municipal van is in sight, shouts of "committee *ki gaadi*" warn hawkers down the street. Often there is loss of goods in the hurry to flee and hide. When a particular hawker refuses to pay the *pradhan's* 'fee', he is identified by the *pradhan* and reported to the NDMC official; his goods damaged. The same happens to his neighbour to make it seem like fair play. Thus, the charade continues.

Recovery of goods: Rarely do hawkers try to get their goods back from the municipal godown because the *baledaars* (those who pack the goods into the municipal vans) often pocket most of the seized stuff like watches, clothes, purses etc. in the process of packing. Often the *baledaars* release the goods on the spot to the hawker, for a price, when senior officials are not watching. Further loss of goods happens at the godown. So, it is not worth paying the requisite fine amount, which is at least Rs. 500. Then there is the wait of at least 7-15 days. Hence the hawkers prefer to buy their goods again because of the loss of income for the days spent to recover the goods. Thus for the tea-hawker, the loss of his utensils and food (like bread and biscuits) would be far less than the amount to be paid as penalty and the time required for recovery of his goods.

The police: The police "control" the entry of hawkers onto the stretch, which is mediated by the *pradhan*. In fact, while speaking to different hawkers across the city, it became more evident that no hawker can have a *rehri-patri* anywhere in the city without paying the police official and the municipal authority of that area, a particular monthly amount. However, the hawkers do not mind paying the police as long as they are allowed to carry on their trade undisturbed. In fact, there were not many reports of police picking up goods and not paying for them, at least on this stretch. Usually, they pay the cost price for whatever they buy, but they routinely "expect" gifts during festivals. Once in a while an odd policeman takes a book from a bookseller, reads and then returns it.

Hawkers are ready to pay for legality: To ward off the harassment of municipal raids which affects their business adversely, the hawkers are willing to pay the government a monthly rent. The non-food-item sellers are ready to pay to the tune of Rs. 300-500 at least, and the amount scales to a high of Rs. 1000-1500 in the case of tea-stall owners and fast-food stalls. It must be mentioned here that a few of the food hawkers are even ready to buy the site they occupy for about Rs. 20,000, indicating the economic value of the space and their activity.

The average incomes: Daily incomes range from Rs. 60 for a peanut seller, about Rs. 100-150 for a clothes seller and over Rs. 150 for fast-food sellers.

Street Hawkers in Central Market, Lajpat Nagar

The total number of unlicensed hawkers in this 124m×91m market (we covered only the main block of the market) under the jurisdiction of the Municipal Corporation of Delhi is about 355. This number does not include the *pucca* shops in the market. It only includes the *rehri-patri wallahs* (stationary hawkers) and the ambulatory hawkers. The *pucca* shops are assumed to be licensed, though for many, the claim is suspect. Moreover, almost all of them have encroached on the space outside their shop for display and sale of goods. So much so, that initially we mistook these goods to be those of the hawkers. Also, quite a few shops have sublet a portion of their premises to a key-maker/duplicator who sits in a corner of the shop.

About 25 per cent of the hawkers are involved in selling eatables as diverse as dry fruits and hot sweet-potatoes apart from the usual *chat-wallahs*. Compared to the 45 per cent of hawkers selling eatables on the AIIMS stretch, the number of hawkers selling them here is less because of the presence of a substantial number of *pucca* and licensed eateries in the market. There are about 19 hot sweet-potato sellers on the periphery of the market, because obviously no *pucca* shop would sell this stuff. Since demand for hot sweet-potatoes is evidently high and capital input for their sale is quite low, it is a niche market that is filled by the hawkers. The other three-fourth of the hawkers are involved in selling articles like clothes, jewellery, purses etc., and providing services like applying *mehendi*. In fact, the market has 30 *mehendi wallahs*. About 105 hawkers sell clothes/sweaters/bedsheets. An important point to note here is that at least one-tenth of the hawkers in the market do not occupy any space to display their goods – the items they sell are slung across their shoulders or draped on their arms. They walk in an approximate radius of about 12ft displaying their goods and trying to catch the attention of prospective customers. The opportunity to make money in this market of limited space is hard to miss. To understand better, look at the photo given above, showing sale of trinket jewellery from the back of the car.

Aaja meri gaadi se kharid jaa

In contrast to the AIIMS market stretch, the clientele here is evidently upmarket and consists mostly of upper and middle income groups who visit both the permanent stalls and the hawkers, though the lower and middle income groups mostly frequent the hawkers.

Eliciting information here was tougher than the AIIMS stretch. Primarily, because of the ubiquitous presence of police in the area and the nearby police station. Yet in the course of our survey of about 53 hawkers, the following facts emerged:

The players: The hawkers in this market do not have any *pradhan* or union leader. Still there are three other principal players in the "hawk-osystem" here, the municipal authorities, the police authorities, and the shopkeepers with their *pucca* shops. Each shopkeeper, by default or convention, "owns" the immediate public space in front of the shop. Any hawker who wishes to 'use' that space has an informal contract with the shopkeeper, whereby paying daily or monthly rent, he gets to erect a basic stand to sell his goods (Understandably, the hawkers owe allegiance to the shop owner). This amount paid to the shopkeeper may or may not include the amount to be paid to the municipal authority. However, each hawker has to pay the police daily or monthly. As a hawker succinctly put it: *"police ke permission ke bagair, yaha parinda bhi par nahi maar sakta."* Interviews revealed payments of about Rs. 200-500 to the municipal officials even for putting up overhead banners across the street, as these frequently violated municipal regulations.

The payments: The payment amounts here are extremely varied and any averaging would only serve to distort the true picture. Here are a few examples to illustrate the same.

- A clothes-seller occupying an 8ft×8ft space pays about Rs. 1000 monthly to the shopkeeper, which includes the payments to the police and municipal authorities.
- Another clothes-seller occupying an area of 7ft×6ft pays about Rs. 300 daily to the shopkeeper and about Rs. 1000 monthly to the police.
- A toy-seller occupying 3ft×4ft space pays about Rs. 1000 monthly to the shopkeeper and about Rs. 250 monthly to the police.
- Another toy-seller on a 6ft×4ft space pays about Rs. 250 daily to the shopkeeper, about Rs. 800 monthly to the police and Rs. 200-300 a month separately to the municipal authorities.
- A wallet-seller occupying a space of 2ft×4ft, which is not in front of any shop, pays about Rs. 1000 monthly to the police and Rs. 100 monthly to the municipal officials.
- A *mehendi wallah* occupying an area of 1.5ft×1.5ft pays Rs. 800 monthly to the police and about Rs. 100 to the municipal official.
- A *chat-golgappa* seller occupying an area of 6ft×4 ft pays about Rs. 500-600 monthly to the police and about Rs. 100-200 monthly to the municipal authorities.
- A sweet-potato-seller on a 3ft×5ft *rehri* (cart) pays about Rs. 30 daily to the police and about Rs. 400 monthly to the municipal authorities. In fact, the police collect daily payments of at least Rs. 20-30 from the ambulatory hawkers at the end of the day.

- A temporary tea-stall owner who supplies tea to most of the shopkeepers, occupying an area of 3ft×4ft pays Rs. 100 daily to the police. And he claims he never pays anything to the municipal authorities because information of any impending raid reaches him beforehand.

However varied the rates may be, they are constant with respect to collection and are only subject to fluctuation depending on the amount of business profits during the day or month. For example, on a rainy day or on a day when raids are conducted, the shopkeeper and the police are "understanding" enough to take less than the usual amounts.

The raids and nexus: Municipal authorities carry out raids once or twice a month. They usually happen when shopkeepers who compete with hawkers register a complaint, or when complaints of traffic congestion increase beyond a limit. It must also be mentioned that all encroachments are removed by the police when senior officials or ministers come visiting.

During raids, municipal officials ask the police to accompany them because, sometimes, when tempers run high during "serious" raids, they may need police protection. The police in turn, often inform the shopkeepers and hawkers of the impending raid, giving them enough time to move their wares to a safe place. Sometimes, the municipal officials may even raid without the police. Yet the hawker grapevine is pretty strong. Information reaches a substantial number of hawkers by the time the officials appear on the scene. Since the market is a big place to raid in one go, many hawkers get the chance to save their goods. And it is made quite clear by the municipal and police officials, that at the time of raid, there will be no chances of remission if caught.

For a hawker, saving the goods and hiding them till the raid is over is "normal and usual". And once the raid is over, they put up their temporary structures again, the goods are back on display and they are back to business.

Recovery of goods: In this market too, the hawkers concurred that there is no point trying to get their goods back after the raid. For example, a guava-seller will have a fine of at least Rs. 1800 imposed on him if his *rehri* (cart) is caught by the municipal authorities. Also, there is the 7-10 days time that it takes to get the cart back and the storage charges of Rs. 100 per day imposed by the municipal officials.

▲
MCD truck with hawkers' confiscated wares after the raid at the Lajpat Nagar Market

Empty pavement just after the raid
▼

▲

Two hours after the raid — business as usual for the hawkers

Shopkeeper helping to hide the goods of hawkers during a raid alert

▼

▲

One hour after the raid — already setting up shops

Hawkers back in business two hours after the raid

▼

After all this, there is still no guarantee of recovering the *rehri* in proper condition. Throw in the extra possible bribes needed to recover the cart, and you will begin to understand why the guava-seller would rather buy a second-hand rickety *rehri* for about Rs. 1200, than go through the whole rigmarole of retrieving the confiscated one. This is also why he does not invest and buy a good, long-lasting, stable and easily maneuverable cart which is available for about Rs. 4000.

Hawkers are ready to pay for legality: The hawkers here were initially flummoxed at the prospect of buying public space. However, persistent questioning elicited the following responses:

- A clothes-seller occupying a space of 7ft×7ft is ready to mobilise about Rs. 5 lakh to buy the space or pay a rent of Rs. 2000 per month for legalising his presence.
- A seller of jewellery, beads, etc. occupying 1.5 ft×1.5 ft is ready to pay Rs. 1 lakh to buy the space or pay a rent of about Rs. 1000 per month.
- A toy-seller occupying 3ft×4ft is ready to pay Rs. 2 lakh to buy the space or pay a rent of Rs. 1500 per month.
- A bookseller occupying 10ft×6ft offered to pay about Rs. 1.5 lakh for the space or a rental charge of Rs. 700 per month.
- A flower-seller will not mind paying Rs. 1500 per month as rent for the 2ft×4ft space he is occupying.
- An ambulatory hawker selling hangers (displayed on himself) will not mind paying Rs. 50 daily to ward off the raids and consequent insecurity and disruption of his business.
- At the lower level, the *mehendi wallah* who, while expressing his inability to buy the space, said he was ready to offer a monthly rent of Rs. 250, and the decorative bottles' seller was ready to pay about Rs. 600 per month as rent.

Given the fact that this survey was conducted immediately after a municipal raid, the desire for legality, and resentment against disruption of business was quite high. Informal surveys conducted among unlicensed hawkers in other markets in the city revealed that the rates progressively increase as one moves to more posh markets like Sarojini Nagar, where hawkers are even ready to pay a monthly rent of Rs. 10,000 for a 3ft×3ft space where they can put up their revolving hanger of clothes. In fact, at Central Market in Lajpat Nagar, a vendor interestingly pointed out that a hawker would be averse to disclosing to his fellow hawkers the true and total amount of illegal payments he makes, for fear of them offering to pay more to the authorities and usurping "his" space.

The average incomes: Incomes range from a daily Rs. 100 for those occupying about 3ft×2ft space for wallet-sellers or *mehendi wallahs,* to a high of about Rs. 500 for clothes-sellers in larger spaces of 7ft×6ft. Hawkers have been conservative while disclosing the amounts for obvious reasons.

Other Parts of the City

1. Hawking in front of a trade fair at Pragati Maidan for 15 days would require you to pay at least Rs. 100 to the police. For a larger set-up like a water trolley, the amount may go up to Rs. 2000 and one would have to pay to the municipal officials as well. The high amount is due to the high earning potential. Most of the smaller vendors do pay to the police but prefer not to pay to the municipal officials. So they either hide during raids or end up being displaced every now and then.
2. The shopkeeper–hawker "friendly" relation is in vogue at the Karol Bagh market as well. However, most of them pay their *"mahina"* (a monthly payment), as they call it to the police and municipal officials directly. For purposes of illustration, a clothes-seller there pays about Rs. 1000 to the beat inspector and Rs. 300 to the municipal official. Nevertheless, in case of traffic bottlenecks, the traffic police forces them to close shop.
3. An unlicensed clothes seller in Karol Bagh spoke of how he was allotted alternate places at the time of issuing *tehbazari* permits. All three options given were equally unfeasible as they were in far off and unviable places like Naraina.
4. A *chole-bhature wallah* in Chandni Chowk, who evidently has a large sale, pays Rs. 4000 to the municipal officials and Rs. 1000 to the police on a monthly basis. A belt seller near him does not have to pay any money to the police since the constable of that area is his relative. However, he mentioned, he did have to give him "gifts" regularly.

5. The weekly markets are very popular in Delhi. A survey of the Govindpuri Budh Bazaar, held on Wednesdays, revealed that these vendors have specific markets to cater to on specific days: Sunday-RK Puram; Monday-Saket; Tuesday-Jasola; Wednesday-Govindpuri; Thursday-Okhla; Friday-Madangir and Saturday-Sarita Vihar. There was no mention of harassment, yet there were the mandatory unofficial payments to be made to the police of about Rs. 5-15 per shop, per day. Also the municipal authorities issue temporary permission on an official slip costing Rs. 5-7 per shop/set-up/table. If a vendor has five shops, the municipal official may take official payments from him for three shops only and unofficial payments at less than the prescribed rate for the remaining two shops. Thus, the process works well for both of them. Almost all the vendors have their own autorickshaws to move their goods everyday to the different markets. Quite a few of them employ helpers at the rate of Rs. 100 per day.
6. A vehicle mechanic in Hauz Khas has certificates from Piaggio and LML, based on which he provides advice to customers regarding availability and suitability of spare parts. Though the presence of a *tehbazari* permit enables him to ward off eviction, yet he has to pay the municipal and police officials or at least provide free repair services to them. Other hawkers nearby have to face physical eviction now and then, though they make regular monthly payments of Rs. 200-250 to the police and Rs. 150-200 to the municipal authorities. As he put it: *"sarkar garibi nahi hatana chahti; woh garibon ko hatana chahti hai"* (They don't want to remove poverty: they want to remove the poor).

The famous Sunday Book Bazaar at Daryaganj, Old Delhi, offers everything from Cookery to Classical Literature. There are about 150 bookstalls on the *patri* which stretches from Delhi Gate to *Lohe Ka Pull* (iron overbridge at the end of the market), a stretch of approximately 1.25 km on Netaji Subhash Marg. Each hawker pays Rs. 50-100 per Sunday (a conservative estimate) to the police for "permission" to sell. A new bookseller, to have his own *patri*, has to contact the local police and pay the requisite amount. The police then allot him space to sell the books. A particular bookseller's place remains fixed if he "squats" consecutively for a few Sundays. There are many instances of sellers who have been operating for more than 10 years in this market.

Conclusions from Studies in Delhi

Insecurity: The issue that troubles most unlicensed hawkers is, surprisingly, not the illegal payments. They resent it but are not as concerned about it as about the lack of security regarding their business, despite having spent more than 25 years and even after making "protection payments." Continuous eviction threats force them to not only make payments, which are a drain on their income, but also limit expansion of their business. Most of them are ready to pay for business security and to legalise their enterprise, but no government has evolved any satisfactory solution so far.

That is the reason why a watch repairer on the AIIMS stretch, who started with an initial investment of Rs. 1000 about 13 years back, now has a business capital of only Rs. 5000. Or a hawker of diaries, who started with an investment of Rs. 3000 about six years back, still has goods with a net worth of Rs. 3500 only. Cleanliness becomes a victim of this insecurity in most areas. However, in posh markets, most of them recognise the value of clean surroundings to attract customers and do keep it optimally clean.

Loans are usually taken without interest, from friends. However, taking loans with an interest of Rs. 5-10 for every Rs. 100 borrowed for 2-3 days is also not uncommon.

Desire for legality: The hawkers' desire to pay the authorities for continuance of business and to ward off raids is clearly evident. The intended payments are nevertheless higher than the actual permit fees charged by the government. The conclusion is that hawkers are not the typical encroachers who wish to make a free living from public spaces. Their dilemma is primarily due to poorly-designed urban spaces coupled with urban regulations, which look upon hawking as a criminal activity and not as an economic activity.

Change of trade: Most hawkers who sell eatables with low investments change their goods, depending on the season. It is not uncommon to find a hawker selling hot sweet-potatoes in winter and *nimbu pani* in summer, or another hawker selling flowers in winter and mangoes/watermelons in summer.

Market for trade of hawkers' permits: A *tehbazari* permit costs Rs. 30. The *tehbazari* permit is highly valued because of the twin advantages of security and space that it provides. Any person hawking without a *tehbazari* permit is illegal. However, since they are not being issued any longer, they can be bought in the black market for a price of Rs. 30,000 to Rs. 3 lakh, depending on the location. Location and space are the most crucial factors for this business. Inspite of the high premium for the *tehabazari* permit, there are enough aspirants for it, considering that the initial investment can soon be recovered. Officially, there are only 24,000 *tehbazaris* in Delhi. Hawkers often talk about filing applications only to find that the permits have been issued to someone else with political "connections".

Protection payments: These have to be made to the municipal authorities and police. Rates vary depending on the following factors:

- Location of market: The rates are low at AIIMS market; they go up in Central Market and go further up in markets like Sarojini Nagar. Usually this factor depends on the class of clientele frequenting the place, or the scale of business in the particular market.
- Type of trade: Fast-food hawkers make more money on the AIIMS stretch due to the absence of shops selling food; in case of Central Market, clothes-sellers make the most money.
- Size of site occupied: The rates vary as per size of site.
- Period of stay in the market: The older ones pay less though not necessarily. Often, when a new police official comes into the area, the rates may be increased.
- Useful contacts: Contacts in the police or municipal body help in bringing down the rates.
- Weather: During rainy season, business is down and hence payments, too, go down.

Role of state government: The Delhi State Government officials do not deal directly with the hawkers. The hawkers' only interaction is with the municipal and police authorities and neither of them are under the clear and direct authority of the state government.

These case studies do not capture the suffering of the hawkers, especially the poorer ones. They emphasise only on the economic processes and consequences, as such accounts have not been studied in detail before. We have not mentioned the tension they suffer when subjected to the raids or even the threat of a raid. As a hawker put it: the very mention of a *gaadi* i.e. the municipal van is enough to make their hearts skip a beat. Or the long hours they put in for their work regardless of the heat, rain and cold. The only motivation for them to go on is providing sustenance for their family. It is not surprising that the hawkers spoken to, in different parts of the country; reacted in the same manner. They said they would prefer the colonial rule of the *angrezi hukumat* (British rule) to the Indian governance. Because, there is the continued perception that however colonial and cruel the British were, they were still law-abiding and fair.

There are certain sections of the Police Act and Indian Penal Code (IPC), which are the main deterrents to the profession of vending.

- Section 283 of the IPC (Danger or obstruction in public way or the line of navigation)-Whoever, by doing any act or by omitting to take order with any property in his possession or under his charge, causes danger, obstruction or injury to any person in any public way or public line of navigation, shall be punished with fine which may extend to two hundred rupees. The offence punishable under this section is the nuisance of causing obstruction.
- Section 431 of the IPC (Mischief by injury to public road, bridge, river or channel) Whoever commits mischief by doing any act which renders or which he knows to be likely to render any public road, bridge, navigable river or navigable channel, natural or artificial, impassable or less safe for travelling or conveying property, shall be punished with imprisonment of either description for a term which may extend to five years, or with fine, or with both.
- Section 34 of the Police Act - No person shall cause obstruction in any street or public place by
    - Allowing animals or vehicle.
    - Leaving any vehicle standing or fastening any cattle in the street or in the public place.
    - Using any part of a street or public place as a halting place for vehicles or cattle.
    - Leaving any box, bale package or other things whatsoever or upon a street for an unreasonable length of time or contrary to any regulation.
    - By exposing anything for sale or setting out anything for sale in or upon any stall, booth, board, cask, and basket or in any other way, whatsoever.

These provisions create the contradiction between a legal 'licensed' vendor and 'illegal' obstruction or causing nuisance resulting in physical eviction of even licensed vendors.

SECTION II

HAWKING IN URBAN INDIA

The following pages present a snapshot view of the hawking scenario across different cities. The information is based on research conducted by CCS researchers in Mumbai, Kolkata, Chennai, Vijaywada and Cochin; NASVI's study in Ahmedabad, Bangalore, Bhubaneswar, Kolkata, Imphal, Indore, Mumbai, and Patna; and Small Business Service Institute's survey in Guwahati. The cases show that though raids may or may not be frequent, bribes to authorities are common. NASVI's study concludes that in most cities hawking is regarded as an illegal activity. There are municipal and police laws that impose restrictions on the trade. In most cases, these laws do not directly prohibit hawking as a profession. They impose restrictions on the use of urban space for street vending. The NASVI study found that, of all the plans of urban development authorities in the eight cities they surveyed, only two, Imphal and Bhubaneswar, had some provisions for including street vendors in their plans. The plans for Indore and Bangalore have provision for accommodating pavement shops (called *ghumtis*). They could be included as immobile street vendors. These shops/kiosks situated near municipal markets can be given licenses for their trades. The plans of the other cities simply blacked out the existence of street vendors. Imphal is the only city, which has clearly stated rules for street vending. The Manipur Town Planning and Country Planning Act, 1975 provides that in residential areas (which include private as well as government housing), there should be provisions for four to six shops and 10 hawkers per 1,000 people.

The Bhubaneswar Development Authority has reserved three per cent of the public space as commercial zone. Shops are allotted space in this area through draw of lots. Space is also reserved on the pavements for street vendors, which is a positive aspect of the authority's plan. However, the space is not sufficient for the hawkers to ply their trades. In case hawkers operate outside the space allotted to them, the municipal authority can forcibly evict them and their goods can be confiscated.

Chennai (Tamil Nadu)

Chennai has about 1-1.1 lakh hawkers according to the Greater Chennai Small Traders Association (GCSTA). A high level team headed by Justice Abdul Hadi, appointed by the Corporation of Chennai in 2000, declared 49 zones in Chennai as no-hawking zones. All of the no-hawking zones are occupied now. All places exclusive of the 49 no-hawking zones were beyond city limits. The GCSTA collected 60,000 letters of grievance from the affected hawkers. Based on the grievances, the Chief Justice of the High Court questioned the Hadi scheme. In September 2002, Justice Kanakaraj, took over. He visited all 10 zones and met with representations from hawkers, twice. He submitted his scheme on 30 January 2003. The highlights of his scheme were:

- Explicit zone-by-zone consideration of existing hawkers and alternative places are demarcated by the committee for permitting the hawkers to continue their business. In some places, the committee permits them to continue in the place where they are currently doing business, but by providing new stalls to be built by the Corporation of Chennai.
- Slots to be charged at Rs. 10 per sq. feet and each of them given 5×5 sq. feet of space.
- Licenses and photo ID cards to be issued.
- Only hawkers with ID cards be allowed to carry on their business in specified areas in the whole of the city of Chennai. All other hawkers shall be deemed to be unauthorised and shall be summarily removed without any prior notice.
- An unauthorised hawker shall not only be evicted but liable for prosecution before a Magistrate and a fine of Rs. 5000/- or imprisonment for a period of one month shall be levied if found guilty of violation of the scheme provisions.

The Kanakaraj Scheme is yet to be implemented. The civic officials have argued that the hawkers would want to be at places where they would have potential business. If the alternative sites were away from public attention, the hawkers would make their way back onto the roads.

Sugana, a 32-year-old single mother with two children, and sells flowers on Ranganathan Street in Mambalam, one of the city's busiest markets. At the time of interviewing she was also selling earthen 'deepams' since it was the festive season. She has been in the locality for the last five years, initially investing Rs. 10,000. She said that the police regularly raid the street demanding that they move. At each raid, though the police are paid Rs. 20, for which makeshift entries are made in a book, no receipt is handed over to them.

Murugan is a 36-year-old handkerchief vendor in the same locality. He was previously a screen printer but moved to selling hankies to make more money. He started off with an initial investment of Rs. 10,000. His daily earnings are around Rs. 150, and during peak season he can earn as much as Rs. 500. But his woes are the same. There are daily raids in the locality. The raids last for anything up to two-and-half hours and amount to a loss of atleast Rs. 50 for him. There are also several cases registered against him, and every time a case is registered, Rs. 100-150 is paid as fine (no receipts given). About five years back, he was relocated to another place, but he eventually returned because of low earnings there.

Mumbai and Ahmedabad (Maharashtra)

The laws for the two cities are similar as both are regulated by the Bombay Municipal Corporation Act 1950. This was in force when the two states, till 30 April 1960, were under the Bombay Presidency. The municipal laws do not provide for the erection of any structure or stall on the streets, which will obstruct the passage of the public, or impede the working of a drain or open channel. Such a structure is liable to be removed by the municipal commissioner. Also, the person responsible for the creation of the structure is to incur the expenses for its removal. It is imperative for a person to procure a license from the municipal commissioner to be able to hawk his/her wares in any public place. Failure of compliance will lead to the removal of any product being hawked on the streets, without prior notice.

The municipal laws regulate the use of pavements, while the police regulate the use of roads. Hawkers are evicted mainly under Sections 102 and 107 of the Act. These sections stipulate that anyone preventing smooth flow of traffic can be arrested and removed.

Mumbai: During the survey, it was found that though the hawkers resented the highhandedness of the police, yet they considered them as their "trade enablers". According to them, it was because of the police that they were able to carry on their trade on the road despite the Brihanmumbai Municipal Corporation (BMC) warning them to discontinue it. While Imtiaz, who sells towels near Crawford Market claims he pays no bribe to the police, his neighbour reveals that they pay a bribe of approximately Rs. 20 to the police everyday. Many hawkers are petrified to say anything against the protectors of their business, for fear of eviction.

The Mumbai Hawkers Union (MHU) informs that till 2002, the BMC used to collect Rs. 100 in the morning and Rs. 60 in the evening i.e. Rs. 160 a day from every hawker in Mumbai and gave them a *challan* against the money collected. A case was filed against the BMC by MHU and the High Court banned this BMC activity of collecting money from hawkers in June 2002, calling it illegal. Since then, no *challan* is issued for the money collected. The BMC, though, issues a receipt on confiscating the hawkers' goods during their usual mega raid commonly called the 'Commissioner's Raid'.

Approximately 60 per cent of the hawkers never go back to recover their goods, because retrieving the confiscated goods is not worth the fine imposed by the BMC. The fine structure is to collect Rs. 1250 on the spot and return Rs. 400-600 the next day when these people are required to appear before the court. Hawkers claim Rs. 50-100 bribes are given at these "*andha* courts". So called because of the "*andha kanoon*" that works here, wherein they have to appear subservient, head and shoulders bent and accept charges when asked "*jurm kabul hai?*", failing which, the fines will be increased. The hawkers find it difficult to understand how what they do for a living is looked at as a grave offence. Also, they never get back all the confiscated goods. This is especially true for perishable goods, electronic goods etc. BMC workers, especially from the lower rung, steal, damage or lose the goods, says a hawker from Vile Parle, an upper middle class suburb in north Mumbai.

Raids take place despite the regular *hafta* paid to municipal authorities and police. What bothers the hawkers most is regular harassment such as paying less money for goods purchased, or walking away with the goods without paying, etc., by the police and municipal authorities.

In Andheri, a suburb adjacent to Vile Parle, there is a small group of hawkers, which is under the protection of a local *pradhan*. These hawkers pay him Rs. 3000 per month. When there is a raid, these people simply cover their wares for some time; they are not required to hide the material as there is an assurance from the *pradhan* that no goods will be confiscated. This is not true for another group of hawkers in the same area who do not pay the 'protection money' and suffer regular harassment.

In the northernmost suburbs of Mumbai, like Dahisar and Borivili, largely consisting of middle class families, the problem is not so much the municipal corporation as the police. Here the police do not confiscate the goods but arrest the hawkers themselves under the Obstruction of Traffic Act.

In Mumbai, where there are around 2 lakh hawkers (4 lakh according to the Mumbai Hawkers' Union in 2003), the municipal corporation has granted only 14,000 licenses. Moreover, the municipal corporation has stopped granting new licenses for the past two decades; hence most of these license holders do not ply their wares, as they are too old or have died. The census undertaken by TISS-YUVA on hawkers in Mumbai found that only 5,653 hawkers, out of a total of 10,2,401 hawkers covered, had licenses. Notwithstanding the harassment, there are several strategic locations in Mumbai city where a hawking pitch may fetch a price of Rs. 5 lakh or more.

The NASVI study found that street vendors in Mumbai, especially those in the central business district and the affluent residential areas in the city and the suburbs, work under constant threat of eviction. Their study showed that a majority (76 per cent) of the street vendors paid bribes daily to the police and the municipality. All the vendors operating in south and central Mumbai paid *pavti* (cleaning charges) to the municipality before this practice was stopped by a High Court order. The BMC had introduced this system as charges from hawkers for keeping the pavements clean. Male hawkers had to pay Rs. 2 per day while female hawkers paid Rs. 1 per day. Interestingly, they did not come across any hawker who had paid the actual charges. All of them had paid between Rs. 5 to Rs. 20 per day as *pavti*. When asked why they paid more than the required charges they said the excess amount was in fact a bribe to prevent eviction. In addition to this they paid the local police a separate amount ranging from Rs. 2 to Rs. 10 per day. After the *pavti* system was stopped, these vendors began to pay money on a weekly or monthly basis to the authorities for conducting their business.

In the suburbs, the survey found that street vendors pay daily or weekly bribes to the police and the municipality. These are not camouflaged as *pavti*. Even in areas where they are unionised, vendors have to pay bribes. In general it was the male hawkers who usually had to pay bribes, and the amount was higher compared to the bribes paid by female hawkers. Food vendors tend to pay more bribe to the municipality, because they face a constant threat of having their goods destroyed, due to lack of hygiene.

In the central business district in south Mumbai, they found that some of the unions act as associations for collecting money to be given as bribes to the authorities.

> Mohan Rama Pawar migrated to Mumbai in 1985 for employment because of famine in his native place in Solapur, Maharashtra. Today Mohan sells toy windmills to kids. It is a work of skill and labour. He earns around Rs. 2500 per month, out of which Rs. 100 is paid to the police every month. On top of it, the municipal raid occurs at least once a month and his average loss per raid is Rs. 1000, when all his goods get scattered on the footpath.

However, the Supreme Court, on 9 December 2003, allowed hawkers in Mumbai to sell their wares on the pavements of 236 streets of the city.[2] The bench passed the orders on the appeals of several hawkers' groups under the banner of Maharashtra Ekta Hawkers' Union and the Bombay Hawkers' Union. However, the judges limited the size of each hawker's trading site, business hours and the type of goods in each area.

- The bench also stipulated that hawking activities would not be carried out within 150 metres of railway stations and market places. It also imposed the condition that no hawking would be allowed within 100 metres of educational institutions and religious places.
- Vending of costly items, e.g., electrical appliances, video and audio tapes and cassettes, cameras, phones etc. were to be prohibited. In the event of any hawker found to be selling such items, his licence would be cancelled forthwith.
- Hawking would be only between 7.00 a.m. to 10.00 p.m.
- Licences for the trade will be given on the basis of draw of lots.

2. "Mumbai hawkers win road space". Accessed online at http://www.telegraphindia.com/1031210/asp/nation/story_2663242.asp on 18 February 2004

- Any person/organisation which feels that any road/street designated as hawking zone should be a non-hawking zone may apply to the Committee having that road/street designated as a non-hawking zone or vice versa.
- Existing cobbler pitches in non-hawking zones could be continued but no further pitches may be added.

It was estimated that some 38,000 hawkers will benefit from the order. However, a survey by the municipal corporation put the figure conservatively at 1.05 lakh.

Ahmedabad: The NASVI study found that harassment and bribery is less prevalent for female hawkers who are members of SEWA. As per their study, 75 street vendors were members of SEWA and they did not pay bribes. The police constables were wary of taking bribes from these vendors. At the same time, the remaining 225 street vendors in their sample who were not unionised complained that they faced regular harassment and had to pay bribes regularly to the municipal authorities and the local police to ward off harassment. The vendors pay around Rs. 10 per day to these people, irrespective of their daily earnings. Hence, at a rough estimate, between 10 per cent to 20 per cent of their income is given as bribes.

Vadodara (Gujarat)

On 2 May 1986, the Supreme Court passed an order by writ petition no. 657, directing the Vadodara Municipal Corporation to formulate a scheme for hawking and non-hawking zones in each ward of the city. All the areas, which hold good potential for selling wares, were marked off as non-hawking zones. For example, the area around "R.C. Dutt Road" which also has the biggest market complexes in the city is marked as a non-hawking zone as vendors 'obstruct traffic and cause vehicular accidents'. Nevertheless, the food vendors on this spot attract many customers.

There are a number of rules in the report concerning the recovery of 'license fee' from vendors on a daily basis. It goes to the extent of specifying what kind of vendors should be assigned to a particular spot. For instance, it says that vendors selling flowers, coconuts etc. be assigned areas around temples and mosques. Not much of this seems to be in practice these days, considering more than 90 per cent of vendors are doing business illegally. The report mentions that there were 10,000 hawkers in Vadodara in 1987. At present (2003) there are at least 20,000-30,000 vendors in the city. Since none of the VMC officials could give even an approximate number, there are probably more.

So what happens to the vendors doing business without licenses? They are easy prey for the municipal corporation officials and the omnipresent traffic police.

Vadodara is divided into wards, and each ward is divided into hawking and non-hawking zones. The officials of each ward office are responsible for the regulation of street vendors in their respective area. Street vendors who have licenses pay Rs. 150 every six months to retain the validity of their licenses, and vendors without licenses have to pay 'administrative charges' to the VMC officers.

Ultimately it all boils down to harassment. Many of the vendors do not have licenses and the officials can pick up their goods at will. They remove the goods and often damage them and cause great losses to the vendors in the process. Vendors in the old city areas run at the sight of any VMC officials. A VMC official mentioned that license renewal costs Rs. 150 every six months, but the licensed vendors said that they had to pay Rs. 200 every month. Wonder where the rest goes?

The extortion is mostly done by the traffic police. They are the ones who keep a regular 'check' on the vendors. Officially, traffic police officials are supposed to give *challans* to the vendors, in case they are 'obstructing traffic'. They can also get the *larris* (cart) picked up. But, according to a ward officer, no traffic police official ever picks up any *larris* or even hands out any challans. They have fixed rates actually called *'hafta'* (the ward officer used this term too), which the vendors pay them on a weekly basis. About Rs. 10-20 is enough for this particular requirement, but on Sundays the rate goes up to Rs. 60. On payment of *hafta*, the vendor can get 'permission' from the cop to take some liberties like putting a few chairs on the roadsides.

> Amar has been plying a chat *larri* in the old city area of Raopura. He has been doing business here for the past ten years without a license. His site of business is on the side of the Sur Sagar lake, which is a non-hawking zone but has at least 60-70 street vendors. On the last occasion of raid, VMC officials picked up his *larri* and threw the eatables away. He had to go to the VMC office, and pay Rs. 500 to get his *larri* back from a place about five km away called 'Moochmowda' on Padra road. Needless to say, the *larri* was in a damaged state.

Vijayawada (Andhra Pradesh)

The hawkers here are mainly on Besant Road and Eluru Road, though the Vijayawada Municipal Corporation (VMC) has banned both these roads for hawkers. Ironically, Besant Road area has the highest concentration of hawkers. About 300 of them ply their trade from this no-hawking zone. This illegal trade is of course courtesy the "informal payments" to the local traffic police.

Besant Road is just a case in point. There are about 935 roads in Vijayawada of which 13 are "no-hawker zones" and all 13 of these banned roads are the economic nerve of the city. Making a living here however, comes with a price. Hawkers here pay Rs. 2.50 per basket of fruits or vegetables put up for display. Collection of this bribe has the tacit approval of the VMC, which charges an excess of Rs. 2 per day called *aseelu* in the local language, from the hawkers in the banned zones. The VMC collects this cess through contractors, who in turn post look outs all day long to keep a record of vendors in the area.

Most of these vendors are from Vijaywada city and neighbouring districts. They earn about Rs. 50-60 per day which comes down to Rs. 10-20 after paying off the police, VMC contractors and the moneylenders. If their goods are seized during raids they have to pay a penalty of Rs. 250 to retrieve their goods. So they don't even bother.

Vendors of food need Prevention of Food Adulteration licenses (PFA) from the state government. These licenses have to be renewed annually. They need to show an address as proof of residence. The process normally takes a week but with informal payments, it can be hastened. A PFA inspector can check the carts any number of times but normally does so, once in two months. If the vendors are found violating norms, their carts can be seized. However, this can be avoided by paying a bribe of about Rs. 100.

Kolkata (West Bengal)

Hawking or street vending in Kolkata is controlled by the Municipal Commissioner under the provisions of the Calcutta Municipal Corporation Act of 1980. This Act prevents any type of vending on the streets. It was under these provisions that on the night of November 16-17, 1996 that the infamous Operation Sunshine took place. More than a hundred thousand hawkers were forcibly evicted from the streets that night and property worth several crores of rupees were destroyed or confiscated. This action was, by all accounts, the most brutal action taken against the urban poor in any city in the country.

Matters did not end with Operation Sunshine. In 1997, the states government proposed an amendment to the Calcutta Municipal Corporation Act. This was Bill No. 33 of 1997 and was known as The Calcutta Municipal Corporation (Second Amendment) Bill, 1997. This later became an Act. Section 371 of the Act was amended as this section contains regulations on street vending. The original section prevented the use of any pavement for hawking goods. The amendment expanded this to include, "any basket, receptacle or goods on pavement, street, park or garden for display or sale" (Section 371, sub-section 1). This section further states (sub-section 1A) that any hawker contravening or abetting in contravening sub-section 1, shall be punished with rigorous imprisonment for a term extending upto three months or a fine of Rs. 250.

In the Statement of Objects and Reasons, the Act states in 2(*ii*) that in order to prevent encroachment in public places, "it has been decided to declare any such encroachment by the hawkers, stall holders and other organisations as cognisable and non-bailable offence." It is ironic that alleged rapists and murderers, in some cases, are granted bail, but a hawker selling wares on the street is regarded as a more dangerous criminal by the state government!

Fortunately for street vendors in the city, the municipal corporation has not been able to enforce the provisions of this amendment, mainly due to the resistance put up by the Hawkers' Sangram Committee. This organisation comprises 26 hawkers' trade unions in the city, which represents different political and ideological leanings. After Operation Sunshine, which saw the strengthening of the Hawkers' Sangram Committee, extortion from the local authorities has decreased. It still continues in areas where the hawkers are not unionised. While conducting the study, it was found that hawkers in some parts of the city preferred to pay regular bribes to the police rather than join a union.

Patna (Bihar)

The Patna Municipal Corporation Act of 1951 lays down certain rules relating to street vending. Section 527 of the Act states that the only competent authority for permitting sale through street vending is the Chief Executive Officer (viz. Municipal Commissioner). No stalls can be set up, no goods can be displayed or sold on public streets without prior permission of the CEO. This permission has to be in the form of licenses for a specific period of time (not exceeding one year) and with a specific fee. The vendor cannot construct a permanent structure. In case these rules are flouted (i.e., in the case of unlicensed street vendors or those who construct permanent structures), the CEO may remove the impediments without prior notice and charge rent for the use of the space.

Even when licenses are provided, the vendor has to fill in elaborate details in a form. Section 138 states that the licensed vendor has to, among other details, state the kind of articles to be sold. They also have to provide a description of the place of sale, time of sale, state the validity of the period of his/her license, describe the booth or stall through which the sale will be conducted. If these are not done, a magistrate can fine the person for violating the rules of his/her license. Given the low level of literacy among the vendors, one wonders, how an average license holding street vendor can complete such minute details.

A highly arbitrary and authoritarian act can be found in the Bihar Police Act. Section 34 states that the police can punish any one causing obstruction, annoyance or inconvenience to the public. Two actions come under the purview of this section, namely, slaughtering of animals in public and displaying goods for sale. The section further notes that a person indulging in these activities can be arrested without a warrant and can be convicted or fined. Bihar perhaps is the only state in the country that gives the police the right to arrest street vendors. In all other states, municipal authorities deal with street vendors with the assistance of the police, if needed.

The NASVI study found that the police, the municipal authorities and local musclemen all extort money from the vendors. It is common practice for the police to charge Rs. 2 per day from each vendor. A fruit vendor at the Income Tax Roundabout told us that he sells his wares at seven road crossings and he has to pay Rs. 2 to the police at each crossing, failing which he will be beaten by the constable. Vendors at Rajendra Nagar over-bridge referred to the police as 'licensed goondas'. These vendors had to pay not only Rs. 2 each day but occasionally a police jeep would pull up and the policemen would pick up fruits and vegetables without paying for them. Any sign of protest and they would be beaten.

The municipal authorities are close on the heels of the police in harassing street vendors in the city. Street vending is illegal and the Patna Municipal Corporation levies fines on vendors. These fines are collected by individuals who have been given the contract to do so. Another finding was that the contractors charge different fines from different hawkers because the hawkers are not aware of the exact amount of the fine. At the same time, payment of fines was not a protection against eviction by the municipality. Even after paying fines, the hawkers could have their goods confiscated by the *'Halla Gari'* (local name for the truck used by the municipality to conduct raids).

The vendors escape harassment from police and municipality when local musclemen control their area. Like in Antaghat markets, the vendors are forced to pay Rs. 2 per day to these goons as protection money, popularly known as *'Rangdhari Tax'*. These goons too pick up fruits and vegetables from the vendors under their 'protection' without paying for them.

Bangalore (Karnataka)

Street vending in Bangalore is regulated by certain acts of the Karnataka Government. The Karnataka Municipalities Act, 1964 states that municipal councils/corporations in the state are obliged to make adequate provisions for constructing, altering and maintaining public streets and markets and provide suitable places for vegetable vending.

The Karnataka Municipalities (regulating the conditions by which permission may be given for temporary occupation) Bye-laws, 1966 make special provision that on certain streets or public roads, specified by the municipal council/corporation, sale of goods like vegetables, fruits etc., may be permitted temporarily. For this, a monthly or daily fee may be charged.

In 2000, as a result of a High Court judgement, the Bangalore Mahanagarpalike (Municipal Corporation) had issued a draft notification stating that hawking can be carried on only in the hawking zones between 8 am and 8 pm. Hawkers are not permitted to sell their goods at busy traffic circle intersections. Besides, only one hawking license per family was to be issued, which may be renewed at the discretion of the commissioner.

However, street vendors do face harassment from the police and the municipal authorities. Mobile vendors, or those operating in the suburbs face less harassment unlike those working in the city centre. This harassment is reflected through continuous eviction by police and fines ranging from Rs. 50 to Rs. 110. Yet the vendors feel that the municipal authorities are not as corrupt as the police. These vendors have to pay Rs. 2 or 3 every day to the beat constable in order to ply their trade.

Tavamani, a vegetable vendor in City Market, has been selling vegetables from the same place for the past 15 years. Prior to that, her mother had occupied that place. She borrows money daily from a moneylender to buy two baskets of vegetables and has to pay an interest of Rs. 10 daily. She leaves her house at 5 a.m. and goes to Kalasipalyam where she buys the vegetables and later sits for the whole day from 7 a.m. onwards. She has to pay Rs. 3 twice a day to the beat constable as bribe. It appears that the police here collect bribes in shifts. If a vendor works for half a day she/he has to pay Rs. 3 as bribe. Since Tavamani sits for the whole day she has to pay twice. In case she does not pay, the policeman can beat her up and throw her vegetables on the pavement. Since this has happened to her in the past, she pays up without protest. Despite regularly bribing the police, she lives under constant fear of eviction by the municipality.

Fayaz Ali stays in the Shivajinagar area and sells footwear (mainly slippers) at the City Market. He migrated to Bangalore from his village five years ago as one of his three children was deaf and needed treatment. Since he could not find any other employment he took to street vending. He works during the afternoon and evening, as he needs time to attend to his child. He has to pay between Rs. 3 to Rs. 5 daily to the beat policeman in order to ply his trade. However, thrice in the past municipality has confiscated his goods and he has had to pay Rs. 100 for their release. He cannot understand why, after paying 'tax' to the police, he is harassed.

Imphal (Manipur)

In Imphal the unlicensed vendors face problems from the police. Imphal municipality provides legality to unlicensed street vendors only if they pay the "obstruction fees" of Rs. 31. All licensed vendors in Khwairamband Bazar pay Rs. 7 a month as obstruction fees. In other markets the fee is Rs. 5 per month. These amounts relate to the time of the study in 2001. The study showed that there were 642 unlicensed vendors and half of them did not pay the fee, as they found it steep. These vendors sit at north of Uripok Road, Naga Mapal, Alu Gali Road, Samuma Khong and Sagolband Road. The municipality refuses to grant them licenses as it claims there is no space in the markets. Those who do not pay the obstruction fees are harassed by the police. They are arrested and their goods taken away. They have to withstand verbal abuse from police constables daily and they live in constant fear of eviction. They told us that their daily earnings were meagre and if they paid the steep charges, they would be left with hardly any money to feed their families.

An interesting feature of the hawkers in Imphal is that an overwhelming majority of them are women. There are male hawkers too but they are from outside the State (Bihar, Assam and West Bengal). The women street vendors are all Manipuri. Women exclusively run Khwairamband Bazar, situated in the city centre. Most of the women vendors complain that, though obstruction charges are collected from them, the municipal authorities do not employ the requisite number of sanitary staff to remove garbage.

Bhubaneswar (Orissa)

Street vending in Bhubaneswar is regulated by the Orissa Municipality Act, 1950. Section 295 (2) of this Act provides that a municipality has the right to provide places for use as public markets while levying certain fees as deemed necessary for a maximum period of three years and subject to certain prescribed conditions. It is imperative for a person to obtain the permission of the municipality for the sale or exposition of goods, failing which the Executive Officer (municipal commissioner) may expel him/her.

The study found that the harassment vendors faced at work are mainly related to their illegal status. Municipal authorities and police raid their places and confiscate their goods. They have to pay fines to release their goods but there was no rampant extortion by the police or the municipal officials as in other cities. However, the vendors did complain of local groups extorting money from them under different pretexts, such as pujas, festivals etc.

Guwahati (Assam)

The Small Business Service Institute conducted a survey of 8850 street vendors (*paan* vendors, *chaiwallahs*, venders of garments, sugarcane juice etc.) mainly in Guwahati city. About 12 per cent of them were mobile and the rest stationary. *Paan* vendors formed the majority with about 72 per cent and 44 per cent were *chaiwallahs*. This is not surprising considering that *paan* and tea vendors often form part of the same set-up.

None of the street vendors paid any legal tax to the Guwahati Municipal Corporation. However, 35 per cent of them said that they paid bribes to the policemen, 15 per cent paid to the GMC officials and 20 per cent to the local mafia. The average amount paid varied from Rs. 5 to Rs. 50 per day. Only about 10 per cent of them had a turnover of about Rs. 3000. About 30 per cent had a turnover of about Rs. 1000 and the rest had a turnover of about Rs. 400.

Key Lessons from Findings All-over India

- There are huge numbers of hawkers in urban areas.
- They fulfil an economic need of various sections of the population.
- A great percentage of their economic surplus ends up in the pockets of officials of the law and order machinery.
- Urban plans do not have provisions to accommodate these hawkers, and in the rare case that they do, it is not implemented.
- Hence the issue that hurts them most is the insecurity over one of their major "factors of production" – the space they use.
- As a result of the insecurity that plagues them, they are unable to invest in expanding their business.
- This "factor of production", that is, the space used by the street vendors is often not designed or intended for their use, but has been paid for by the tax-payers' money and designated for other uses – streets or pavements for example. By using these spaces to hawk their wares, a "public good" is getting diverted to private use and a rent is being charged by those who have not invested in the public good. This represents a diversion and deprivation of the tax payer's rights.

Passport to livelihood

Mehendi on mobile

Find vacant land and sell vacancy forms

MCD Technical Instruction for ice cream hawkers. "Thou shalt not shout to attract customer nor will thou sit or lie on the trolley at any time"

Overall Conclusions

To be fair, it would be wrong to paint the municipal and police machinery as one big greedy fellow feeding on poor hawkers' earnings. Quite a few of them are very much aware of the hardships faced by the hawkers. Some do empathise with them, but being part of a system they also have to perform their "duty." The situation could have been a lot worse, but for the "co-operation" of these officials who are not always sincere in their "duty" and do employ their discretionary powers. It would also be a mistake to look on the hawkers as a poor community. There are a sizable number of hawkers who have managed to make it big despite the problems. They would indeed have expanded their businesses and generated employment and income (most of the present shopkeepers did start out as hawkers or with tiny shops) but for the consequences of urban regulations and constraints of urban market space – for which government policies are responsible.

Obviously, senior economists and government officials who talk of jobless growth, and liberalisation not trickling down to the urban poor do not know how these street entrepreneurs' efforts are stifled or stymied through regulations. No wonder, only 36 per cent of the urban population is gainfully employed, according to the data of the 57th round of NSSO.[3] Every year, one million Indians join the jobseekers' queue. A significant fact is that 60 per cent of the workforce in India is self-employed, which is a high proportion compared to most countries. And if street-entrepreneurship is not seen in an entirely new perspective, we may be in for worse times. Already, the Planning Commission task force report has warned that unless urgent steps are taken, unemployment will reach 40 million in 2007 with severe socio-economic impact.

If we consider the fact that hawkers sustain certain industries by providing markets for their products, the total employment figure becomes larger. A lot of the goods sold by hawkers, such as clothes and hosiery, leather and moulded plastic goods, and household goods, are manufactured in small-scale or home-based industries, which employ a large number of workers. The manufacturers could hardly have marketed their products on their own. The hawkers in turn provide a valuable service by helping sustain employment in these industries. While most gain from affordable costs and reasonable quality of these products, the greatest beneficiary are the poor who gain from these low-cost products sold by the hawkers.

Where the government draws up grandiose urban and rural employment programmes with few actual beneficiaries, these hawkers get self-employed by trading on urban space and meeting market/societal demands. It is time to see hawking in an entirely different light. When the government and media speak of

---

3. The Job Circus. 2004. *Outlook*. 2 February, p 44.

liberalisation benefits not trickling down to the poor, they forget to pay attention to the fact that liberalisation has not occurred at the micro-level of regulation framing. Migration to cities shows that government efforts to eradicate poverty in rural areas have not been successful, and cities have become the engines of growth and prosperity. A large number of hawkers have in fact, been displaced from the jobs of the organised sector. A study finds that around 20 per cent of the hawkers in Mumbai were once permanent employees in the organised sector. In Ahmedabad, around 30 per cent of the male hawkers surveyed were previously working in large factories, and in Kolkata, half the street vendors covered were permanent workers in the formal sector. In these cities, a large number of factories, especially textile mills and engineering industries had closed down and the decline in the manufacturing sector led to a sharp increase in the services sector.

If the government continues to ignore their problems, it would obviously result in large-scale unionisation of the hawkers. Nothing wrong in that. Only, once this happens, this powerful lobby could well attract political interests as a potential vote-bank. The hawkers could begin to extract privileges from the political class through various benefits and possible distortionary funneling of tax payers' money. And hence the state will end-up creating one more political lobby.

Approaches to Deal with Street Hawking within the Context of Delhi

It should be remembered that space is not the primary constraint. The main issue is market space. If only were an issue, then half of the 354 acre Rashtrapati Bhavan itself would suffice to accommodate more than three lakh hawkers of Delhi with an area of 6ft×4ft each (the standard *tehbazari* permitted area). Hawkers are attracted to locales by virtue of the demand felt there; just any urban space would not do for them.

Hawking and No-hawking Zones

Government and municipal policies demarcate hawking and no-hawking zones within the city through static parameters of the prevalent traffic congestion, pedestrian convenience and hawkers' presence. Invariably, some of the most profitable zones for hawking will lie within the no-hawking zones. And the hawker will keep returning there and will be willing to pay requisite amounts in the form of illegal payments to the regulatory authorities to enable them to start or continue their trade. The returns generated from the profitable hawking there would enable them to tide over the illegal payments, even the high fines. The market generates its own economic value of the space whose utility is too valuable to be left unexploited by the vendor and taken advantage of by the immediate regulatory authorities. Also, it is not possible to have a posse of policemen around a market to ward off hawker encroachment. Even if one did, these policemen may probably take to hawking! It is far more profitable than the pittance that they receive as salaries. It is also worthwhile to mention the enforcement costs to deter hawking, at a time when there are so many other serious crimes that merit police attention, especially the crimes against women.

The four categories of *tehbazaris* mentioned below were laid down by the Supreme Court in 1992, in the specific context of conditions in Delhi.

Regular Tehbazari: This license to squat and carry on business in a fixed spot on a yearly basis was to be granted to those whose names are contained in the survey report conducted in 1982 and who had proof of operating at a particular spot between 1970 to 1982. They were entitled to have covered stalls in semi-permanent structures.

Casual Tehbazari: This involved licensing people who sell goods in weekly bazaars, on holidays, festivals and melas. At the time of the Supreme Court judgement, there were about 67 weekly markets in Delhi. They have increased to several hundred today, indicating the rate at which this sector is growing.

Open Tehbazari: Squatters who had started hawking from 1983 onwards and who were not found on the date of the 1982 survey were also to be considered for grant of open *tehbazari* (meaning they were not to put permanent or semi-permanent roofs over their heads) of 6 ft×4 ft subject to the production of continuous squatting and proof of residence and nationality.

Pheri or Mobile Hawking: Persons who did not fall within any of the above three categories were permitted to apply for hawking licenses under Section 420 of the Delhi Municipal Corporation Act of 1957. Their applications were to be considered on merit for permission to hawk—not squat—by moving in specified areas with their goods on their heads or on bicycles.

So it can be argued that every government-designed scheme to curb hawking will fail as enforcement authorities have more to gain from the illegal payments by allowing encroachment. In fact, it works to the authorities' advantage that the hawkers are in a constant state of insecurity and illegality. That is the only way they can gain. As the experience of Manushi Nagrik Adhikar Manch (a forum involved in developing schemes to accommodate hawkers in the areas of Sewa Nagar, CGO complex and Dhaula Kuan) shows, such experiments have invariably run into rough weather from vested interests of police, municipal authorities and even the local sweepers who saw evident loss of their power.[4]

Construction of separate buildings also will fail, as hawking is not done in a multistoried building. These customers who frequent hawkers do not climb flights of stairs to buy from them. Think of the absurdity of going to the third floor of a building to buy peanuts!

The raids will be carried out on orders from above or public pressure. The charade will continue; the general public will still expect the government to deliver solutions and the authorities will continue to flout the rules.

Take the case of allotment and implementation for provision of urban space for the informal sector in Delhi as outlined in the box given on the next page. Agency 'A' plans the utilisation of urban space and Agency 'B' is supposed to allot the specified space to hawkers. Both 'A' and 'B' are in charge of monitoring and enforcement of the norms. Both fail to do so and each blames the other. As a result, the hawkers pay for the authorities' failure. 'A' is the Delhi Development Authority which is in charge of the development of land in Delhi and 'B' is the Municipal Corporation of Delhi responsible for the maintenance of civic services.

For example, according to the DDA Master Plan, hospitals have a provision of three or four informal units for every 100 beds. Both the AIIMS and the Safdarjung hospitals have a capacity of over 1500 beds each. That would mean a total number of 90 informal units at least. However, the actual number of informal units is much more and the number of *tehbazaris* is 17. Who is to be blamed? If the plan provisions are enough, as claimed by a faithful few, what about the actual number of 161 hawkers that the market's natural propensity has created. "Natural markets" as these places are called, have vendors identifying consumer demand and fulfilling it.

---

4. Kishwar, Madhu. "Working under constant threat: Some setbacks and some steps forward in Sewa Nagar". Accessed online at http://free.freespeech.org/manushi/130/threat.html on 18 February 2004.

INFORMAL SECTOR (excerpted from the Master Plan of Delhi) 2001

Large sections of unemployed and under-employed in rural areas and small towns look forward to the metropolitan cities like Delhi for employment and enter the city to move up the economic ladder. This brings forth a multitude of small enterprises, petty trading and casual labour. Thus a metropolis like Delhi has (i) modern wage-paid sector and (ii) equally large if not larger traditional bazar-type informal sector. This sector with highly reduced needs of equipment and buildings is important as a source of employment and also for the economic functioning of the city.

The informal sector units locate themselves strategically near work centres, commercial areas, outside the boundaries of schools, colleges and hospitals, transport modes and near large housing clusters) As a single item, eatables constitute the highest number (35.14 per cent) followed by personal services (14.36 per cent). Walled City and Trans Yamuna area particularly show a very high percentage of this activity. The Municipal Corporation of Delhi charges a certain fee termed as *tehbazari* for continued use of particular space by such units. However, a large number of units are either mobile or not covered under the tehbazari.

It is proposed to incorporate the informal sector in trade in the planned development of various use zones. The norms are given below:

i)	Retail trade: Central Business District Sub-Central Business District District Centre Community Centre Convenience Shopping Centre	Three to four units per 10 formal shops. As specified in the norms separately.
ii)	Government and Commercial Offices	Five to six units per 1,000 employees
iii)	Wholesale Trade and Freight Complexes	Three to four units per 10 formal shops
iv)	Hospital	Three to four units per 100 beds
v)	Bus Terminal	One unit per two bus bays
vi)	Schools	
	Primary Secondary/Senior	Three to four units
	Secondary/Integrated	Five to six units
vii)	Parks	
	Regional/District parks	Eight to ten units at each
	Neighbourhood parks	major entry two to three units
viii)	Residential	One unit/1000 population.
ix)	Industrial	Five to six units per thousand employees
x)	Railways Terminus	To be based on surveys at the time of preparation of the project.

The above activities may need suitable location of taxi stands.

It would be desirable if few standard, efficient and colourful designs for mobile as well as stationary units are evolved and are placed all over the city. It would add to the cityscape and would bring in lot of richness and experience of the city in a developing country.

At the time of sanction of the building plans/layout plans, the provision of informal sector trade units should be ensured so that (a) the poor clientele to which informal sector serves are not exploited and (b) informal sector units are developed to cater to the target group.

Licencing

At the same time, the policy, in its good intention to provide legality to hawkers, will issue them licenses and photo ID cards for the hawking zones. The relocation of the hawkers will fail because they would only be provided unprofitable far-off places, which will not be acceptable to them. Therefore, it is back to square one: encroachment, protection payments and raids will continue in the no-hawking zones.

Alternatively, the government may go about issuing licenses to hawkers in a particular zone based on factors like tenure, proximity to residence and possession of previous *challans*. None of these are market-compatible parameters. Allowing two clothes sellers, three toy sellers and four fast-food makers in front of a hospital, just because they possess evidence of tenure, leaves the demand for a water trolley unfulfilled. Obviously, a smart water-trolley vendor will slip in to fill the need. But he is actually illegal. Slowly, more such 'illegal' vendors will come in and each of them will make illegal payments to the authorities and encroachment will continue.

> Only those edible food articles shall be carried for sale, which are manufactured in premises licensed and approved for this purpose. (According to the Technical Conditions for Street Hawkers, Section 420 of the Delhi Municipal Corporation Act, 1957)

Again, licences may not be issued for hawkers cooking food as in Delhi. One would have to only walk a few of the hawker-dominated streets in Delhi to understand the disconnect between policy and reality.

Micro-finance Schemes for Hawkers

This is one more banal scheme of the government akin to the "liquor-wash" scheme of the government [The Delhi government has one department (Department of Prohibition) advocating alcohol prohibition and three other agencies (DTTDC, DSIDC and DSCSC) engaged in selling the same]. Are these schemes for establishing a hawking stall or for expanding one's present business of hawking? Neither makes sense, especially in light of the regulations framed to deter or criminalise hawking.

Judicial Decisions

a) In M. A. Pal case where the petition was filed for directing the authorities to remove encroachment and obstruction made by unauthorised hawkers, the Madras High court held that allotment of space to hawkers should be properly done under the law. Further the Court said that the trade so long regulated in a proper manner can never be a public nuisance; rather it is beneficial for the public at large. [M.A. Pal & Others Vs. R. K. Sadarangam, AIR1985MADRAS23].

b) In a case relating to removal of excess of hawkers from the streets of the city, the Supreme Court held that the power conferred upon the commissioner under Section 313 of Bombay Municipal Act to grant license to hawkers is in the nature of discretion coupled with duty and it should be exercised by consulting all concerned interests and guided by consideration of what is in public interest. The Court also gave guidelines for creating hawking and non-hawking zones and also consider creating hours for hawking activity.[Bombay Hawkers Union Vs Bombay Municipal Corpn.AIR1985SC1206]

c) In the famous Olga Tallis case, the Supreme Court held that pavement dwellers should be given alternate accommodation before removal of encroachment who have been staying at these places for a long time and also been given census cards.[Olga Tallis Vs. MCD AIR1986SC18]

d) The right to carry on trade or business mentioned in article 19(1)(g) on street pavements if properly regulated cannot be denied on the ground that the streets are meant exclusively for passing or repassing and for no other use. [Sodan Singh Vs NDMC,AIR1989SC1988]

e) In a case where Municipal Authorities refused to petitioners to continue with their trade while they were permitted earlier to carry on trade on payment of charges described as *tehbazari*, the court held that the authorities should help the petitioners to earn their livelihood. It further held that all public streets and roads vest in the State but holds them as trustee on behalf of the public, and the members of the public are entitled to use them as a matter of right. [Sodan Singh Vs NDMC, (1989)4 SCC155]

f) In a case where the Authorities made sub-classification on the ground of possession of survey receipt report, the Court held that in allotment of tehbazari sites/stalls/kiosks, MCD is not justified in making sub-classification among hawkers/squatters on the basis of who possessed survey receipt report and those who did not possess the same. [Gainda Ram and Ors Vs MCD Town Hall and Ors,(1993)3SCC178]

g) In this case, the hawkers were allotted space on the basis of proximity to their residence which rendered their present trading place redundant. The Court directed the committee to get preferences from the applicant and decide taking in to consideration their seniority and length of presence.[Gainda Ram and Ors Vs MCD and Ors,(1994)5SCC52].

h) In a case where the petitioner, a registered society, filed a petition requesting for removal of squatters and encroachers from a Road adjacent to the road leading to a temple to allegedly avoid inconvenience to the devotees and decongest the area. However, the authorities

Contd...

...Contd...

contended that the squatter are the lawful allottees of tehbazari sites. The court held that in view of the decisions of Supreme Court, no case is made out for their removal. [Shakti Mandir Society Regd. and ors. Vs MCD and Ors,93(2001)DLT415]

i) In this case, some sites were demolished to make land available for Metro Rail. In the petition for direction for allotment of alternate viable sites by the hawkers of the demolished sites, the court directed the parties to make representation to the corporation if there is any other site which the corporation can allot them for carrying out their business. The sites earlier given by the corporation were not found viable for trade by the tehbazari hawkers. [Anil Kumar & Ors Vs MCD,92(2001)DLT209]

j) In this case the petitioner was granted tehbazari for open to sky but the petitioner constructed a *pucca* shop which was demolished by the MCD. In these circumstances, the court held that the demolition was not illegal as the petitioner had violated the condition for grant of tehbazari by constructing pucca shop. [Hira Lal and Ors Vs. MCD2002IIIAD(DELHI)413].

The Outcome of these Policies

They will and have given rise to the following consequences:

- Encroachment resulting in pedestrian inconvenience on pavements and/or traffic congestion on thoroughfares. The elite then blame the hawkers for the resultant sullying of the beauty of the city.
- Citizen-customers who miss out on desired products and a portion of the manufacturing industry that makes these products.
- Harassment of hawkers by government authorities and/or payments to them to ward off harassment.
- Utilisation of urban space not reflective of the tax-payer's interests. It is in the interest of the tax-payer to have access to hawkers as well as freedom from their possible nuisance, none of which finds expression in the government's objective of spending.

Reforms

The two fundamental questions here that need to be answered are:

1. In the already congested urban spaces, how can hawkers be accommodated?

2. And how can hawkers be accommodated in emerging urban areas?

In view of the performance-nuisance conflict inherent to the issue, a framework involving private property rights offers us the most effective policy solutions. Remember that most encroachments that happen - from hawkers to slums - are usually on public space owned by the government, spaces not vested as private property. Anything other than a property rights based approach will not work in the long term and will serve only as a temporary solution. It is only private parties that have every incentive to seek negotiable and voluntary solutions for unforeseen problems.

For the effective solution to accommodate street hawking and many other professions, especially in emerging urban areas, the chapter on urban land management would elaborate on the private property rights approach. Here we delineate measures to accommodate hawkers in built-up urban spaces. Collective ownership of property rights as in the ward-based ownership of urban public space would also work as an interim solution, even if the entire private property rights approach is not adopted.

In advocating ward-based ownership of public space, we build on the Draft National Policy on Street Vendors's recommendation of regulating hawkers by Ward Committees (WC).[5] This is also in tune with the 74th Constitutional Amendment, which mandates the formation of Ward Committees and permits the conception of a local government as a community governing itself. Such participatory governance enables the people of a specified area to know its problems, to identify its needs and prioritise them, and take decisions on subjects which can be best handled at that level.[6] The model builds on the conclusion from studies and random surveys that hawkers are not out to take a free ride on public space but are willing to pay for

5. Government of India, 2002. Draft National Policy on Street Vendors. Department of Urban Employment and Poverty Alleviation, Ministry of Urban Development and Poverty Alleviation. Accessed online at http://urbanindia.nic.in/mud-final-site/policies/policy USV.htm on February 5, 2004

6. Urban governance in India and especially Delhi is severely confusing, what with Councillors, MLAs and MPs taking care of the same area. No wonder, arguments among them are common as to who does what and where. City governance models have dramatically improved and it does not make any sense to stick to the present ones any longer.

it given the chance. They might even pay market rates if sufficient returns are perceived at that place. And it is a myth that hawkers occupy the space for free. They already pay costs in terms of bribes or loss of goods—the costs of illegality.

The principal players in this model would be:

1. Hawkers' union in that particular ward or one that might be chosen based on conditions elaborated later from among the several hawkers' unions that might be formed. Mumbai already has union leaders for hawkers of each ward.
2. Ward Committee (WC) that in addition to other issues handles the issue of hawking and negotiates with the hawkers' union as just another service provider, and/or a benefactor of that ward's space. Ward Committee would have elected and not nominated representatives from the Resident Welfare Associations, Market Trade Associations, Housing Societies/Cooperatives etc.
3. Citizens of that ward who elect the members of the Ward Committee.

The WC will have ownership of the public space within the ward and have rights to lease the space to interested parties. The transferee will have only user rights to the leased space. The WC's interests and rights to the space will be supreme, subject to certain basic constraints. The citizens of the ward shall have the right to decide, apart from other ward-related issues, where and how many hawkers they need, if they need them at all.

Usually, the middle and lower classes have the greatest need for hawkers, so they might be more willing to accommodate them in their areas and bear the resultant traffic congestion, unlike the richer classes. However, the rich might prefer to have mobile hawkers in the mornings/evenings or even in weekly markets. Resident Welfare Associations can also have a say in the spatial/temporal restrictions on hawkers. The public space in and around a market can be given to the Market Trade Association (MTA). That would give leeway to the MTA to provide hawkers with non-conflicting goods for sale. But then this may not always be true. *Dilli Haat* bereft of all other stalls save one would not attract the same number of people that an assortment of stalls would do. MTAs may in fact, find it profitable to offer different goods of the same category (e.g. books, clothes) at a variety of prices or even allow for food stalls on the periphery of the market to attract more visitors.

The solutions are diverse at the ward level and subject to change according to needs. Even these stipulations can change with time unlike regulations, which are indifferent to local concerns and take time to change. The WC can also take the advice of urban space consultants or traffic experts to take care of the technicalities. In case of traffic congestion from an excess of hawkers at particular points, the transport authorities would know exactly with whom to deal and do so with the union/WC through negotiations.

Each WC could deal with the hawkers' union of a particular area through contracts. Any hawker setting up his wares in that area would have to be a registered member of that union. The WC may demand a particular amount from the union. The individual rents to be paid by the hawkers may be left to the union. A WC may have the discretion to sign a contract (with any condition) with any of the several ward-level hawkers' union leaders, for maintenance of the road or to prevent further encroachment.

The hawkers' union acts in self-regulation and is responsible for the categories and number of hawkers there, maintenance of food quality etc. It is also its concern whether or not to allow any more hawkers in the area or any further encroachment of public space. Spatial allocation and demarcation rules may be part of the contract drawn up by the union or WC. Sub-contracting/sub-letting of space might also be allowed. It is important to allow the prices for the particular spaces to be decided by a free play of market forces and that there be competition among the different unions/cooperatives for maximum economic benefit to all. A reasonable demand for a potential hawker may be to have appropriate certification when he joins the union.

Admittedly, we have outlined a simplistic model. However, approaches carried out on these lines in various wards will only enable to strengthen the functional modalities. The leaseholder of the pavement as a private property will try different methods of including hawkers, whereas a government will want to issue the most suitable on the basis of market incompatible factors like tenure. The second one will only lead to increased encroachment, as demand at that place will still exist. In the first case, it may actually be profitable to have a corporate/ward citizens'-sponsored hawker-free proper sidewalk and not the poorly designed ones that we have which are a "challenge" for the physically challenged and old. Private players have every incentive to offer better services.

Other measures include repealing of uniform municipal rules for street hawkers across the city. The Ward Committees and the transport authority may decide on any of the rules that need to be followed by the street hawkers.

Ward Committees know their areas and are aware when a trader is causing problems for other traders or who is responsible for garbage dumping. So they are able to micromanage specific street locations better. A mega-city with over 10 million people and hundreds of streets cannot possibly compete with such localised management. Any signs of encroachment or breach of terms of the contract can be immediately brought to the notice of the union or WC and further action be taken. It will be easier for WCs to negotiate with hawkers at the ward level rather than for governments to deal with hawkers at a national level where the complexities are infinite. Also, situational conditions vary from area to area and only localised approaches can work.

Alternatively, hawkers could form cooperatives and pool in enough money (either through self or micro-financing from SHGs) to buy private space for their hawking purposes. This is because, individually each of them would not be able to buy the patch of space as no property owner sells land in such fragmented parcels.

Instead of becoming a dead end, street trading can become the incubator for vibrant, growing businesses.

The solutions may seem surprising, but the fact is that hawkers are willing to pay and private property approaches do work. And this is going to have to happen sooner or later. Just which politician would be willing to initiate it and take the credit is the moot question.

Background Regarding the Municipal Laws in India

The municipal corporation laws, based as they are on 19th century British practice, are outdated and detrimental to the peaceful conduct of business by vendors.

From ancient times, hawking and vending have been an integral part of Indian trade and commerce. However, as the British started gaining administrative control over India, they began introducing their own institutions and legal frameworks. For the hawkers, the Bombay Provincial Municipal Corporation Act (1949) and its adaptations for various Indian cities, the Bombay Police Act (1951) and its adaptations for various Indian cities, the Indian Railways Act (1819) are some major legislations which were formulated by the British and retained in essentially the same form by the Indian government. Unfortunately these laws, based on England's experience in dealing with urban poor and migrants, were designed to facilitate control over Indian people, regulate the economy to suit their administrative skill and to enhance their sense of security.

The following sections from Halsbury's Laws of England show how the laws passed in India were almost word by word based on English laws. Halsbury: Volume 16 Section 616. Metropolitan councils are empowered to deal with persons who erect or place any post, rail, fence, bar obstruction or impede the traffic for which it was formed or laid out, or who place any temporary obstruction such as goods, barrows, stalls etc. in any street. Vol. 22 Section 185: A hawker is required to take out annual excise licence and any person who hawks without having or without immediately producing upon demand a current licence granted to him is liable to fine and imprisonment.

Volume 31 Section 1016: Every person who places, hangs up or otherwise exposes to sale any goods, wares, merchandise, matter, or thing whatsoever that the same project into or over any footway, or beyond the line of any house, shop or building at which the same are so exposed so as to obstruct or incommode the passage of any person over or along the footway is liable to a penalty not exceeding 40 *shilling* to imprisonment for a period not exceeding 14 days and may be arrested by any constable witnessing the offence.

The Bombay Municipal Corporation Act (1882)

Section 313: Except under and in conformity with the terms and provisions of a licence granted by the Commissioner in this behalf, no person shall hawk or expose for sale in any public place or in any public street any article whatsoever whether it be for human consumption or not.

Section 314 (b): The Commissioner may without notice, cause to be removed any article whatsoever hawked or exposed for sale in any public place or in any public street.

Section 229: No person shall, except with the permission of the Commissioner under Sections 227 or 234, erect or set up any wall, fence, rail, post, step, booth or other structure whether fixed or movable and whether of a permanent or a temporary nature, or any fixture in or upon or over any open channel, drain, well, or tank in any street so as to form an obstruction to or an encroachment upon, or a projection over, or to occupy any portion of such street, channel, drain, well or tank.

(*Source:* Excerpts from *Legal Status of Hawkers in India* by Usha Jumani and Bharati Joshi.)

Bibliography

Austin, Regina 1994. "An Honest Living: Street Vendors, Municipal Regulation, and the Black Public Sphere." *Yale Law Journal*, June, pp. 2119-2131.

Aiyer, Swaminathan S. Anklesaria. 2001. "Street Hawking Promise Jobs in Future", *Times of India*. 25 November.

————. 2002. "Freedom & growth: No Siamese twins", *Economic Times*, 27 November.

Bunsha, Dionne. "Targeting hawkers", *Frontline*. Volume 19 - Issue 02, Jan. 19 - Feb. 01, 2002. Accessed online on 18 February 2004 at http://www.frontlineonnet.com/fl1902/19020940.htm

Cross, John C. "Street Vendors, Modernity and Postmodernity: Conflict and Compromise in the Global Economy". Accessed online on 18 February 2004 at www.openair.org/pub/IJSSP/postmod.htm

Cross, John. 1998. *Informal Politics: Street Vendors and the State in Mexico City*. Stanford: Stanford University Press.

Dyrness, Grace R., 2001. *Policy on the Streets: A Handbook for the Establishment of Sidewalk-Vending Programs*. University of Southern California: Center for Religion and Civic Culture. Accessed online on 18 February 2004 at www.usc.edu/dept/LAS/religion_online/pdf/sidewalkvending.pdf

Gewertz, Ken. Outlaw entrepreneurs: Urban design professor supports street vendors use of public space. Accessed online at http://www.news.harvard.edu/gazette/2000/11.30/01-outlaw.html on 5 February 2004.

de Cunha, Gerson. "Steering clear of icebergs", Accessed online on 18 February 2004 at http://www.india-seminar.com/2000/491/491dacunha.htm

Ela R. Bhatt, Founder, Self Employed Women's Association, interviewed by Mirai Chatterjee, General Secretary, SEWA, Ahmedabad. Accessed online at http://www.india seminar.com/2000/491.htm on 5 February 2004.

Hindu. 2001. "A hawkers paradise turns pedestrians nightmare", Chennai, 31 October.

————. 2002. "MCD launches drive to remove hawkers", New Delhi, 23 June.

Joshi, Sandeep 2002. "Displaced hawkers await rehabilitation", *Hindu*, September.

King, R. and Dinye, R., 2004. *A Core Economic Sector: Governance, Context & Experience of Use of Public Space for Economic Activities in Kumasi*

Kanth, A.K. 2000. "Vendors, police and governance", paper presented at, Street Vendors: A Symposium on Reconciling People's Livelihood and Urban Governance, India, July, Accessed online at http://www.india -seminar.com/2000/491.htm. on 5 February 2004.

Leduka, C. 2001. *Contested Urban Space: The Local State versus Street Traders in Maseru's CBD West.*

Mavundla, Lawrence and Mesotho, Mehlaleng 1991. *Freedom to Be Enterprising: The Informal Economic Agenda.* Johannesburg: Pavement Books.

Nnkya, T. 2003. *A Rights-Based Approach: Governance, Context & Experience of Public Space and Livelihoods in Dar Es Salaam.*

Peron, Jim. "Why the poor need property rights", Accessed online at http://www.liberalvalues.org.nz index.php?action=view_article&article_id=89 on 28 January 2004.

Pratt N. 2002. Literature Review: Making a Living on the Street- Public Space as an Asset for Sustainable livelihoods in Nepal, Ghana, Tanzania and Lesotho. Prepared for Engkar funded research project.

Jhabvala, Renana. "Roles and perceptions", Accessed online at http://www.india-seminar.com/2000/491 491r.jhabvala.htm on 28 January 2004.

Reddy, M., Naidu, V., and Mohanty, M. "The Urban Informal Sector in Fiji: Results from a Survey", Accessed online at http://www.fijianstudies.org/dload/vol1no1 urban_informal_sector.pdf on 20 January 2004.

Sharma, R.N. 2000. "The politics of urban space", paper presented at, Street Vendors: A Symposium on Reconciling People's Livelihood and Urban Governance, India, July, Accessed online at http://www.india-seminar.com/2000/491.htm. on 5 February 2004.

Singh, A. 2000. "Organising street vendors", paper presented at, Street Vendors: A Symposium on Reconciling People's Livelihood and Urban Governance, India. July, Accessed online at http://www.india -seminar.com/2000/491.htm. on 5 February 2004.

Shrestha, S. 2003. *Modern Influences on an Historic Tradition: Public Spaces and Sustainable Livelihoods in Kathmandu.*

Sharit K. Bhowmik, Professor of Sociology, University of Mumbai. "A raw deal?" Accessed online at http://www.india-seminar.com/2000/491/491s.k.bhowmik.htm on 18 February 2004.

Shaktiman Ghosh, President, Calcutta Hawkers Men's Union, Kolkata. "A Question of Survival", Accessed online at www.india-seminar.com/2000/491/491shaktiman%20ghosh.htm on 18 February 2004.

S., Vivian. "Private guards may keep hawkers away", Accessed online at http://ww1.mid-day.com/metro/thane/2003/october/65351.htm on 25 February 2004.

Sharma, Aruna P. "MCD moots new vending policy", *Hindustan Times*. New Delhi. 10 October.

Tiwari, G. 2000. "Encroachers or service providers?" paper presented at, Street Vendors: A Symposium on Reconciling People's Livelihood and Urban Governance, India, July, http://www.india-seminar.com/2000/491.htm.

The Delhi Police Act, 1978. Delhi: Universal Law Publishing.

The Delhi Municipal Corporation Act, 1957. Delhi: Allied Book Company.

Tiwari, G. 2001. "Pedestrian Infrastructure in the City Transport System: A Case Study of Delhi", *World Transport Policy & Practice*, 7:4, 13-18.

Vittal, N. "Corruption – Its impact on human rights". Accessed online at http://cvc.nic.in/vscvc/cvcspeeches/sp1aug01.pdf on 28 January 2004.

Vijapurkar, Mahesh. 2000. "When pedestrians won the day", Mumbai. *Hindu*. 29 June.

Appendix A

Guidelines for Grant of Tehbazari[1]

In consultation with the Delhi Administration, the following guidelines are laid down for the purchase of grant of *tehbazari* and for conducting traffic clearance operation in future:

(i) No *tehbazari* should be allowed on either side of a road with a right-of-way of 60 ft. or above, within a distance of 22 ft., provided that if the storm water drain is within 22 ft., tehbazari will be allowed beyond the storm water drain.

(ii) In case of roads with a right of way of less than 60 ft., no *tehbazari* will be allowed on either side of the road within a distance of 6 ft. from the edge of the road, but in cases where there is a storm water drain within a distance of 6 ft. from the edge of the road, *tehbazari* may be allowed on the land beyond the storm water drain.

(iii) Wherever *tehbazari* is granted, it should be enquired that a 6 ft. wide foot-path is kept clear on either side of the road.

(iv) No *tehbazari* will be allowed on roads which are visited by VIPs., like Bahadur Shah Zafar Marg, Subhash Marg, Indraprastha Marg, etc.

(v) While granting *tehbazari,* it should be ensured that the metalled portion of the road, foot-paths, cycle tracks etc., are kept completely clear.

(vi) On roads where adequate open site is available between the building line and the storm water drain, *tehbazari* may be allowed provided it does not interfere with the entry gates of the residential house and the owner/occupant of the house does not make a request for use of the land in question for granting purposes at the prescribed rates. *Tehbazari* holders may be allowed to put up chabutras or takhats but without enclosing them on a written undertaking being furnished by each *tehbazari* holder that these *chabutras* and *takhats* confer on them no rights whatsoever and that those will be removed immediately on the Municipal Corporation requiring them to do so, without any compensation etc.

(vii) The rates for levy of *tehbazari* for land between the storm water drain and the building line will be as laid down in the Schedule of Rates for temporary occupation of land, circulated with office order No. F.10 (7) – Law-Corp./25 dated 10-10-1967. These will also be subject to the conditions laid down in Para 9 of office order No. F. 6(8)/65-Law Corp./2 dated 20th January, 1968.

(viii) To segregate the *tehbazari* licencee/*khokhwalas*/stall holders from the thin flow of traffic, railings should be fixed at a distance of 5 ft. to 6 ft. of the *tehbazari* line of *khokhas*, stalls, *tehbazari* site etc.

---

1. Issued vide Office Order No. 87/T.C.O. dated 31-1-1969 by the Deputy Commissioner Municipal Corporation Delhi *Source:* R.S. Verma. 2003. Delhi Municipal Corporation Act, 1957, Third edition. Delhi: Allied Book Company.

This work should be phased and priority given to major roads, such as Najafgarh Road, GT Road, etc. Persons encroaching on public roads beyond the railings should be prosecuted vigorously.

(ix) No action for prosecution will be taken against tarpaulin which are put against rain or sun, where such tarpaulin are put up outside regular shops no saleable wares will be allowed to be placed under them. In the case of tarpauline put up either above licensed *rehries* or *tehbazari* sites, prosecution should be launched only where the area exceeds the permissible *tehbazari* area. Tarpauline should not extend to footpaths which should be kept free of all encroachments.

(x) Licensed *chabutras* or *takhats* should not be challenged unless these extend beyond the permissible limit or violate the *Takhat* Bye-laws.

(xi) *Tehbazari* may be allowed in lanes if sites are available between the building lines and the storm water drains and the grant of tehbazari does not create a nuisance for the houses or shops, opening on those lanes.

(xii) Licensed *rehriwalas* and *tehbazari* holders will be prosecuted if they extend themselves beyond the permissible area or violate other conditions governing the grant of licencee/*tehbazari*.

(xiii) Pre-July, 1969, *tehbazari* squatters will be proceeded against, only if they occupy land in excess of *tehbazari* permission or violate any other conditions of the *tehbazari*, including compliance with general traffic rules and regulations. Before such clearance is undertaken, the licences/*tehbazari* sanctioned in such cases should be cancelled.

(xiv) *Khokhawalas* who are able to produce proof of their sites prior to 1st August, 1960, will be allowed to continue till such time as they are given permanent rehabilitation sites, but prosecution action against them should be taken if they violate any conditions of the Municipal Licence/*tehbazari* permission, including non-payment of rental/*tehbazari* fee.

(xv) *Khokhawalas* who claim occupation between 1-8-1960 and 31-12-1965 should not be disturbed provided they produce proof of their continued existence from 1-8-1960 and they do not cause traffic congestion and interference with the right of way of the road.

(xvi) Recovery of *tehbazari* should be affected from all *khokhawalas* put up before 31-12-1965 for the past three years. In cases where evidence is produced by the *khokha* owners about their existence for a period less than three years, a decision for recovering *tehbazari* for a lesser period will be taken by the Z.A. personally.

(xvii) Unlicensed *rehriwalas* and *khokhawalas* should be proceeded against vigorously. Similarly licensed *rehriwalas* who have been provided stalls or stall-items but keep on carrying on their business at places other than the new stall sites, should be prosecuted.

(xviii) Zonal Assistance Commissioners should supply to SP (Traffic) and the SDM of the area concerned, from time to time, lists of licensed rehriwalas who are allotted permanent inhabitation sites to ensure that they are cleared out from the old sites speedily after the allotment of stall-sites be given to them.

(xix) There the SP (Traffic) and the SDM of the area are of the view that some of the licensed *rehriwalas* on certain roads, created a traffic hazard or add to traffic congestion, the ZAC, SP (Traffic) or his representative and the SDM should jointly inspect such sites and agree to their shifting to selected adjacent areas, pending allotment of regular stall-sites to them.

(xx) Holiday Bazars should not be allowed in purely residential areas. These should be held only in the Bazar areas on days on which the Bazars are closed.

It is again emphasised that vigorous efforts should be made to regulate the grant of *tehbazari* on the lines of the above order and the orders issued earlier on the subject, and recovery made on a campaign basis.

Appendix B

Street Hawkers: Technical Conditions
(Section 420, DMC Act, 1957)

Hawking of Food Articles

1. All articles of food carried by the Vendor shall be kept in glass cases and clean sanitary vessels, protected from dust and flies.
2. Only edible food articles shall be carried for sale, which are manufactured in premises licensed and approved for this purpose.
3. The Vendor shall have to declare the name of the licensed premises where the food stuffs are prepared. The Vendor shall wear clean dress and head gear. He/she shall pay special attention to personal hygiene.
4. The Vendor shall be free from contagious or infectious diseases. He/she shall have to produce a certificate of medical fitness at the time of issue/renewal of licence.
5. The licence shall always be carried by the Vendor and he shall produce it for inspection whenever required to do so, by the licensing authority or any other person authorised on its behalf.
6. The Vendor shall be immunised against Cholera and enteric group of fevers at the time of issue/renewal of license.
7. No articles considered unfit for human consumption shall be sold by the Vendor.
8. Failure to comply with any of these instructions shall entail legal action against the Vendors and may even result in revocation of license.

Sale of Ice-Cream by Hawking

1. Carts will not ply in the prohibited areas as may be notified to licensees from time to time.
2. Design of the Ice-cream Box will be such as will not permit ice or spillage from the ice chamber coming in contact with ice-cream. Trolley shall be frequently painted and maintained in a perfect stage of repair at all times.
3. Every authorised trolley will show the serial number of the trolley and the total number of authorised carts of the factory as 1/10, 2/10, ...,10/10 and the name of the firm. This may be done by painting or with help of a number plate. The size of each figure and letter will not be less than 16 sq. inch.
4. The authorised salesman will wear clean dress and a head gear (Cap/Turban etc.) Salesman shall maintain a high standard of personal hygiene. Nails will be kept short and hair trimmed at all times.

5. The trolleys will not ply in a manner which may cause obstruction to the traffic.
6. The salesman will not shout to attract customers nor will he sit or lie on the trolley at any time.
7. Medical Fitness Certificate of the Salesman and license will be displayed on the trolley in a proper frame. Salesman shall be protected against Typhoid and Cholera, at all times by appropriate inoculation. These facilities will be provided free by the Zonal Health Officer.
8. A neat container with cover will be suitable with each trolley for the collection of used cups, waste paper and spatulas etc. Vendor will see that unsanitary conditions, which can be attributed to his trade, do not arise.
9. Only the Ice-Cream prepared in a licensed factory will be put up for sale.
10. Following instructions will be observed to ensure that Ice Cream is not contaminated during the process of sale:-
    (a) Temperature of the ice box will not be allowed to rise above freezing point at any time.
    (b) Only pure freshly manufactured Ice-Cream will be put up for sale every day.
    (c) Only properly sterilised spoons/spatulas will be offered to customers for use. These will be carried in a clean container to safeguard them against contamination from dust and flies.
    (d) Candies will be kept wrapped in clean glazed paper.
    (e) A pair of long handle tongs shall be normally used to take Ice-Cream out of the box. The pair of tongs should be kept dipped in bleach solution.
    (f) The composition of Ice-Cream will conform to the standard laid down in the Prevention of Food Adulteration Rules, 1956.

Refrigerated Water Trolleys

The trades of manufacturing of ice-cream and water cooling through refrigeration process, come within the purview of the licensing of the Health Department. Rigid control over both the trades is very necessary since consumption of both items have got a great bearing on the incidence of water-borne diseases. Because of the very nature of these products, their sale has necessarily to be through the retail vending i.e. through the trollies. However, their consumption is seasonal and the sales are confined to about nine months in a year. In fact, the number of rehries in the entire Corporation area and in the Zones is fixed by the Corporation and the same cannot be exceeded.

However, in case of the ice-cream and water trollies there is no such limit and issue of licence to them mainly due to the fact that this trade is seasonal. The Health Department has been considering and issuing new licences to the ice-cream factories as well as refrigeration water plants and the trollies subject to number of limitations. M.H.O. is the licensing authority for these trades. After the number of trolley licences are prescribed by the M.H.O., the sites in case of water trollies are fixed by the Z.H.O.s in consultation with their respective Z.A.Cs.

The Enforcement staff of the Health Department is supposed to keep vigilance over the sale of wholesome water to the public. If the sale of refrigerated water through licensed trollies is not encouraged, then all sorts of hawkers will sell unwholesome water through earthen pots, tins and other unhygienic and filthy containers, with the result that there is likelihood of spread of Gastro-Enteritis and other communicable diseases. The Health Department, therefore, encourages the sale of refrigerated water through the water trollies.

Large number of ice-cream factories and water cooling plants in different zones have already been issued licences and it would be proper from the health point of view to stop the sale of these products. In fact, the consumption of water, cooled through mechanical process without addition of ice needs to be encouraged specially during summer months. In the absence of reasonably safe drinking water at low price, the people, especially floating population, are bound to be exploited by the unscrupulous traders and road-side vendors dealing in sale of cheap brand of aerated waters and syrups. The guidelines suggested for grant of licences for the trollies dealing in the above trades may be as under:-

(1) The parking space for which licence is applied should be available in the premises itself;

(2) The number of water trollies may be fixed according to the cooling capacity of the plant, which depends upon the horse-power, size of the storage tank and the compressor unit. While deciding the number of trollies, the parking space and number of compressor units fixed should be taken into consideration. Roughly, one horse-power load can provide sufficiently cold water for three trollies. One compressor unit with minimum capacity of 3-5 tons can roughly cool water for 10 trollies.

(3) While sanctioning the trolley licensees, the standard conventional trolley may be taken into consideration. The size of this trolley is about 4½ ft. × 2½ ft. (box including wheel). The trollies of bigger size should not be allowed.

(4) Under no circumstances ice will be added to the water for cooling purpose.

(5) The business of ice-cream and refrigerated water will not be carried out in the same premises;

(6) The power to sanction or rejection of licences for plants and trollies shall continue to vest with Municipal Health Officer;

(7) The old licensees will also have ultimately to implement these instructions. Since immediate implementation will cause hardship to old licensees, they will be given only one year to implement these instructions.

Latest Policy Regarding Issue/Renewal of Licence of Water Cooling Plant Trade by Mechanical Refrigeration and Refrigerated Water Trollies:

(1) Number of Water Trollies: Prior to the year 1976, number of water trollies depended only on the availability of space for parking of trollies within adjoining the premises of the water cooling plant. In the absence of adequate cooling capacity of the plant holder, this practice apprehended the contamination of water and as such French Technical instructions were framed to avoid the chances of contamination of water according to the Circular No. 1193/LCI/DHO (PH) dated 27-4-76 the parking space of trollies for which licence is sanctioned should be available in the premises itself. This circular is in vogue at present for such water cooling plants which have come up after March, 1976. Yard stick of 10 trollies to a compressor of 3.5 H.P./3 trollies per H.P. sanctioned A.C. (Factories) has also been fixed. Regarding renewal of licence for water cooling plant established prior to 1976, it has already been decided that each case shall be decided on its merits and if the adequate suitable space for storage of the trollies in such case is available within the immediate vicinity of the plant besides in the premises itself, renewal of licence shall be considered. Wherever there are any chances of contamination of the water, no relaxation is to be given.

(2) Standard size of Trollies: The size of water trollies shall be 4½ ft.×2½ ft. excluding the wheels. Trolley of bigger size shall not be allowed.

(3) Radius of operation of Water Trolley: The distance of three km radius from the water cooling plant to the parkings sites should be by shortest route by road and not as the crow flies.

(4) Token System: The case for providing tokens for licenced water trollies is already under action and is likely to be finalised shortly.

(5) Distance between Trollies: It has been decided by the Commissioner that distance of 50 metres between two water trollies in congested areas of City, Sadar Pahar Ganj, Civil Line and K.B. Zones and 100 metres in less congested areas of Shahdra, New Delhi, South, West and Rural Zones be observed. However, this shall not hold good in case of parking of water trollies near Cinemas, Markets and other places of recreation etc. Even at such places a distance of about 10 metres shall have to be maintained.

*(6) Unlicensed Water Trollies:*The unlicensed water trollies should be rounded up by the Food Hygiene staff and a composition fee of Rs. 500/- plus prior charges as already circulated be charged in order to discharge the nuisance.

3

Setting up Shop: Shopping for Legality

After dealing with street hawkers, in this chapter we will study the dynamics of another livelihood option - that of starting a concrete/ *pucca* shop selling articles like sweetmeats or services like hairdressing. Opening a shop obviously means more capital - for buying or renting the space, to maintain an inventory stock and also for the maintenance charges of the premises - than what a hawker would need to launch and operate his trade. But we focus here primarily on shops that need a low amount of capital to start.

Let us first take a look at the Acts and Rules that these shops would have to follow and also the primary agencies involved in legalising various aspects of shop keeping in Delhi.

- Municipal Corporation of Delhi (MCD) grants a Trade License. The shops merchandising in eatables and a few other categories of shops have to get a Health Trade License.
- Labour and Labour Welfare Department lays down certain provisions regarding opening and closing timings to be followed by the shops and establishments in Delhi for apparent purposes of labour welfare.
- Sales Tax Department registers the shops for their liability of paying taxes.
- Every weighing and measuring apparatus in any of the shops or other establishments in Delhi is required to be certified annually by the Weights and Measures Department.
- Prevention of Food Adulteration (PFA) Directorate regulates the food quality by laying down certain standards to be followed.
- Delhi Development Authority (DDA), in its capacity of being the custodian of the Master Plan of Delhi (MPD), lays down

the zoning regulations for the city. There might seem to be no direct linkage between the shops and the Master Plan, but indirectly the Plan provisions actually have an impact on the legality of the shops and their operation.

The common perception is that starting and running a small shop may be an undemanding task, but our research results point to the opposite. We interviewed a few government officials from the departments concerned for a clear picture of the regulations for shops. While some were quite forthcoming about the information orally (on condition that they would not be quoted), many others complained of unavailability of data/documents to support. We interviewed many shop owners in the Hauz Khas Market in South Delhi, Lakshmi Nagar Market in East Delhi and also the Pratap Market in South Delhi. Besides, a few sample studies were also conducted in other parts of Delhi - Bengali Market and Patel Chest - which corroborate the survey findings. We found that most shops were illegal on one count or the other: for instance most shops did not have MCD Trade License, yet almost all were paying their Sales Tax. The licensing inspectors did admit that more than 70 per cent of shops in Delhi do not have the MCD Trade License. Inspectors from various departments are supposed to make rounds of the shops to ensure that the rules and regulations are properly followed. The shopkeepers and the officials chalk out their own 'informal' arrangements regarding these inspections. And the arrangements vary, depending on the location value, profitability of the shops, clientele catered to (Greater Kailash market vs local market in Shahadra), greed of the officials and various other factors. Thus, even this apparently mundane affair is mired in extra legal norms. The MCD grants Trade License to the shops on the basis of the area in which the shops are situated, i.e., as per the MPD provisions which demarcate the areas where shops can be opened.

PROCEDURES

Trade Licence

The Eleventh Schedule of the DMC Act, 1957 specifies a list of items for which the premises may not be used without a license. The list is exhaustive (Appendix-A) and covers almost all kinds of trades. The Licensing and Enforcement Department of MCD issues a General Trade License under Section 417 of the DMC Act. Apart from the

General Trade License, MCD's Health Department also issues license for the shops dealing in eatables or other commodities or services (see Appendix-B).

Ironically, a shopkeeper can get this license only after he begins the trade and remains in the same for some time (*illegally*). This is because, as opposed to the convention usually followed - of granting the license before the launch of the trade - the MCD issues the license only after the trade has actually begun. One of the requisite documents is the 'proof of establishment of the trade'. This means that in case the license is rejected, the government expects the entrepreneur to either withdraw his capital from the trade that he envisages to be a profitable one (and the government would then probably go on to announce an employment generating scheme financed by the taxpayers' money to employ this entrepreneur) or to continue illegally without the license, which in turn means that the government is actually creating room for illegality itself.

Opening a Shop in a Commercial Area

According to a Licensing Inspector we interviewed, if the shop is situated in a 'commercial area', the shopkeeper has to make an application to the Deputy Commissioner of that zone with the following details:

- Name of the shopkeeper
- Premises number
- Trade
- Partnership/sole proprietorship
- Owner/tenant
- Address
- Floor on which the trade is running

The following documents must also be attached along with the application:[1]

1. Documentary proof of legal occupancy
    - If the applicant owns the shop, he has to attach a copy of the sale deed and the house tax receipts.

1. Sourced from Municipal Corporation of Delhi Trade License (General) [official website]. Accessed on 25 February 2004 at http://www.mcdonline.gov.in/mcd/tradefaq.jsp.

- If the shop has been allotted by the DDA, the applicant has to attach a copy of the allotment letter.
- For those who intend to set up shop in a *rented* premises, the following have to be submitted:
    - Copy of the lease deed.
    - Copy of the rent agreement.
    - NOC from the landlord (Most applicants fail to give this, said the Licensing Inspector).

2. Two copies of the Key Plan (It is a map/layout plan of the location/position of the shop in the market) prepared by an architect.
3. Two copies of the Site Plan (It gives the measurements of the area of the shop) prepared by an architect.
4. No Objection Certificate (NOC) from the Building Department of MCD regarding non-existence of unauthorised construction. The Executive Engineer inspects the site and submits his report — on the basis of which the NOC is granted. The process may take from a minimum of seven days to may be more than six months.
5. To prove the date of establishment of trade the applicant has to submit the following documents:
    - Copy of the Certificate of Registration under Section 7(1)/7(2) of the Central Sales Tax Registration & Turnover Rules, 1957 (Form-B).
    - Copy of the Certificate of Registration under the Delhi Sales Tax Rules (Rule 16, Form–ST-8).
    - Telephone Bill of the shop.
    - Invoice of the purchase of raw materials.
    - Bank statement of the shop/firm.
6. A copy of the Partnership Deed – if there is any – also has to be furnished.
7. Documentary proof of existence of fire fighting equipment at the unit: the applicant has to submit a copy of the bill of purchase of the fire fighting equipment for the shop.

Cinemas, gas agencies, petrol pumps and the restaurants have to also get an NOC from the Delhi Fire Service Department.

8. Affidavit on Rs. 10 stamp paper duly attested by the public notary.
9. Indemnity Bond on Rs. 100 stamp paper duly attested by the public notary.

The application, along with the required documents and the prescribed license fees, has to be submitted at the Citizen Service Bureau of MCD. Section 417 (3) of the DMC Act specifies that the license fee shall not exceed Rs. 500. The applicant must sign all the document copies mentioned above; or else the application may be termed 'incomplete'. But this detail is not made public by the MCD on the official website. As corroborated by a Licensing Inspector, these are common occurrences.

Once the application is submitted, the Licensing Inspectors check the authenticity of the documents submitted, for which they visit the site. The officials have ample authority and discretion in deciding the successful applications. Rarely do the applications get approved without bribing the officials. The bribe amount depends on many factors. Often the shopkeepers are also in violation of one rule or the other. To cite a case from our survey, the condition of planting a fire extinguisher was not followed at a shop in Munirka market which had a Trade License. When questioned, the shopkeeper told us that he had submitted a fake purchase bill of the equipment with his application and during inspection managed to 'appease' the officials.

Fate of the Application

Most applicants fail to submit all the documents and their applications get rejected. Any of the three fates may befall an application at the MCD:

- Application is verified and approved and license granted.
- Application is verified, found incomplete and therefore a letter forwarded to the applicant requesting him to furnish the rest of the documents. The application in the meanwhile is called a pending case.
- Application is verified, inconsistencies found on inspection and hence rejected.

According to the Licensing Inspector, only about 20 per cent of the applications that the Department receive actually move to the next stage! He said most applicants find it very hard to submit all the documents required and therefore, their applications never get approved.

Common Grounds on which the Applications are Rejected

The most common reasons, as per the licensing inspectors interviewed, for not granting approval for the license are:

- The traders setting up shop in rented premises usually fail to get the NOC from the landlord.
- Most of the shops have undertaken unauthorised construction in their premises and therefore, they are unable to get the NOC from the Building Department of the MCD.

Once the Inspectors approve the application, the Licensing Committee comprising the Assistant Commissioner, Deputy Commissioner, licensing inspectors and Deputy Health Officer of the concerned zone review it. The license is issued once the review is over.

The Administrative Officer sends the approved application back to the Citizen Service Bureau (CSB) from where the applicant can collect the license on showing license fee payment receipt. The MCD has actually tried to simplify the procedure by making it a single-window access, as the dealings between the shopkeepers and the MCD technically occur only at the CSB - to apply and collect the license. But the purpose of simplifying the procedure still remains defeated, as the CSB staff informed us that most of the applicants for the license submit their applications directly at the office. This happens because the power of clearance is still vested with the inspector, who functions on arbitrary norms.

Process Time of Application

The entire process should, as per official claims, take 20 working days.[2] But the ground reality is different. The Inspector himself admitted that the process usually takes much longer, from six months to even a year sometimes. And the shopkeepers corroborated the same.

---

2. Sourced from Municipal Corporation of Delhi Trade License (General) [official website]. Accessed on 25 February 2004 at http://www.mcdonline.gov.in/mcd/tradefaq.jsp

Snip!

Brijender Kumar, a barber, has been running Modern Hair Saloon, in North Delhi for over a year now. Ten months earlier he applied for the Health Trade License with the requisite documents. He awaits a reply till date. He is also aware that the only possible way of getting the license will snip a hole in his pocket! Ironically, he never got the license for his previous shop in Kamla Nagar Market. Another barber's shop, Menz Saloon, in the Bengali Market, has been also operating without a license for the last two years. This one works totally on the principle of bribes - a hefty amount of bribe is paid every month for operating the saloon.

Opening a Shop in a Residential Area

For starting a trade in a residential area, no license is granted but temporary registration is required under the 'Ad-hoc Trade Registration Scheme'. Registration happens once in several years based on the policy decisions. Usually the scheme is declared around election time to garner votes. A notification about the scheme is published in the city's leading newspapers and interested applicants are allowed to apply only at that time. The last time such licenses were released was in 2001. Hence all the shops that have opened in residential areas after 2001 are actually "illegal."

The procedure of applying for registration under this scheme is similar to getting a license for running a shop in a commercial area.

Is the ad-hoc Registration Scheme an Illegal one?[3]

MCD is legally bound to issue licenses to trade and industries in accordance with the provisions of the Master Plan, which demarcates nine categories of land uses. Violation of the Master Plan is a legal offence. But the Delhi Government started a new scheme in 1994 to grant ad-hoc registration to traders to operate in non-conforming areas. This scheme was illegal *ab-initio* because according to the Master Plan, commercial use of land demarcated for residential purposes is not approved. Despite this, the Delhi Government directed MCD to issue licenses under this scheme. MCD also obliged and issued thousands of licenses under this scheme saving their skin by saying that since registration is only ad-hoc in nature, no rights would accrue to the trader and MCD will revoke the same any time in future if the party is found violating any law. Neither the Delhi government nor the MCD are legally authorised to modify the land use of a particular area, without specific clearance of the DDA or the competent authority as defined under the Delhi Development Act. It is the legal duty of DDA to prevent any violations of Delhi Master Plan, but the DDA took no action regarding the issue.

3. An excerpt from Sisodia, Manish. Industrial relocation: Who are the Real Culprits? [article online]. India Demands. Accessed on 25 February 2004 at http://members.tripod.com/indiademands/industrial_relocation.htm.

Health Trade License

Apart from the General Trade License, MCD issues license under Section 417 of the DMC Act. The trades that are licensable by MCD's Health Department are mentioned in the Technical Conditions.

The procedure for applying is similar except that a few more documents are to be attached with the ones mentioned above. These are:[4]

1. Structure Safety Certificate of the building from a registered architect.
2. Proof of commercial water and electricity connection i.e. the bills. For this, first, a commercial water connection has to be procured from the Zonal Engineer of the Delhi Jal Board. In order to get this, the following have to be submitted:
3. Copies of the rent receipt (in case of tenancy).
4. NOC from the landlord.
5. Ownership proof of the premises.
6. Affidavit stating the resolution of the applicant along with a request letter on the letterhead or receipt book of the undertaking.
7. NOC from DCP Licensing in case of cinema halls, gyms, lodging houses, swimming pools etc.
8. In case of mobile catering vans-

   NOC from ACP Traffic.

   Copy of RC, Insurance.

   Updated Road Tax, Fitness, Commercial Number.

   Medical Fitness and Vaccination Certificate against Typhoid of food handlers in eating establishments.

It is interesting to note that only the Health Licensing Department requires the structural safety certificate whereas while applying for a General Trade License, the applicant does not need to submit this.

---

4. Sourced from Municipal Corporation of Delhi Trade License (Health) [official website]. Accessed online on 25 February 2004 at http://www.mcdonline.gov.in/mcd/healthtradefaq.jsp.

Regulations on Paper

Once the application is submitted, the Health Inspectors examine the site to check for technical conditions. Even a cursory look at the technical conditions reveals their impracticality for compliance and subjection to harassment on account of them. Some of the regulations are:[5]

- The premises of an eating house or a baking unit shall be completely fly-proof, preferably with double doors, with the outer door opening outwards and fitted with springs to ensure their self closing. The baking units are also required to make the premises rodent and bird proof, whereas the eating houses are not stipulated for the same! No pets shall be allowed in the baking unit at any time.
- Adequate number of hand basins made of porcelain/stainless steel shall be provided along with soap and a nailbrush for thorough cleansing of hands. Clean and dry towels shall be kept for the use of customers.
- A refuse bin of an adequate size with a pedal operated cover shall be provided in the premises for collection of waste material. This shall be emptied, and washed daily with a disinfectant.
- No personal belongings like clothing, bedding, shoes etc., shall be kept in the premises.
- No food shall be served to the customers outside the premises, nor on leaves and paper except white unprinted paper plates.
- There will be no smoke nuisance in the kitchen.
- Chipped enamelled containers will not be used. Stainless steel/aluminium containers e.g. mugs, jugs, trays, etc., shall preferably be used.
- The floor area of a barber's shop shall be a minimum of six square meters for one chair, and two square metres for every additional chair. Sufficient number of fans shall be provided to keep the premises cool and comfortable. Furniture shall be clean, comfortable and free from bed bugs and vermin.

---

5. Health Trade License, Technical Conditions. Section 417. Delhi Municipal Corporation Act, 1957.

- All workers at the barber's shop shall wear clean overalls and headgear while at work.
- All implements in the barber's shop shall be kept clean and sharp. Razors, scissors and clippers shall be kept in 22 per cent Cresol, Dettol, or Chlorosol lotion when not in use during working hours. Before use they shall be washed with clean water. The rest of the time they shall be kept clean and protected with Vaseline. Combs shall be kept clean and dry. Shaving brushes, after each shave, shall be washed in 1 per cent soda solution and then washed in water. Razors shall be wiped with a clean towel every time.
- Customers suffering from communicable skin diseases shall not be entertained at a barber's shop.
- The food stuff for sale at a *kirana* shop shall be kept in suitable containers duly provided with proper cover. The same shall be kept on a wooden trestle with minimum height of nine inch and dry fruits should be kept for sale in glass jars or show cases.

Some of these conditions might well offer you mirth (see Appendix-C). How the officials actually check for all these conditions is still a mystery to us. Being well aware of how quixotic some of these conditions are, the officials maintain a smart balance between their 'duties' and ground realities by accepting bribes.

Once the Health Inspector inspects the site, verifies the documents, the hygiene and sanitation conditions, the Deputy Health Officer gives his report. If the report is satisfactory, a license is issued to the candidate. Incidentally, the Health Department does not issue licenses for meat shops. The Veterinary Department of MCD is responsible for that.

Running the Shop

Renewal of the MCD Trade License

The story does not end at acquiring the license. This license, once acquired, has to be renewed annually. The date of validity of the license is 31st March of each year and the application for renewal can be submitted till 30th April of that year.

For renewal, an application has to be submitted at the CSB along with the original license and the renewal fee. The documents to be submitted are:[6]

- Original License copy
- Any other documents, if asked for

No late fee is to be paid if license is renewed between 1st March and 30th April. If it is renewed after 30th April, then late fee is charged @ 20 per cent per month. And if renewed after one year, late fee is charged @ actual fee for each year or part thereof.

In case of eating-houses, the food handlers have to undergo a medical check-up at the time of renewal.

Penalties

Shops running without an MCD license are *challaned* by the Inspectors. The *challan* slip mentions the date on which the shopkeeper has to appear at the Municipal Magistrate's office, where the amount of the fine is decided on a case by case basis (the amount of the challan may vary from Rs. 100-10,000). Some of the violations as per the Act and the fines imposed thereon are mentioned in Table 1.[7]

A mannequin outside a clothes store or a table with some articles for sale outside a shop is a common sight in a market. This encroachment by shops beyond their space limit is illegal. In fact, this is one of the most common violations that the shops are penalised for by the MCD.

Therefore, the shopkeepers feel it is fine to not obtain a license as they would be fined for something or the other whether they have a license or not. In fact many shopkeepers who have licenses never get them renewed as they feel it is a waste! It is more cost effective to operate without one as innumerable delays and bribes can then be avoided. Hence, they incur the cost of bribing the inspectors during the time of checking.

Over 70 per cent shops in Delhi do not have a Trade License, as per guesstimates made by the inspectors in informal talks. Survey results endorsed that these guesstimates might be close to the truth.

---

6. Sourced from Municipal Corporation of Delhi Trade License (General) [official website]. Accessed online 25 February 2004 at http://www.mcdonline.gov.in/mcd/tradefaq.jsp.

7. Twelfth Schedule. Delhi Municipal Corporation Act, 1957.

Table 1

Section	*Subject*	*Fine or imprisonment*	*Daily fine which may be imposed*
321	Deposit, etc. of things in streets	Simple imprisonment for six months or fine upto Rs. 5000 or both	10
382	Selling or making of food, etc. or washing of clothes by an infected person	50	-
406 (1)	Sale in municipal markets without permission	200	-
407 (1 & 2)	Use of places as private markets without a license	500	25
417	Certain things not to be kept and certain trades and operations not to be carried on without a license	1000	100
421	Keeping eating house, tea shop, lodging house without a license or contrary to license	100	-
430 (5)	Failure to produce license or written permission	50	5

Master Plan of Delhi (MPD)

The Master Plan demarcates nine categories of land uses namely Commercial, Residential, Manufacturing, Recreational, Transportation, Utility, Government, Public and Semi-Public and Agriculture and Water Body. Commercial use of the premises in a residential area is not allowed under law except under mixed land use provisions specified in the Master Plan. But over the years, despite the laws residential areas have been put to commercial uses extensively throughout Delhi. The number of shops in residential areas in Delhi is estimated to be around four lakh.[8] One of the reasons for this massive violation could be attributed to the fact that DDA has not developed even the commercial areas that had been envisaged in the Master Plan (see Table 2).

8. It's illegal shops now in DDA residential areas. [article online]. Accessed on 30 March 2004 at http://www.calonline.com/news/Jan01/11/del1.html.

Table 2

Commercial Centre	*Target in the MPD*	*Developed*	*Work-in-progress*
District Centre	29	7	3
Community Centre	124	27	7
Local Shopping Centre	-	125	6
Convenience Shopping Centre	-	429	6

Source: MPD-2001 and DDA Annual Report 2003

MCD is legally bound to issue licenses to trade and industries in accordance with the provisions of this Plan. Violation of the Master Plan is a legal offence. If a shop is situated in an area not meant for commercial use, the shop would be illegal irrespective of the fact that it may be following all the other rules and regulations. As a result, businesses that are easy to start up and require little capital are mired in the restrictions that also limit the ability of small businesses to expand and force them to stay out of the legal framework.

Zoning imposes additional restrictions on the same. DDA oversees zoning restrictions, ensuring that all activities are undertaken in compliance with the zoning requirements as laid down in the Master Plan of Delhi. Mixed land use has been allowed subject to certain conditions. It is specified that commercial activity in residential areas is permitted only if the resident of the unit runs the establishment. In addition, certain activities are prohibited in residential premises like repair shops, retail shops, selling coal, firewood, timber, etc. Strictly earmarking the use of land in areas and then creating exceptions by way of piecemeal changes in the land use regulations results in gains being reaped by a few powerful lobbies. The needs of the people vary from area to area. A shop selling groceries may be a nuisance in a posh residential area, but some kind of commercial activity may be welcome in some other area/neighbourhood. In such cases, zoning restrictions have a negative effect.

Registration Under Delhi Sales Tax Act

Every dealer selling taxable goods whose turnover exceeds the prescribed taxable quantum (Rs. five lakh) at any point of time during the financial year is liable to be registered. Besides, every dealer who is liable to get registration under the Central Sales Tax Act shall also be liable to be registered under the Delhi Act.

Registration Procedure

Application

The Registration Application has a prescribed form, which has to be filed before the Sales Tax Office (STO) of the concerned Ward (Delhi has been divided into 106 wards by the Sales Tax Department).

- Registration may be applied in form No ST-5 if the dealer has only one place of business.
- The application should bear a court fee stamp of Rs. 25 on application.
- A copy of the latest rent receipt as proof of legal possession of the business premises is also required to be filed along with.
- The application is to be signed by the proprietor.
- The verification at the bottom of the application is to be signed by the proprietor.
- A list of items required by the business is also to be given in relevant columns of the application form.

List of Documents Required[9]

1. First purchase Bill.
2. First inter-State Sale Bill.
3. Copy of Draft/Cheque received as sale-price of the goods despatched/sold.
4. Copy of Goods Receipt/Railway Receipt under which goods despatched for sale outside Delhi.
5. Bank statement for the above.
6. Rent receipt up-to-date, if business premises are taken on rent, else proof of ownership.
7. Ration Card/Passport/Election Card.
8. Items required for resale/manufacturing/packing.

9. Sourced from Delhi Sales Tax. [official website]. Accessed on 25 February 2004 at http://www.delhisalestax.com/taxpayer_advocate/registration_procedure.htm.

9. Income Tax/Wealth Tax Order, if any.
10. Sale Deed/House Tax Receipt.
11. Photo, two each of all partners and surety dealer.
12. Affidavit regarding:
    a) Amount and source of investment.
    b) No proceeding pending relating to past liability.
    c) Details of immovable property, if any.
    d) Sales and Purchase up-to-date.
    e) Past Activities.
    f) Details of firm/person who introduced during opening of bank account.
13. As per amendment, w.e.f. 1997, surety is not required to be filed till the dealer does not require statutory form for his purchases.
14. Surety/Bank Guarantee as prescribed by ward officer.
15. In addition to above:
    a) In the case of partnership
        (1) Partnership Deed.
    b) In the case of private/limited company
        (1) Memorandum and Article of Association.
        (2) Certificate of Incorporation.
        (3) Resolution authorising one person to deal with the Sales Tax Authorities.

Before a Sales Tax Registration Certificate is issued, a Sales Tax Inspector (STI) visits the business premises of the dealer to verify facts.

Steps through which the application passes:

- Once the application is submitted, it reaches the Sales Tax Officer (STO) of the concerned ward.
- The STO then marks the application to the STI in the ward for physical verification of the details mentioned in the form.
- The STI is officially given a period of 7 days in which to visit the site of business and verify the facts. Often the STI needs incentives to make the visit.

- Once the STI inspects the site and is satisfied/dissatisfied about the authenticity of the claims of the dealer, he submits a report to the STO.
- If the report is positive, the STO grants approval for the Registration Certificate (RC) to the dealer.
- The RC, can be collected from the Computer Cell.

As per information given by a taxation consultant outside the ST office, the file has to be pushed to the next stage. Usually the 'rates' vary depending on various factors. For instance, a shopkeeper may have to pay around Rs. 1,000-3,000 to the STI, another Rs. 2,000-4,000 to the STO and may have to spare Rs. 500 for even the typist who types out the RC! Besides, the peon would need his *kharcha-paani* while he shuffles the file from room to room. Thus, one ends up paying around Rs. 3,600-7,600 to obtain an RC.

Time Limit for Registration

The registration must be applied for within 30 days from the date of the dealer becoming liable to pay tax. The entire process should officially take 15-20 days.

Common grounds on which the applications are rejected:

- Books of accounts not being maintained properly. The books that the STIs check are the ledger, cash book, bank statement, day book, etc.
- In some of the cases, the trade/business mentioned in the application is not actually being carried out on the site. There are a few cases where more than one firm is operating from the same premises and thus, the demarcation of space for each firm's operation becomes difficult for the STIs.
- In most cases, the business site is a disputed property and the traders either cannot furnish an NOC from the landlord or give a false one.
- In some cases the traders do not meet the liability limit.

It was noticed, during the survey, that informal systems have been worked out between the shopkeepers and the various government officials that come for inspections. One market trader's association head elaborated on how it worked for the Sales Tax Department officials. Usually, the officials come for inspections once in a year.

Instead of inspecting all the shops situated in the market, they conduct dummy checks on some and as per their agreement with the market *pradhan*, they withdraw from the market. Then the market *pradhan*'s boys move in and go from shop to shop collecting money. At the Munirka Market, where the survey was conducted, each shopkeeper has to pay Rs. 200 per annum. Imagine the amount the officials make at that rate from over 2000 shops in that market. As usual, the shopkeepers pay money to avoid penalisation for some or the other clause they are violating. Interestingly, these payments are termed 'weakness taxes' by the *pradhan*.

Delhi Shops and Establishments Act

This Act is applicable to all shops and establishments in the entire National Capital Territory of Delhi. Labour and Labour Welfare Department of the Delhi government is responsible for enforcement of this Act. The Act is enforced through the Chief Inspector of Shops (CIS) and various inspectors under the Act, who are posted in nine districts of the capital. All the shops have to get registered with the Department. Registration was mandatory under the Act prior to 1989 since when the same has been kept in abeyance. Even though registration under the Act has been made optional since 1989, the provisions of the Act still apply to all shops.

Provisions under the Act[10]

Opening and closing hours for shops: No shop can be opened earlier than or closed later than the timings fixed by the Act or by general or special order issued by the government in this behalf.

Rest and close days: Every shop has to remain closed for one day in a week, and the Labour and Labour Welfare Department decides the weekly closure day for all the markets in Delhi. Certain shops have been ordered to remain closed on other specified days of the week. For instance, all barber shops have to close on Tuesdays, all the coal retail dealers licensed by the Delhi administration and all flour mills have to observe Monday as their weekly off day. The leather merchants of Karol Bagh have to observe Sunday as the weekly off day. All cotton waste and paint merchants of Subzi Mandi have to close on Sunday.[11]

---

10. Delhi Shops and Establishments Act & Rules, 1954.
11. Appendix 5-I. Delhi Shops and Establishments Act & Rules, 1954.

Legal obligation for keeping the premises clean: The premises of every establishment shall be kept clean and free from effluvia arising from any drain or privy or other nuisance and shall be cleaned at such time and by such methods prescribed under Rule 11 of the Act (Appendix).

Working hours for employees of shops or establishments: It should not exceed nine hours on any day or 48 hours in any week.

Period or interval for rest and meals: No period of continuous work should exceed five hours, which is to be followed by an interval for rest and meals of at least half an hour for an adult person. The employer fixes the time for such intervals and must intimate the Chief Inspector a week before such fixation and it should remain operative for a period of at least three months.

Hours of work of young persons employed: Young persons[12] employed in the shops shall not be made to work for more than six hours a day. They are not to be employed continuously for more than 3½ hours without an interval of at least half an hour.

Records and registers to be maintained: The occupier of every shop shall, in the prescribed form and manner, keep a record of the employees' particulars, work-hours, leaves taken, intervals for rest and meals and overtime paid.

Issuance of appointment letters: The employer shall furnish every employee with a letter of appointment which shall contain particulars such as name of the employer; name and address of the establishment; name, father's name, and age of the employee; hours of work and date of appointment.

Time and conditions for payment of wages to employees: Every employer or his agent or the manager of any establishment shall fix periods of wages payable to the employees, which shall not exceed one month. Wages must be paid before the expiry of the seventh day from the last day of the wage period.

Different types of leave available to an employee: Every person employed in an establishment shall be entitled to 15 days of privilege leave for one year of service, which can be accumulated to 45 days and 12 days of sickness or casual leave in a year.

---

12. Section 2 (34). Delhi Shops and Establishments Act & Rules, 1954, 'young person' means a person who is not a child (younger than twelve years) and has not completed his eighteenth year of age.

Restriction on working hours of women/young person: No woman or a young person can be required to work, whether as an employee or otherwise in any establishment between 9 P.M. to 7 A.M. during summer season and between 8 P.M. to 8 A.M. during winter season.

Employment of children: Children of 12 years and below are prohibited to work in shops.

Inspections

The inspectors are supposed to examine the premises, records, registers and notices to ensure that all the provisions of the Act and Rules are being properly observed. If the shop is found to be violating some provisions of the Act and Rules, a *challan* is issued which needs to be settled in court.

Most of the inspections are done to check the shop timings and payment of minimum wages. Other stipulations are rarely checked. But it is very easy for shopkeepers to ignore all rules and regulations or break them because the fine can only go upto Rs. 250. As far as timings are concerned, some shops like the ones in the residential areas are given exemptions and hence can remain open for longer periods. Also, the timings are relaxed during festival seasons.

Inspections are often random or on the basis of complaints. There are 72 sanctioned posts for inspectors in the department of which only 42 are filled and 30 lie vacant. It is naïve to even expect that these 42 inspectors would be able to ensure that all the provisions of the Act are enforced on all shops in Delhi, and needless to comment on the effectiveness of these laws in ensuring labour welfare.

The market is a witness to how redundant these laws are as far as timings and rest hours are concerned. Also, these laws are hardly a relief for the labour. The best solution would be to allow more commercial activity to flourish by withdrawing needless restrictions. This would entail greater employment generation than any of the other government efforts. The stimulation of market demand for labour will mean increased bargaining power for the labour, which will ensure better working conditions and higher wages for them.

Regulations regarding Extension of Trade into Night

There are three agencies involved in determining and monitoring the closing hours of shops and commercial establishments — Delhi

Police, MCD, Labour and Labour Welfare Department. The rules laid down by each of these are often in contradiction with each other. Recently the rules have been relaxed concerning shop business at night but confusion still prevails on the ground.

Delhi Police

The Delhi Police Act empowers the Commissioner with the ability to control working hours of an eating house.[13]

Laws regarding closing time: The officials were quite vague about the timings despite the fact that they receive circulars from the Police Headquarters. The Licensing Inspectors of Licensing Branch, Delhi Police, are supposed to make sure that the restaurants, *paan* shops and *dhabas* close at the stipulated time. They can ask the district police to inspect and ensure that the outlets close on time. The officials interviewed said they already have too much work on their hands to bother about these inspections. Generally, they carry out inspections only if there is a complaint. The closing timings as told by an official in the Department are given in the following table:

Type of public place	*Closing Time**
Restaurants	11 pm
Paan shops and *dhabas*	11 pm

*: Grace period of half-hour in case of restaurants to serve the last customer. Timings in summer and winter differ by half-hour.

Source: Deputy Commissioner of Police (DCP), Delhi Police

Penalty: In case eating houses without bars are found operating beyond the stipulated time, the inspector can impose a challan, which is then submitted in the court of the Metropolitan Magistrate. The amount of fine imposed is at the discretion of the Magistrate.

Rationale behind the Laws: The Police regulates the closing hours of eating houses because these are places where people get together. This raises the issue of public security. They govern the activities to keep a check on the crime rate. The same holds true for *paan* shops and *dhabas*.

MCD

The Trade Licenses granted by the MCD also mention the permissible working hours:

---

13. Section 28, Delhi Police Act, 1978.

Type of license obtained by shop	*Closing Time*
Commercial Trade License	7 pm
Ad-hoc Registration	6 pm

Source: Office of the Municipal Corporation of Delhi.

Labour & Labour Welfare Department

Section 15, Rule 7A prescribes the working hours for various establishments, as given in the Table:

Nature of Establishment	*Closing Hour*	*Opening Hour*
Shops (during summers)	7:30pm	9:30am
Shops (during winters)	7pm	9am
Commercial Establishment	6pm	8am

Some commercial establishments are exempted from closing hour rules. Barbers, hair dressers, *halwais*, retail shops dealing in meat, fish, poultry, milk and milk products, ice cream, cooked food, flowers, tobacco products, beverages, fruits and vegetables, medicines and newspapers are all exempted from the time stipulations. For the entire list, refer to the Appendix.

Legislation of Laws: From time to time, various changes are made in different clauses of the Act but there has been no change in Section 15 of the Act. There are times when the government passes a special order and asks all shopping areas to stop working after a certain time on security grounds. For instance, when BJP was in power in 1998, it had stipulated that shops should close at 7 P.M. However, this happens if there is a marked increase in incidents of crime, or in the case of a terrorist threat.

Enforcement of Laws: According to Delhi Shops and Establishments Rules, the Chief Inspector and other inspectors under him have to inspect that the provisions of the Act relating to the opening and closing hours are duly observed.

Penalty: If any shop violates the clause of closing time of the shop, the inspector can impose a *challan*. The *challan* is then submitted in the court of the Metropolitan Magistrate. The amount of *challan* varies from a minimum of Rs. 50 to a maximum of Rs. 250. The amount cannot exceed Rs. 250. The amount of fine to be levied is at the discretion of the Magistrate.

Rationale Behind the Laws: Various clauses under the Delhi Shops and Establishments Act have been formulated keeping labour welfare in mind. The argument being that there is excess supply of labour relative to demand and it gives the employers an incentive to exploit the workers. For instance, the employers keep their shops open for 12 hours or more but employ only one shift of labour. And that most of the time the employers do not pay over-time wages to the workers. The closing time of shops is regulated to ensure that employees do not work over-time, and reach home in time to be with their family.

Imagine the scenario if all the three agencies diligently set out to implement their rules. It would be total chaos for the shopkeepers. They wouldn't know whose rules to follow. Are regulations like these needed if shopkeepers are able to make profit by opening the shops till late? The shopkeepers would open their shops only if they get customers beyond the stipulated timings. Therefore, this regulation becomes a failure where consumers wish to shop over extended hours. As for security, does the presence of more people in markets lead to a higher crime rate? Or are these rules created for the officials to harass the shopkeepers?

Situation on Ground in case of enforcing Closing Timings

Labour Department

Inspectors from the Labour Commissioner's office are supposed to go on inspections on a regular basis. However, that does not happen. The inspector's staff is inadequate to cover all the shops in Delhi. The official strength of inspectors is 72. However, an official said that normally only 38-40 inspectors are on duty at a time. So, the inspectors usually check out specific shops only when there is a complaint.

MCD

MCD Licensing Inspectors are supposed to check whether the shops are closing on time. However, one of the inspectors interviewed gave a very interesting explanation. According to him, there is no reason for them to go for inspection because their working hours end at 5:30 pm. They have no incentive to go out and check the shops after that.

Delhi Police

Most restaurant owners listen to what the local police ask them to do. But the district police remain adequately vague about the actual laws which give them room to fool the owners and extort money.

Random surveys of markets in different parts of Delhi were conducted in order to learn the other side of the story. These showed interesting patterns.

In the Safdarjang Development Area (SDA) Market, quite a few shops stay open till 10 pm. The shopkeepers prefer closing the shops late because there are more customers during evenings, especially in summers. So, they make money by keeping their shops open for longer periods of time. Thus, in a small market like this, shopkeepers are violating the regulations and are functioning according to the market demand. To do this, they either bribe various inspectors to allow them to operate according to their will or become indifferent to the inspectors and pay challans whenever they are caught.

Green Park Market normally remains open till after 9 pm. Interviews with different shop owners revealed that the inspectors make Rs. 15,000-25,000 per month in the form of bribe from the market for not issuing *challans*. Another interesting fact that emerged is that small shopkeepers generally are not cognisant of all the rules and regulations. They do what others do. They do not know under which Act's jurisdiction their shops fall. Some are even under the impression that the president of the Market Association decides the closing time.

Shops in Connaught Place Market are supposed to stay closed on Sundays. Since there are many eating houses and discotheques in the area, it would definitely benefit if the shops remained open on Sundays. The Traders' Association president said that the shops lose approximately four days worth of revenue a week by remaining closed on Sundays. Though, in respect of time regulations, this market is relatively more disciplined - it closes by 8 pm. Hence, they lose revenue once again.

In all cases the market forces determine the closing time. Whether it is an eating house or a shop, the shopkeeper closes the outlet at a time that suits him. His closing time is determined by the demand for the services, by his turnover and by the amount of time he wants to spend with his family. It is not surprising that markets in and around residential areas stay open till late. They generally close around 9-9:30 pm. In other words, regulation has no role to play in reality - those who close their outlets early do so because it suits them. Those who keep their outlets open beyond the legal time do it because it is profitable for them.

Directorate of Prevention of Food Adulteration

The Directorate of Prevention of Food Adulteration is responsible for checking adulteration/misbranding of food articles as per the Prevention of Food Adulteration Rules, 2002.

Prohibitions and Restrictions: There are a number of prohibitions and restrictions imposed by the Directorate. The list is exhaustive but a few relevant ones are:

Prohibition on the Manufacture, Sale, etc. of Certain Food Articles: No person shall manufacture, store, sell or distribute

(i) any adulterated food,

(ii) any misbranded food,

(iii) food articles to be sold under license without fulfilling the conditions of the licence,

(iv) any food article the sale of which is prohibited by the Food (Health) Authority in the interest of public health,

(v) any food article in contravention of any other provision of the Act or the Rules, (see 'Conditions for Sale') or

(vi) any adulterant.

The act of storing an adulterated article of food would be an offence only if storing is for sale. The sale of a part of the stored article constitutes an offence distinct and independent from the offence of storing for sale.

Prohibition on Use of Certain Expressions While Labelling of Edible Oils and Fats: The package, label or the advertisement of edible oils and fats shall not use the expressions Super-Refined, Extra-Refined, Micro-Refined, Double-Refined, Ultra-Refined, Anti-Cholesterol, Cholesterol Fighter, Soothing to Heart, Cholesterol Friendly, Saturated Fat Free or such other expressions which are exaggerations of the quality of the product.[14]

---

14. Rule 37 (D). Prevention of Food Adulteration Rules, 2002.

Prohibition on Sale of Certain Admixtures: For example, cream which has not been prepared exclusively from milk, milk which contains added water, ghee which contains any added matter not exclusively derived from milk fat, a mixture of two or more edible oils as an edible oil, and turmeric containing any foreign substances, etc.[15]

Restriction on Sale of Ghee having less than specified Reichert value except under the "AGMARK" seal.[16]

Prohibition on Sale of Admixtures of Ghee or Butter or on its use as an ingredient in the preparation of an article of food. Any food item resembling honey, but not pure honey, shall not be marked "honey".[17]

Restriction on Sale of Common Salt: No person shall sell or offer or expose for sale or have in his premises for the purpose of sale common salt for direct human consumption unless the same is iodised.[18]

Restriction on Use and Sale of Artificial Sweeteners except that saccharin sodium can be added to carbonated water, *supari*, *paan* masala and *paan* flavouring material within the specified maximum limit and aspartame may be sold for diabetic use under medical advice.[19]

Conditions for Sale of a Food Article: Every utensil or container, used for manufacturing, preparing or containing any food or ingredients, and second hand tin containers for packaging of edible oils and fats meant for sale, shall be maintained in a clean and sanitary condition, away from impure air or dust, properly covered at all times, and such utensils or containers shall not be used for any other purpose. Use of rusty containers, improperly tinned copper or brass containers, containers of aluminium or plastic not conforming to ISI specifications, etc., in preparation of food, is also prohibited. Besides, certain special conditions for sale of certain articles such as asafoetida, salseed fat, lactic acid, edible oils, katha, margarine, milk powder have also been laid down.

No person shall sell powdered spices except in packed form. No person shall sell or serve food in any commercial establishment in plastic articles used in catering and cutlery, unless the plastic material conforms to the food grade plastic.

---

15. Rule 44. Prevention of Food Adulteration Rules, 2002.
16. Rule 46. Prevention of Food Adulteration Rules, 2002.
17. Rule 46 & 45. Prevention of Food Adulteration Rules, 2002.
18. Rule 44 (h). Prevention of Food Adulteration Rules, 2002.
19. Rule 47. Prevention of Food Adulteration Rules, 2002.

Enforcement: Food Inspectors have been posted in 27 sub divisions with the direction to collect samples for analysis in the presence and under supervision of Local (Health) Authorities (LHA) of that sub division. Three Divisional Local (Health) Authorities coordinate the fieldwork in districts allocated to them. In such cases where adulteration/misbranding is noticed, prosecution is instituted in the court of the Metropolitan Magistrate.

The Directorate of Prosecution of Delhi government appoints the prosecutors of the PFA Department. Once appointed, they become a part of the department and their salaries are paid by the PFA Department. In addition to the Departmental Local Health Authorities (LHAs), the Lieutenant Governor of NCT of Delhi, in August 1998, appointed 27 Sub-Divisional Magistrates (SDMs) of government of NCT of Delhi as LHA for the purpose of PFA Act.

Implementation of the Act: Various steps involved in inspection and follow-up action are:

The food inspectors under the supervision of the SDM go to the field and collect samples at random and also on complaints from various food article outlets. The food inspector gives a notice in writing to the seller, of his intentions to have the sample analysed, and takes his signature on the form. Every sample is divided into three counterparts and each counterpart is properly sealed, marked and fastened as per law and bears the slip of the LHA/SDM bearing his signature and code number. One counterpart of the sample is sent for analysis to the public analyst by the next working day. The public analyst sends a report of analysis within 40 days from the receipt of the sample to the concerned local authority.

If the sample is found genuine and LHA is satisfied with the report of the public analyst, intimation is sent to the person from where the sample was lifted. If the LHA is dissatisfied with the report, he may send the second counterpart of the sample to another public analyst. If the sample is found adulterated, then the LHA asks the food inspectors to investigate the case.

On completion of the investigation, the Local (Health) Authority asks for the grant of consent from the Director for initiating the prosecution. On receipt of consent, the LHA institutes the criminal proceedings against the vendor house and intimation is sent to the concerned vendor who may approach the court within a period of 10 days for sending the other counterpart to the central food laboratory. The court takes further action in this regard.

Observations: Lack of awareness among consumers:

Section 12 of the Act states that any purchaser of food (that is the common consumer) can also send across a sample of food, which he thinks is adulterated, for analysis and consequently take recourse to law for prosecution of the guilty. However, this is only in name — the sampling procedures to be followed are so technical and elaborate that the very purpose of granting powers to the consumers is defeated. A random selection of 32 consumers from different areas of Delhi brought the following responses when quizzed about the step they would take if the food they purchase turns out to be adulterated:

Response	*Number*
Will report to a consumer grievance forum	15
Will report to the police	06
Will tell food inspectors	04
No response/no idea	07

Source: Gaurav, Kumar and Singhal, Mayank. 2003. "Delhi's Food: How Safe?" Accessed online at www.ccsindia.org/informs2003/chap3.pdf on 23 February 2004.

Even the four who said they would report the matter to the Food Inspectors had no idea about the procedures to be followed. Thus, it is evident that there is complete lack of information among consumers when it comes to reporting food adulteration.

The average number of samples collected is around 800 per year, insufficient for Delhi, considering there are almost 1.5 lakh registered food establishments in Delhi (based on Sales Tax Department report 1998-99). A figure of 800 is undoubtedly too small to ensure food safety in Delhi.

Weights and Measures

Every weighing and measuring[20] apparatus in shops or other establishments in Delhi is required to be certified annually. The W&M Directorate aims at ensuring that the consumers are not given less than what they have paid for, and that traders don't use inaccurate

20. The terms "Weights & Measures" generally mean an object/instrument/apparatus or device which is used for the purpose of weighing or measuring while selling any goods or service to a consumer.

weighing or measuring equipment. The Delhi Weights and Measures Directorate conducts its functions through nine zonal offices. The Directorate also issues license to the manufacturers, repairers and dealers of weights and measures. Various acts and rules enacted by the government are:

- The Standards of Weights & Measures Act, 1976.
- The Standards of Weights & Measures (Packaged Commodities) Rules, 1977.
- The Standards of Weights & Measures (Enforcement) Act, 1985.
- The Standards of Weights & Measures (General) Rules, 1987.
- The Delhi Standards of Weights & Measures (Enforcement) Rules, 1988.

To prevent over-charging of the consumers by traders on the pretext of local taxes, the previous system of declaring the 'sale price excluding taxes' have been dispensed with. Now the sale price of the package has to be declared in the form 'MRP' - inclusive of all taxes. Charging a price higher than the MRP declared on the package is prohibited under the rules. Penal provisions have been made under the rules for any violation in this regard. Similarly, affixing of 'price stickers' on the package is also prohibited in the interest of the consumer.

Certifications

The weighing and measuring apparatus in shops or other establishments is certified annually. There are two kinds of certification that are issued:

On-site Certification: Zonal officers are supposed to go to the concerned site, inspect and stamp the weighing and measuring apparatus involved. On-site inspection is done for two kinds of weights and measures: petrol pumps and weighbridges. In case of petrol pumps, inspectors are to check the dispensing units. An error margin of 15ml. is given, as petroleum products tend to evaporate.

The stamp consists of tying a lead piece with two wires and then tying this to the four ends of the assembly of the unit. The lead piece has the concerned zonal officer's number and an alphabet signifying the quarter in which it was certified. This kind of stamp, as is apparent, can also be self-made.

Off-site Certification: This involves engaging the services of a repairer and booking the weights with him. The repairer then examines the weights and repairs them, if necessary, and takes the weights to the zonal office and gets them certified for a fee as determined by the zonal office. For cast-iron weights, the stamp consists of a lead piece that contains the zonal officer's number and the alphabet signifying the quarter in which it was certified. The rest of the weighing apparatuses are issued a Verification Certificate.

All instruments of weights and measures are not to be verified/ checked every year. The electrical instruments are the only ones that need to be stamped annually, and the mechanical apparatus and steel metres are stamped every two years. After each verification, the visiting inspector issues a verification certificate that specifies the validity period and the date of verification. On violation of any rules or norms, the shopkeepers can be *challaned* upto a maximum of Rs. 5000 (for the first offence) and a maximum of five years of imprisonment for the second and subsequent offences. The time taken to resolve cases is normally three months for shops.

While on inspection, the inspectors check all the various apparatus used for weighing and measuring purposes. In addition, they are required to check the previously issued verification certificates before issuing a new one. The zonal offices have fixed 'lab' days on which the movable measuring instruments are brought in for correction and certification. As per rules, the verification certificates have to be prominently displayed in shops. If not adhered to, the inspector can impose a *challan*, which could be up to Rs. 2,000.

Any complaints regarding weights and measures including short measurement can be made to the inspector, Legal Metrology, in the area where the incident has occurred.

As told by the officials, maximum violations in Delhi has been found in packaging of Vanaspati Ghee. They were found to be short of delivery, i.e. the weight indicated on the package was often more than the actual content weight.

Inspection

Every zonal office has a staff of inspectors whose main function is to conduct quarterly checks on all shops, vendors, and jewellery stores and to see whether these businesses are using stamped weights. In case these businesses are found not to be using stamped weighing machines and cast iron weights, they are *challaned* a fine that is forwarded to a two-member special court situated in Karkardooma in the trans-Yamuna region.

Violations found by the Department:

- A famous weight loss clinic: Violations were found in the weighing machines, technically known as miscalibration, to the tune of five kilos off the normal.
- A prominent sweetmeat shop: The weighing machines are often tampered with. Even, while measuring individual orders, the weight of the box is also included in the total weight, which is illegal.

Synopsis of the Survey Results of Shops

We interviewed a few shopkeepers in the Lakshmi Nagar and Hauz Khas Main Market. Though the surveys were not comprehensive since the shopkeepers seemed apprehensive about divulging information, there were a few shopkeepers and market association chiefs who gave more details of the matter and also specified that the entire market functions in the same manner.

Lakshmi Nagar Market: It was found that a large number of shop owners have not bothered to obtain a license for their operation. According to them nobody comes for inspections. Some of the shopkeepers interviewed were not even aware that a license had to be obtained to operate a shop. One barber said that none of the barbers in the entire market would have the MCD Health Trade License and that they had never faced any problems either. In the words of another shopkeeper, "First, the inspectors do not come to check anything. And even if they do, we can handle them very easily with our resources."

Another interesting point was that some of them did not even have commercial electricity connection. According to them, the landlord takes care of everything.

The above situation prevails because first, the rules and regulations are so stringent that nobody can comply with them all, and second, the number of inspectors is well short of the requirement. There are a large number of shops in Delhi. Since inspections are not regular, shopkeepers get the leeway to operate without a license.

▲ *Certification for weight*

▲ *Stamp into the weight*

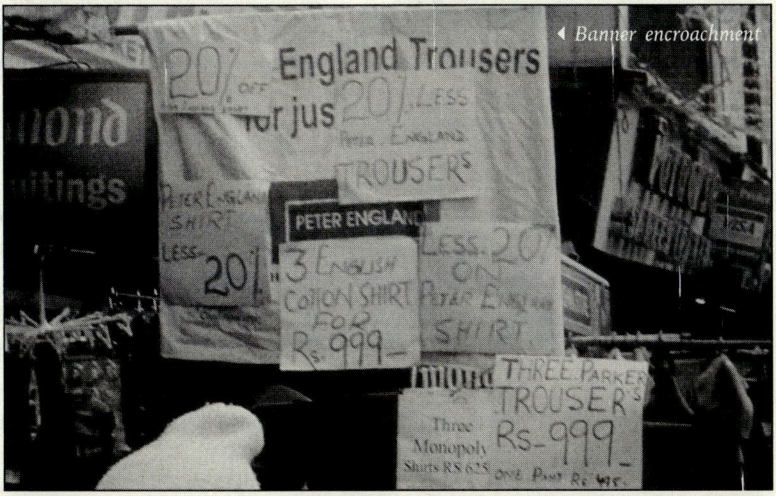

◂ *Banner encroachment*

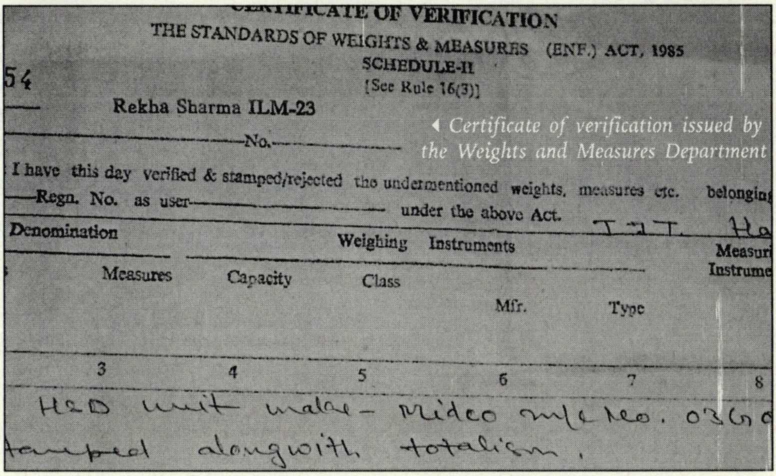

CERTIFICATE OF VERIFICATION
THE STANDARDS OF WEIGHTS & MEASURES (ENF.) ACT, 1985
SCHEDULE-II
[See Rule 16(3)]

54

Rekha Sharma ILM-23

————No.————

I have this day verified & stamped/rejected the undermentioned weights, measures etc. belonging
—Regn. No. as user———— under the above Act.

Denomination		Weighing Instruments			Measuring Instruments
Measures	Capacity	Class	Mfr.	Type	
3	4	5	6	7	8

H&D unit make – Midco m/c no. 0360
stamped alongwith totalism.

◂ *Certificate of verification issued by the Weights and Measures Department*

Encroachment on public space

On the other hand, in the *Hauz Khas Main Market* most shopkeepers were aware of the various licenses and other rules and regulations. Most shops here had the required licenses and various documents essential for running a shop. In fact, one shopowner said, "Inspectors give the required amount of time to fill all the required formalities. They nab the shopowner who fails to do so."

In the Munirka Market, we interviewed the head of the Market Traders' Association, who owned a shoe shop. Largely, the shops in this market are small and the clientele is mainly the middle class. According to the shopkeeper interviewed, there are over 2000 shops in the market. As far as he knew, he said, most shops in the market did not have the MCD Trade License and the visits by MCD inspectors were very rare. All the shops that were liable to pay sales tax were registered with the Sales Tax Department and were paying taxes. But since it is commonplace for the shopkeepers to be tampering with their accounts books, the sales tax inspectors have to be bribed whenever they make the checks. These inspectors usually make annual visits. Inspections made by officials from the other departments concerned with the shops are altogether too rare to bother the shopkeepers or stop them from violating the rules. When asked about the amount of money paid to the officials to hush up issues, they said it generally varied.

Most shops did not have an MCD Trade License and they had no plans to get one in the future since it was simpler to get one when needed by greasing several palms. Clearly, the cumbersome procedure leaves no easy avenues for private individuals to start a shop legally.

And the numerous restrictions on release of licences have not prevented the market forces from operating. Where the need is felt, shops have opened, with or without the requisite licenses. The 'informal arrangements' have helped both shopkeepers and officials go about their work without problems. In any case, inspections are rare and even when they do take place, the checks are random – more a formality than a duty.

During the research, many officials were interviewed, and their common complaints were:[21]

- Lack of adequate and efficient staff
- No formal job training. Everything had to be learnt by conferring with others or through sheer experience
- No orientation to the Acts and Rules to be implemented
- Improper documentation. No inspection proformas
- No guidelines on complaint handling. Lack of database on public complaints that could be analysed
- Frequent transfers. Inspectors are usually transferred from their posts within three years. So, by the time they get familiar with their jobs, they are transferred
- Transfers without merits
- Inefficient supervision

Conclusions

The municipal and state departments responsible for shop enterprise do not possess a market-oriented approach whereby entrepreneurship for shops can be encouraged to satisfy consumer demands or enable shop-owners to further their employment in a country which is high on self-employment (61 per cent) and short on employment. Shops represent one of the easiest entry professions for the poor and the middle-class who may not possess enough education, capital or skill-sets. Yet shop enterprise and its consequent benefits to the poor and unemployed have been undermined. The attitude of municipal and state departments has been one of control rather than encouragement. These controls manifest themselves through the

21. Public Grievances: Departmental Processes, Activities, Information Needs and Problem Areas. Tata Consultancy Services.

innumerable regulations that present unnecessary obstacles to entrepreneurship. We elaborate on the effect of these rules in the hope that the policy-makers take a renewed look at municipal licensing and the role of the departments of the State government for shop enterprise.

Licensing Restricts Entry

Licensing is not the most effective way of ensuring that businesses deliver what they promise. By increasing the entry costs to meet the qualifications of the licensed activity, licensing laws impose a restriction on the number, thereby stifling entrepreneurship. Some licensing laws require installation of costly health and safety equipment, some involve absurd provisions, while other limit entry into the activity. As a result, there are fewer practitioners and the cost of the service in question is higher. Because of weak enforcement machinery, some consumers resort to sub-standard alternatives and do-it-yourself methods—resulting in lower quality. Also, by imposing higher standards, the consumers are forced into buying high quality goods or services when a lower quality is required. Thus, unintentionally, consumers are worse off.

> An intern in our Centre (Centre for Civil Society) was assigned a research project with a one-line objective: what are the procedures required to be followed by a foreigner for opening a chocolate delicacies' shop in Delhi. She spent innumerable hours scouring through tedious documentation, visiting every possible office which may be relevant to it and meeting officials who could guide her on the objective. After two long months we found the information – there is none! She could not find out what the procedures are or in the least, any person who would know about them. Though, most of them did mention the sheer impossibility or deterrence (unofficially speaking) of a foreigner opening shop in Delhi due to the rules regarding land, loans and legality.

Focus on Compliance with Rules

The existing regulations focus on compliance with rules. These rules and regulations rarely address performance, quality, safety or public health in a direct way. The rules to be followed by the shops are long on inputs but low on performance criteria. Though these rules are formed with the stated purpose of protecting public health and welfare, the specifications and requirements carry little relationship to performance. Moreover, inspectors could cite shops for infractions of the rules even though the infraction may have little impact on the quality of service provided. The Kentucky Fried Chicken (KFC) restaurant in Delhi was given a closure order as the Health officials found two flies in the outlet's kitchen and a garbage can outside the premises.[22] Rules regulating barbers detailing largely irrelevant criterion for operation are another example. Often, a business that might otherwise easily provide a high quality product to a satisfied customer is potentially thwarted by the maze of local regulations that are not always market-compatible.

Micromanagement by the State

Issues that are best left to markets still thrive on the roster of rules regarding shops. Micromanagement by the state deciding the day of closure of a shop or the working hours for employees in shops is no longer in sync with the liberalisation path undertaken by the state. It is not to say that better enforcement of these rules will lead to intended results. On the contrary, they would only lead to increased costs of illegality, greater harassment at the hands of the authorities and further deterrence to shop enterprise.

Difficult Access to Enterprise Information and Multiplicity of Agencies

Bureaucratic permits and licensing have dominated the local regulatory framework: all the shopkeepers have to negotiate a lengthy application process. Access to "enterprise information" is difficult and has to be obtained from multiple sources. There are various agencies involved in regulating the shops in Delhi and specific regulations vary with business type. MCD broadly regulates all the shops. The DDA oversees land-use and zoning issues. The PFA as well as the MCD Health Department regulate eating houses. The labour issues in the shops and commercial establishments are governed by the Labour and Labour Welfare Department whereas the Weights and Measures Department oversees the accuracy of the weighing and measuring apparatus used in shops. Identifying the appropriate agencies for obtaining the various licences and clearances is a daunting task, particularly for those unfamiliar with the local regulatory framework. Apart from the diversity of agencies involved in regulating these

---

22. Delhi's Fried Chicken Blues [article online]. Accessed on 18 February 2004 at http://www.asiaweek.com/asiaweek/95/1124/nat2.html

shops, there is also at times a conflict in the rules framed by the different agencies for the same kind of establishments, as was the case for regulating the opening and closing timings for shops.

Complicated Procedures Hinder Entry for the Uneducated

Even for accomplishing and maintaining complete legality of the shops, the shopkeepers either have to master the subtle legalities regulating their specific business or have to go through the agents who get their work done for a price. By virtue of the complicated application process, established ones have an advantage over upstarts. Licensing and other requirements create significant obstacles to new entrepreneurs less familiar with the regulatory system, particularly those with less education and experience in running a business. Thus, the regulatory system complicates the process of starting a small shop and at the same time adds to the cost of starting the trade. The regulatory burden is usually borne by the low-income, less educated and low skilled applicants because of the time, resources and knowledge of the system required in order to legalise their business.

It is also a common complaint that the municipal policies with regard to licensing of shops are subject to frequent change but the information is not adequately disseminated among the people. Documentation available is inadequate. The innumerable circulars and notices that flow through the departments are not always incorporated into the rulebooks available to the public, thus, resulting in further ignorance and harassment.

Land-use Regulations Restrict Commercial Activities in Residential Areas

Zoning imposes additional restrictions. The DDA oversees zoning restrictions, ensuring that all activities are undertaken in compliance with the zoning requirements as laid down in the Master Plan of Delhi. These zoning regulations restrict the commercial activities in residential areas irrespective of the local needs of the people and the positive impacts from the business. Again, people violate these regulations which are then arbitrarily legalised later on under political pressure. The result is a disesteem for the laws. We shall expound further on the issue of zoning in the chapter on urban land management.

Government Regulations fail to Meet the Objectives

An important ground cited for government regulation of product quality and safety is that of consumer ignorance. Keeping in mind the interest of the general public, various standards have been detailed by the government, which need to be observed in order to obtain a license. The objective behind this is apparently to ensure that the shops are maintained in good and desirable conditions, so that the consumer gets value for the money he pays. However, in view of the prevalent market conditions, it is evident that despite their noble intentions, these regulations hardly meet their objective. The shopkeepers conveniently find a way around the lengthy and cumbersome application procedures through agents who negotiate a price for the violation of rules by both the parties.

But Regulation is Desirable...

Rules and regulations are often desirable as they provide regularity in the market place, reduce search costs for consumers, help them make informed decisions, reduce uncertainty, and help people protect themselves from dubious products. However, in our country, regulations almost always involve the government. Their laws and regulations greatly increase costs by preventing entry and raising entry costs (through lengthy and unnecessary application procedures), thus unintentionally debilitating economic growth and entrepreneurship. Small shops involving narrow profit margins, and less capital and other resources, are especially affected by these regulations.

Arguably, regulation is important for both the consumers and the firms. Consumers value the quality of goods and services, but this is difficult for them to measure. For instance, a customer at a restaurant can easily tell if the food tastes good, but it is virtually impossible for him to tell whether the food was prepared in hygienic conditions. The customers are willing to pay for the certification that the food is being prepared in sanitary and hygienic conditions. The shops would also find certification beneficial as they ensure potential customers that the firm does not compromise on quality. Since the parties benefiting from regulation are the shops and the consumers, the market should be providing it without government intervention. But with the government regulatory framework in place, there is little incentive for private regulatory agencies to develop. Moreover, when the government regulation is present, it gives the consumers a false sense of security. It leads them to assume that they are being protected by the government, reducing the incentive to do their own checking. Market regulation, in contrast, gives consumers a greater incentive to acquire information about the quality of the product. Consequently, they are likely to be more alert to potential problems of food safety.

Reforms

We propose regulatory reforms that rely on market incentives: a model of private regulation by any for-profit or not-for-profit agency. Private regulation is effective. Even though compliance with private regulation is voluntary, most firms perceive the compliance costs of private regulation as a necessity for survival rather than a burden. Moreover, the process consumes less time and resources and is more flexible. Following are the proposals in this regard:

Private Certification

The first step is to recognise that the government is not the only source of standards and rules. The alternative model of private regulation would work better. Private organisations could oversee regulation of the shops by certification, brand approval, and standard setting. There could be private regulatory agencies that would be setting the standards and the rules. These rules would be enforced through independent third parties, and all the shops that are currently regulated would be obtaining certification from these agencies. Competing independent parties would prepare updated performance standards based on scientific research, and provide effective monitoring and inspections. Some agencies may perform only inspections on the shops, or some may be setting standards. Such flexibility would create specialisation and would increase the effectiveness of regulation.

An example in this regard is that of USA-based Underwriters Laboratories (UL). It is a not-for-profit organisation that sets safety criteria for a wide variety of manufactured products, systems and components. Besides testing, certification, and quality assessment services, UL also develops national and international standards that are widely used by manufacturers, other certification and testing laboratories, and many government agencies.[23] Though similar to what government regulation attempt to do, the UL also keeps up with the market needs in its area of expertise and delivers results in a more effective and less costly manner. Each year, more than 19 billion UL Marks are applied to products world-wide. UL holds the reputation as the leader in US product safety and certification.

Competition in Standard Setting

The regulatory agencies face problems in identifying and collecting data, and that result in a time lag between policy implementation and achievement of results. A solution to this problem would be to allow regulatory agencies to compete with one another in standard setting. Competing independent parties prepare updated performance standards based on scientific research, and provide effective monitoring and inspections. They also tend to avoid costly and impractical procedures without lowering the quality of existing standards. Enabling competition would also create an incentive for development of more performance-based and result-oriented standards. In addition, competition between the agencies would require them to prove their independence from the firms that they regulate.

In the USA, Green Seal[24] is an independent, non-profit organisation that strives to achieve a healthier and cleaner environment by identifying and promoting products and services that cause less toxic pollution and waste, conserve resources and habitats, and minimise global warming and ozone depletion. It develops environmental standards for leadership products in specific categories and certifies products that meet them. Certified products carry labels that tell consumers about significant environmental attributes, like the amount of certain toxins used in manufacturing and recycling characteristic of a product.

Branding

Quality standards can also be established by way of branding. Consumers may be willing to pay a premium for a branded product.

---

23. Sourced from Underwriters Laboratories Inc. Accessed online on 19 February 2004 at http://www.ul.com/.

24. Sourced from Green Seal. Accessed online on 19 February 2004 at http://www.greenseal.org/about.htm.

Also, those consumers who are satisfied with a low quality product wouldn't have to pay for higher standards. This model will avoid "one-size-fits-all" approach and generate more consumer satisfaction. Since the retail shops are small and fragmented across the market, branding would mean that the brand owning companies might authorise the small retailing shops to sell their products, requiring the shops to maintain certain standards. Soap retailing is one example in this regard. Earlier, *naulakha* washing soap was mostly used which has now been replaced by the branded soap and detergent industry. It is also evident that the soaps are made for consumers from all income groups.

The Kosher food industry is another relevant example in this regard. The Hebrew word "Kosher" means fit or proper as it relates to Kosher dietary law.[25] During the 1970s, companies used a generic letter, K, to indicate that a certain product has passed the Kosher certification test. Today, not only does each independent agency have its own symbol, denoting the source of certification, but there are also industry-wide codes that classify Kosher products. In 1996, 8,100 companies produced 38,000 types of Kosher certified products. Around seven million consumers strictly looked for Kosher approval, and the total market share of Kosher certified products reached $3 billion.[26] Despite there not being health or safety rules, detailed inspections have turned the Kosher symbol into a sign of reliability and cleanliness for consumers.

A shift of emphasis from rules to performance is absolutely necessary. Complex application procedures, which have little impact on the quality of service provided, have to be done away with. As discussed earlier, they inevitably lead to a reduction in quality by restricting entry, thus making the consumers worse off. Also, these procedures create scope for agents to function and often applicants find an easy way out by bribing the officials. Most of the rules mentioned for obtaining a license are difficult or impractical to follow and only provide a ground for further harassment of the shop-owners by the inspectors.

---

25. Sourced from OU Kosher. Accessed online on 19 February 2004 at http://www.ou.org/KOSHER/primer.html.

26. Yilmaz, Yesim. 1998. "Private Regulation: A Real Alternative for Regulatory Reform". In *Self-Regulation in the Civil Society*, edited by Ashok V. Desai, 5-29. New Delhi: Centre for Civil Society.

Tort Law and Product Liability

Tort law is considered a favourable option as providing an incentive to produce safer products. Torts are civil wrongs recognised by law as grounds for a lawsuit. The primary aim of tort law is to provide relief for the damages incurred and deter others from committing the same harms. The injured person may sue for an injunction to prevent the continuation of the tort conduct or for monetary damages. Among the types of damages the injured party may recover are: loss of earnings capacity, pain and suffering, and reasonable medical expenses. They include both present and future expected losses.

Product liability is derived mainly from Tort law. Product liability refers to the liability of any or all parties along the chain of manufacture of any product for damage caused by that product. This includes the manufacturer of component parts (at the top of the chain), an assembling manufacturer, the wholesaler, and the retail store owner (at the bottom of the chain). Products containing inherent defects that cause harm to a consumer of the product are the subjects of product liability suits.

Product liability is generally considered a strict liability offense. Strict liability wrongs do not depend on the degree of carefulness by the defendant. Translated to product liability terms, a defendant is liable when it is shown that the product is defective. It is irrelevant whether the manufacturer or supplier exercised great care; if there is a defect in the product that causes harm, he or she will be liable for it.

Zoning Regulations

The issue of where a shop or enterprise can be opened and whether it constitutes a nuisance is best decided after subjecting it to common law processes rather than on a legislative basis. This issue has been further expounded in the chapter on urban land management.

Livelihood Freedom Test

The Livelihood Freedom Test is applied to all existing and new rules and regulations. Does any law restrict a person's chances to earn an honest living, particularly in case of businesses involving low capital or skills? If the answer is yes, then the approach is Review, Revise or Remove.

The key rule here is 'First, do not obstruct.' The license-permit raj still exists in most areas, characterised by its absurd rules and lengthy procedures. Also, in certain cases licenses are limited, so people trade without them. This leads to regular harassment and extortion by the officials and the police.

The same government which pours money into the *rozgar yojnas* and subsidy schemes prevents people from earning an honest living. Ironically enough, the money for these schemes comes from the poor since indirect taxes contribute more to the exchequer than the direct taxes. Instead, the government should first allow the poor to earn an honest living themselves.

Appendix A

List of Trades

The Eleventh Schedule (Section 417)

Part 1

Purposes for Which Premises May Not be Used Without a License

Carrying out any of the following trades or operations connected with trades—

1. Baking
2. Cinematograph films. Shooting of—
3. Cinematograph films by any process whatsoever. Treating of—
4. Chilies or masala or corn or seeds. Grinding of by mechanical means—
5. Cloth yarn or leather in indigo or in other colours. Dyeing or printing of—
6. Cloth or yarn. Bleaching—
7. Eating house or a catering establishment. Keeping of an—
8. Grain. Parching—
9. Ground-nut-seeds, tamarind seeds or any other seeds. Parching—
10. Hair dressing saloon or a barber's shop. Keeping of—
11. Hides or skins, whether raw or dried. Tanning, pressing or packing—
12. Laundry shop, Keeping a—
13. Leather goods. Manufacturing of by mechanical means—.
14. Litho press. Keeping a—
15. Lodging House. Keeping of a—
16. Metal Casting—
17. Precious metals, Refining of—or recovering of them from embroideries—
18. Printing Press. Keeping a—
19. Sweetmeat shop except in premises already licensed as an eating house. Keeping—
20. Carrying on the trade or business of or any operation connected with the trade of—
    - (i) Autocar or autocycle servicing or repairing.
    - (ii) Blacksmithy.
    - (iii) Coppersmithy.
    - (iv) Electroplating.
    - (v) Glass bevelling.

(vi) Glass cutting.

(vii) Glass polishing.

(viii) Goldsmithy.

(ix) Marble cutting, grinding, dressing or polishing.

(x) Metal (ferrous or non-ferrous or antimony but excluding precious metal) cutting or treating metal by hammering, drilling, pressing, filing, polishing, heating, or any other process whatever or assembling parts of metal.

(xi) Photography-studio

(xii) Radio (wireless receiving set) selling, repairing, servicing or manufacturing.

(xiii) Silversmithy.

(xiv) Spinning or weaving cotton, silk, art silk, or jute or wool with the aid of power.

(xv) Stone grinding, cutting dressing or polishing.

(xvi) Timber or wood sawing or cutting by mechanical or electric power.

(xvii) Tinsmithy.

(xviii) Washerman's trade.

(xix) Welding of metal by electric, gas or any process, whatsoever.

21. Manufacturing parching, packing, pressing, cleaning, cleansings, boiling, melting, grinding or preparing by any process whatever, any of the following articles-

(i) Aerated water.

(ii) Bakelite goods.

(iii) Bidis (indigenous cigarettes), snuff, cigars or cigarettes.

(iv) Bitumen.

(v) Blasting powder.

(vi) Bones.

(vii) Bricks or tiles by hand power.

(viii) Bricks or tiles by mechanical power.

(ix) Brushes.

(x) Candles.

(xi) Catgut.

(xii) Celluloid or celluloid goods.

(xiii) Cement concrete designs or models.

(xiv) Charcoal.

(xv) Chemicals.

(xvi) Cinematograph films stripping in connection with any trade.

(xvii) Cosmetics or toilet goods.

(xviii) Cotton, cotton refuse, cotton waste, cotton yarn, silk, silkyarn, silk inclusive of waste yarn, art silk waste, art silk yarn, wool or woolen refuse or waste.

(xix) Cotton seeds.

(xx) Dammar.

(xxi) Dynamite.

(xxii) Fat.

(xxiii) Fireworks.

(xxiv) Flax.

(xxv) Ink for printing, writing, stamping etc.

(xxvi) Gas.

(xxvii) Ghee.

(xxviii) Glass or glass articles.

(xxix) Gunpowder.

(xxx) Hemp.

(xxxi) Ice (including dry ice).

(xxxii) Insecticide or disinfectants.

(xxxiii) Leather cloth or rexine cloth or water proof cloth.

(xxiv) Lime.

(xxxv) Linseed oil.

(xxxvi) Matches for lighting (including Bengal Matches).

(xxxvii) Mattresses and pillows.

(xxxviii) Offal.

(xxxix) Oil-cloth.

(xl) Oil other than petroleum (either by mechanical power or by hand power or ghani driven by bullock or any other animal).

(xli) Pharmaceutical or medical products.

(xlii) Rubber or rubber goods.

(xliii) Paints.

(xliv) Paper or cardboard.

(xlv) Pickers from hides.

(xlvi) Pitch.

(xlvii) Plastic goods.

(xlviii) Pottery by hand power.

(xlix) Pottery by mechanical or any power other than hand power.

(l) Sanitary-ware or china-ware

(li) Soap.

(lii) Sugar.

(liii) Sweetmeat and confectionery goods.

(liv) Tallow.

(lv) Tar.

(lvi) Varnishes.

(lvii) Wooden furniture, boxes, barrels, or other articles of wood or of plywood or of sandalwood.

Appendix B

Health License Trades

The list of trade licenses issued by Health Department under orders of various authorities is as under:-

The cases in respect of all the licensable trade except which are to be issued by the Addl. MHO(PH)/Dy.MHO(PH) are required to be sanctioned by zonal DHO after inspection and ensuring completion of all formalities as mentioned in Technical Instructions.

The DHO decides the sanction of the license on the basis of the recommendations of PHI and also after satisfying that the premises in question are conforming i.e. they are situated in the approved market or Commercial areas.

As laid down in various Administrative circulars the following trades can be sanctioned/licensed with the prior approval of the Dy. MHO (PH) Addl. MHO (PH) after the premises are inspected by the DHO In these cases the preliminary action is to be taken by the DHO who gives his recommendations for grant of the license.

1. All 3-5 Star Hotels
2. All Ice-cream Factories
3. All Water Cooling Plants
4. All big Aerated Water Factories
5. All Multinational Company Trades
6. All Industrial Units
7. Mfg. of Pharmaceutical/Medicines
8. All Lodging/Guest Houses with more than 20 beds
9. All Restaurants/Hotels with more than 50 seats
10. All Banquet Halls
11. All Mineral Water Plants (Processed Water Units)
12. Mobile Cater Vans/Chef Carts.

Under Section 417 (1) (a) of the Act:

Carrying out any of the following trades or operations connected with trades not covered by the definitions of a factory.

S.No. Eleventh Schedule for (Part I)	*Name of the trade*
1.	Baking
5.	Cloth, yarn of leather in indigo or in the colours, dyeing or printing of.
6.	Cloth or yarn, bleaching
7.	Eating or a catering establishment
8.	Grain parching
9.	Groundnut seeds, tamarind seeds or any other seeds
10.	Hair dressing salon or a barber's shop.
12.	Laundry shop
15.	Lodging house
19.	Sweetmeat shop except in premises already licenced as an eating house
(xviii)	Washerman's trade.

21. Manufacturing/Parching, packing, pressing, cleansing, cleaning boiling, melting, grinding or preparing by any process whatever, any of the following articles:-

21.	(i)	Aerated water
21.	(xxvii)	Ghee
21.	(xxxi)	Ice (including dry ice)
21.	(xxxii)	Insecticide or disinfectants
21.	(xxxv)	Licensed oil
21.	(xl)	Oil other than petroleum & non-edible oil either by mechanical power or by hand power or ghani-driven.
21.	(xli)	Pharmaceutical or medical products
21.	(Lii)	Sugar
21.	(Liii)	Sweetmeat and confectionery goods.

Supplementary schedule prescribed by the Cm. vide office order No. 1027 SL/L dated 8-9-59 (U)/S417 (A)(b). Any purpose which is in the opinion of the Cm., dangerous to life, health or property or likely to create a nuisance.

4. Cold storage
8. Hosiery manufacturing
13. License grinding
19. Tobacco mfg. and sale

Trade licenseable under section 417 (1) (c) of the Corporation Act:

Keeping horses, cattle or other quadruped animals or birds for transportation sale or hire or for sale of the produce thereof.

Sl. No. of Eleventh Schedule (Part II)

1. Camphor
2. Chillies
3. Copra
4. Oil, other than Petroleum

Section 420 of the D.M.C. Act

Licenses for hawking articles through water-trolleys, Ice-cream trolleys catering vans and also vehicles like Trucks, Three-wheeler, Hand-carts and Reharies.

Trade licenseable under section 421 of the D.M.C. Act.

1. Restaurant
2. Hotel
3. Boarding House
4. Tea Shops
5. Coffee House
6. Café
7. Refreshment room or any place where public are admitted for repose for the consumption of any food or drink or any place where food sold or prepared for sale.

As regards licenses covered under P.F.A. Rules 1956 the same shall be issued under relevant section of the DMC Act. Details of such trades are given as under:-

1. Sec. 417	Preparation of Ice
2. Sec. 417	Sale of Ice.
"	Refrigerated Water Cooling plant
"	Preparation of ice-cream
"	Sweetening agents such as Sugar, Gur or Jaggery.
"	Spices and condiments, whole or ground including saffron, curry powder, mustard seeds.

Sec. 421 Mfg. Sale, stocking, distribution of:

(i) Milk and milk products

(ii) Sweets, pastries

(iii) Dhabas

(iv) Ghee (whole-sale & retails)

(v) Edible oils (whole-sale & retails)

(vi) Atta, Dal

(vii) Aerated Water (preparation)

(viii) Aerated Water (sale)

(ix) Biscuit and Bakery

(x) Fruit/Sugar-cane Juice

(xi) Edible vegetable oil

(xii) Edible fats including margarine

(xiii) Pulses, gram, nuts, starches, sago, suji, flours, such as maida, besan & articles made out of flour including Bakery products (cooked)

(xiv) Non-alocholic beverages such as carbonated water.

(xv) Coca and Chicory.

(xvi) Flavouring agents, anti-oxidants, emulsifying and stabilising, agents & preservatives permitted for use in food and food containers & wrappers.

(xvii) Artificial sweetner

(xviii) Savoury

(xix) Ice candies

(xx) Edible gelatin

(xxi) Molasses

(xxii) Coconut

(xxiii) Silver leaf for human consumption

(xxiv) Any other articles of food and drinks not classified.

APPENDIX C

Shops: Technical Instructions

(As Per Section 417 and 421 of Delhi Municipal Corporation Act, 1957)

Barber's Shop/Hair Dressing Saloon

1. The floor and walls upto a height of one meter shall preferably be made of smooth impervious concrete material.
2. The height of the premises shall not be less than 3 m.
3. The floor area shall be a minimum of six sq. m. for one chair, and two sq. m. for every additional chair.
4. The premises shall be drained into a sewer and where there is no sewer, into a surface drain to the satisfaction of Health authorities.
5. The premises shall be well ventilated and adequately lighted.
6. The walls and ceiling shall be white/colour washed every year and wood work painted every two years. The premises shall be kept in a good state of repairs at all times.
7. Continuous supply of safe water shall be ensured in the premises. In case of intermittent water supply adequate storage arrangements shall be made.
8. A wash-hand basin made of porcelain/stainless steel shall be provided alongwith soap and a nail brush for thorough cleaning of hands. The wash-hand basin shall be kept clean at all times.

9. Sufficient number of fans shall be provided to keep the premises cool and comfortable.
10. Furniture shall be clean, comfortable and free from bed-bugs and vermins.
11. All tables, racks, shelves, boards etc., shall have zinc/aluminium/stainless steel/marble sunmica top to facilitate proper cleaning.
12. The floor and skirted walls shall be thoroughly cleaned daily.
13. Adequate seating arrangements for waiting customers shall be provided in the premises.
14. All workers shall wear clean overalls and headgears while at work.
15. Adequate First-Aid arrangements shall be made available in the premises to attend to minor cuts.
16. Adequate arrangements for storing clean and dirty linen separately shall be provided.
17. All implements shall be kept clean and sharp. Razors, scissors and clippers shall be kept in 22 per cent Cresol, Dettol, or Chlorosol lotion when not in use during working hours. Before use they shall be washed with clean water. The rest of the time they shall be kept clean and protected with Vaseline. Combs shall be kept clean and dry. Shaving brushes, after each shave, shall be washed in 1 per cent soda solution and then washed in water. Razors shall be wiped in a clean towel every time.
18. The head rest of the Barber-chair shall be protected by a clean paper/cloth and fresh piece shall be used for each individual.
19. Separate and clean face towels and sheets shall used for each customer.
20. A waste-bin with a pedal operated cover shall be provided in the premises for collection of waste cotton wool, clipped hair and other waste material.
21. All employees working in the premises shall be medically examined. The certificate of medical fitness shall be displayed prominently alongwith the license.
22. Customers suffering from communicable skin diseases shall not be entertained.
23. The premises shall neither be used for residential purposes nor shall it communicate with any residential quarter. No personal belongings like clothing, bedding, shoes etc. shall be kept in the premises.
24. A high standard of personal hygiene shall be maintained by workers at all times. No smoking, chewing and snuff shall be allowed in the premises.
25. Failure to comply with any of these instructions may entail legal action against the defaulters and even result in cancellation of license.

Eating House or a Catering Establishment

1. Catering establishment is a premises where public is admitted for repose or for consumption of any food or drink or any place where food is sold or prepared for sale. It includes, eating houses, tea shops, refreshment rooms, restaurants, *dhabas*, snack bars, canteens, barbecues, hotel and motels.

2. The premises shall be structurally sound and kept in good state of repairs at all times.
3. The floor and walls upto a height of one meter shall be made of impervious smooth concrete material and the corners rounded to facilitate thorough washing and cleaning of the premises.
4. The floor area shall not be less than nine sq. m. and the height not less than three m.
5. The premises shall be drained into a sewer, and where there is no sewer, into a surface drain to the satisfaction of the Health Authorities.
6. The premises shall be well ventilated and adequately lighted.
7. Continuous supply of safe water shall be ensured in the premises. In case of intermittent water supply adequate storage arrangement shall be made.
8. The premises shall be completely fly-proof, preferably with double doors, outer door opening outwards and fitted with springs to ensure their self closing.
9. Sinks with a draining board, detergent and hot water shall be provided to ensure proper cleaning of utensils, crockery and cutlery. There shall be a separate place for washing pots.
10. Adequate number of wash-hand basins made of porcelain/stainless steel shall be provided along with soap and a nail brush for thorough cleansing of hands. Clean and dry towels shall be kept for the use of customers.
11. The walls and ceiling shall be white/colour washed every six months, and the wood work shall be painted every year.
12. The premises shall be kept cool and comfortable by sufficient number of fans/coolers.
13. A refuse bin of an adequate size with a pedal operated cover shall be provided in the premises for collection of waste material. This shall be emptied, and washed daily with a disinfectant.
14. All tables, racks, shelves, boards etc. shall have zinc/aluminium/stainless steel/marble/sunmica top to facilitate proper cleaning.
15. Sign-board shall be prominently displayed at the premises indicating the nature of cooking medium being used.
16. The floor and skirted walls shall be washed daily with a disinfectant like phenyl at the close of day's business.
17. The premises shall be kept free from all insects by an insecticidal spray having knockdown effect at the close of day's business. No spraying shall be done during the conduct of business, but instead fly swats/flaps used to kill spray flies getting into the premises.
18. The premises shall not be used for residential purposes, nor it shall communicate with any residential quarter. No personal belongings like clothing, bedding, shoes etc., shall be kept in the premises.
19. No person suffering from contiguous or infectious disease shall be employed in the establishment. All persons working in the premises shall be medically examined and immunised against cholera and enteric group

of fevers at the time of issue/renewal of license. The certificate of medical fitness and immunisation shall be displayed prominently in the shop along with the license.

20. A high standard of personal hygiene shall be maintained by workers at all times. No smoking, chewing and snuff shall be allowed in the premises.
21. No food shall be served to the customers outside the premises, nor it shall be served on leaves and paper except white unprinted paper plates.
22. There shall be no smoke nuisance in the kitchen.
23. Chipped enameled containers shall not be used. Stainless/aluminium containers e.g. mugs, jugs, trays, etc., shall preferably be used.
24. Brass utensils shall be frequently provided with inside lining.
25. There shall be proper arrangements for storage of dry rations, tinned stuff and other raw materials.
26. Failure to comply with any of these instructions may entail legal action against the defaulters and even result in cancellation of license.

Baking Unit

1. A baking unit (Bakery) shall mean any building or portion of a building in which baking for sale of bread, biscuits, cakes, pastries or other such food or any operation subsidiary or preparatory to baking is carried out.
2. The premises shall be structurally sound, and kept in good state of repair at all times.
3. The premises shall be rendered completely fly proof preferably with double doors and outer door opening outward and fitted with springs to ensure their self-closing. It shall also be made rodent and bird proof. No pets shall be allowed in the premises at any time.
4. The premises shall be kept free from cockroaches and other vermins at all times.
5. The premises shall be well ventilated and adequately lighted.
6. The floor area shall not be less than nine sq. m. and the height not less than three m.
7. The floor and walls upto a height of one meter shall be made of smooth impervious concrete material and the corners shall be rounded to facilitate washing and cleaning of the premises. The ceiling shall be kept clean and free from cob-webs.
8. The premises shall be maintained in a good state of repairs and cleanliness. Whenever required, it shall be white/colour washed, painted and disinfected. The premises shall be kept free of smell by using deodorants. At least every six months, it shall be white/colour washed regularly or earlier, if required.
9. The walls and ceiling shall be white/colour washed every six months and the wood work shall be painted every year.
10. All tables, racks, shelves, boards etc. shall have zinc/aluminium/stainless steel/marble/sunmica top to facilitate proper cleaning. All surfaces

coming into contact with the goods shall be smooth and free from pits, dents, cracks, crevices and loose sales.

11. The stores for raw materials shall be free from dampness by providing damp proof measures.
12. Adequate measures shall be taken to reduce hazards of heat radiation/condition by using fire proof and heat resistant lining of the oven and chimney, wherever required.
13. The oven mouth shall open inside the bakery premises and not outside. Feeding/stoking operations shall be carried out from within the premises. The chimney from the oven fid with conventional fuel shall be at a height of two m. higher than the highest building in the vicinity.
14. Continuous supply of safe water shall be ensured in the premises. In case of intermittent water supply, adequate storage arrangement shall be made.
15. No ash pit shall be allowed within the premises. A waste bin of adequate size with a pedal operated cover shall be provided in the premises for collection of waste material. This shall be emptied and washed daily.
16. All equipment shall be kept clean, washed and dried at the close of day's business to ensure freedom from growth of mould/fungi and infestation. All equipment shall be placed well away from the walls to allow proper inspection.
17. Sinks and troughs used for washing ingredients shall not be used for washing hands.
18. The containers shall be clean and stacked in a manner that does not allow contamination of products.
19. All food handlers shall be medically examined at initial employment and periodically every three months thereafter including laboratory examination wherever indicated. A record of such examinations shall be maintained. Persons suffering from communicable diseases or who are carriers shall be prohibited from working in premises.
20. All food handlers shall keep their finger nails trimmed clean and wash their hands with soap detergent and water before commencing work and every time after using toilet. Paper/roller towels shall be used for wiping hands dry. Adequate number of wash hand basins made of porcelain/stainless steel shall be provided and kept clean.
21. All employees shall be provided with clean uniforms/aprons headgears while at work. Separate lockers and change room/place shall also be provided.
22. Eating, chewing, smoking, spitting and nose blowing shall be prohibited within the premises.
23. Sufficient and suitable sanitary conveniences shall be provided and kept clean. There shall not be any direct communication with processing unit.
24. Bare hands shall not be used for handling bakery products at any stage. No product shall be kept in the open except in the showcase. Clean grease/butter paper polythene bags shall be provided. Used and printed paper shall not be allowed for any purposes in the Unit.

25. Failure to comply with any of these instructions may entail legal action against the defaulters, and even result in revocation of the license.

Kirana Goods and Dry Fruits

1. The premises should be free from all insects and rat proof.
2. The premises shall not be used for residential purposes nor it shall communicate with any residential quarter.
3. The premises should be well ventilated and lighted.
4. The premises shall be free from dampness by providing damp proof measures.
5. The workers shall be medically examined and immunised against Cholera and enteric group of fevers at the time of issue/renewal of license.
6. The walls shall be periodically white/colour washed and wood work painted.
7. No person suffering form contagious diseases shall be employed in the establishment.
8. A high standard of personal hygiene shall be maintained by workers at all times.
9. Food stuff for sale shall be kept in suitable containers duly provided with proper cover and the same shall be kept on wooden trestle with minimum height of nine inches.
10. A foot operated covered receptacle shall be kept for depositing the waste material.
11. The dry fruits should be kept for sale in a glass jars or show cases.
12. Failure to comply with any of these instructions may entail legal action against defaulter and may result in cancellation of license.

Appendix D

Maintenance of Establishment

Following points need to be considered with regard to maintenance of an establishment:

Cleanliness

1. Every shop and establishment should be kept clean and free from effluvia arising from any drain or other nuisance.[1]
2. It is the duty of the shopkeepers and occupiers of all establishments to have the premises swept and cleaned. All filth and rubbish should be collected and removed to the nearest receptacle or municipal depot.[2]
3. All the inside walls and the ceiling tops of the rooms except the storeroom, the passages and staircases should be limewashed or colour washed, at least once in two years.[3]

---

1. Section 25, Delhi Shops & Establishments Act, 1954.
2. Section 353, The Delhi Municipal Corporation Act, 1957.
3. Rule 11(1)(a), Delhi Shops & Establishments Rules, 1954.

4. All beams, rafters, doors, window-frames and other woodwork except floors, should be painted at least once in four years.[4]
5. No filth, rubbish or debris should accumulate or remain in any establishment. Dustbins/other receptacles should be provided in the premises.
6. The area around the place where drinking water is distributed should be kept clean and properly drained.

Lighting and Ventilation[5]

1. The shopkeepers and owners of the establishments must ensure that the premises is sufficiently and properly lighted, so that there is no casting of shadows on actual place of work.
2. The premises should be adequately ventilated. Ventilation may be either natural i.e. by windows, ventilators, etc. or artificial i.e. by exhaust fans, etc.
3. Inadequate and unsuitable lighting or ventilation in the premises of an establishment is a continuing offence liable to fine upto Rs. 250.
4. Drinking water should be made available at or near the work places for the employees.

Prevention against Fire[6]

All shopkeepers and owners of establishments must ensure that no person in the establishment smokes or uses a naked light in the premises or uses a naked light in the immediate vicinity of any inflammable material.

---

4. Rule 11(1)(b). Delhi Shops & Establishments Rules, 1954.
5. Section 26, Delhi Shops & Establishments Act, 1954.
6. Section 28 and Rule 12. Delhi Shops & Establishments Act, 1954.

4

Urban Land Management Plans: Master Plan for Disaster

A plan for a city is a purported guide to manage future growth outlining the desirable development of the city. It develops a vision for the city and addresses the issue of the appropriate use of urban land. Compare it to the government budget where resources are allocated for competing purposes from competing resources. Needless to add, plans of a "good city" frequently differ among planners themselves where each has his/her own perspective.

Urban land management plans prepared by government predetermine the use of land and thus, fundamentally affect the course of livelihoods in cities. This coupled with poor implementation typical of government machinery exacerbate the situation and mislead citizens to define the problem in terms of over-population, inadequate transportation, land abuse and often as simply, poor implementation of apparently good plans. The present chapter is an effort to understand and look at the usual problem in a different perspective and offer the possibility of there being solutions other than governmentally imposed ones. It would also enable laymen to understand the issues, demystify plans and their implementation, and lead to informed judgements.

The Master Plan of Delhi (MPD) offers a prism to view land management plans, their implementation and their effects on livelihoods and numerous other activities. Its importance is heightened in light of the fact that most other urban development plans in India are modelled on this Plan. The Plan is prepared under a Central Act, Delhi Development Act, 1957 as the National Capital Territory of Delhi (NCTD) is a Union Territory. Therefore, the Government of NCTD is not directly responsible for the Plan. Minor changes are approved by the Chairman of Delhi Development Authority (Lieutenant-Governor of Delhi is ex-officio Chairman of

DDA). Major changes are made by the Minister for Urban Development, Government of India. Zoning/ subdivision regulations are part of the planning process (e.g. Floor Area Ratio, parking, height, coverage, set backs). Bye-laws are part of a municipal process and therefore, resolutions by the State assembly/corporation are meaningless on planning issues.

In 1947, when India acquired independence, Delhi was essentially an administrative city, with a population of about 10 lakh. With the influx of refugees, it began to grow and expand rapidly through the distributive trade, commerce and industry. This in turn began to transform its character from an administrative city to an administrative-cum-industrial-cum-commercial city. In 1957, the Delhi Development Authority was set up to develop Delhi according to a plan. Such a Plan was prepared by DDA and enacted in 1962, henceforth called the Master Plan. The Plan was prepared for a period of 20 years. This Plan is called the MPD 62. This Plan as updated and approved in 1990 for 2001 is called the MPD 2001. This update was ostensibly delayed due to the unplanned Asiad Games (though there is no reason why both of them could not have proceeded concurrently) and other delays that led it to being notified only in 1990.[1] The current update is called MPD 2021.

The hierarchy of land planning has the following structure where the sub-levels offer greater details in terms of the Master Plan provisions.

Master Plan/Zonal Development Plan (ZDP)/Sub-zonal development Plan (SZDP)/Project level Plan.

MPD-2001 divides Delhi into 15 geographical zones. Each zone has specified dominant land uses from amongst the 37 use zones[2] prescribed in the Master Plan. These zones have been grouped under nine broad categories: residential, commercial, industrial, manufacturing, recreational, transportation, utility, government, public and semi-public and agriculture and water body. Each use zone is further subdivided into a number of use premises[3] out of the 136 use

1. Delhi Urban Art Commission. 1986. Conceptual Plan: Delhi 2001.
2. Use zone means an area for any of the specific dominant use of the urban functions as provided for in Clause 4 of the Master Plan of Delhi.
3. Use premises means one of the many sub-divisions of a use zone, designated at the time of preparation of the layout plan, for a specific main use or activity and includes the use premises described in the Development code of the Delhi Master Plan.

premises. The use zones and use premises refer to the activity for which the land is to be used. A ZDP supersedes the content of the Master Plan, as it incorporates the provisions of the Master Plan. Of the total of 15 zones in Delhi, eight ZDPs were made for MPD 2001, of which only six have been apparently approved so far.

The ZDPs are subdivided into SZDPs. They are the descriptive plans that specify the use of each plot of land. There are 137 SZDPs within the eight ZDPs of MPD 62. At an average each of these covers approximately four sq. km. and an approximate population of 65,000. The SZDPs supplement the Master Plan and ZDP stipulation.

Thus, zonal plans detail out the Master Plan, in turn the SZDPs detail out the ZDPs and offer the basis for layout plans. Building plans must fit in layout plans.

For the development of the commercial activities in the city the Plan introduced poly-nodal hierarchical development i.e. the concept of Central Business District, Sub-Central Business District, District Centre, Community Centre and Local Shopping Centre. The Plan also envisaged performance based industrial development like extensive, light and flatted factory.

MPD 2001 envisages the land in the urban extension be distributed approximately as follows:

Land Use	*Percentage of land*
Residential	45-55
Commercial	3-4
Industrial	6-7
Recreational	15-20
Public and semi public facilities	8-10
Circulation	10-12

Source: DDA Guidelines, Vol-I

The plans can apparently be changed only through a due process of law. Over 40 years after the Plan was formulated, there has not been much change from the *concept* of the original Plan. This assumes importance when seen in light of what a prominent planner said – that the basic conditions on which the Plan had been prepared in the sixties no longer hold true for the present scenario and it is time to look at the issue afresh. That the Master Plan has been amended over

220 times since its inception reflects the whims of political processes and as well its disconnection with present ground realities. After every election the municipal corporation and state assembly routinely pass resolutions condoning past violations of Plan bye-laws.[4]

MPD 1962 – A Review

At the time of formulation of the Master Plan in 1962, the Ford Foundation team had carried out detailed surveys of the city, on the basis of which the Plan was prepared. Land use control and land use permissibility was one of the major stipulations of MPD 62. The MPD 62 stipulated development of the city in accordance with the land use. Each use zone had three categories of uses specified as: Permitted uses (were allowed as normal uses in a specific uses zone), Permissible uses (were only permitted when permission under 'special appeal' is given by the competent authority and otherwise it remained a prohibited use), and Prohibited uses. Use of land contrary to the regulations in a particular use zone is called as 'non-conforming use'. As per the MPD 62, all non-conforming uses were to be shifted in stages to the conforming areas, earmarked in the MPD. Establishment of new uses in any case was to be allowed only in the conforming areas.

However, the Plan underwent serious aberrations during implementation. This period saw a rapid population growth overshooting the Plan projections by 11 lakh. Despite the land use controls, mixed land use in the residential areas continued. Besides the inability of the Plan to envisage the requirements, what the Plan provided for was also not developed: Considering this, certain provisions for mixed land use were provided in the Master Plan 2001. But keeping in view the pace of commercialisation coupled with the population growth, these provisions turned out to be only a piecemeal effort. Moreover, efforts to modify the Plan invariably resulted in gains being reaped by particular groups which were strong enough to lobby the policymakers.

The Delhi Urban Art Commission in their review[5] of the MPD 62 pointed out that:

---

4. Kapoor, Coomi. 2000. "If Delhi dies, who lives? - Mastering the plan" [article online]. *Indian Express*. Accessed on 1 March 2004 at sdnp.delhi.nic.in/headlines/dec00/04-12-2000-news3.html

5. Delhi Urban Art Commission. 1986. *Conceptual Plan: Delhi 2001*.

- The population of Delhi in 1961 was 23.6 lakh. By 1981, during this Plan period of 20 years, it went up to 57.7 lakh. The DUAC (Delhi Urban Arts Commission) noted that during these two decades it became abundantly clear that while the intentions of MPD 62 were to rectify the earlier ailments of the city and direct and control its future growth in a far more organised manner, the DDA was not succeeding in achieving these objectives. If anything, problems of the city kept multiplying. Shortage of basic infrastructural facilities, congestion of traffic, pollution and a gradual decline in the quality of life were becoming more and more apparent.
- Land acquisition and development: Concept of a single agency responsible for acquisition, development and disposal of land had encountered delays at every level. This has resulted in undue escalation in land prices (housing monopoly) and encroachment on public land.
- The Delhi Development Act had prescribed the preparation of zonal development plans for translating the concepts laid down in the Master Plan. But the experience in the preparation of such zonal plans has shown that these plans were of marginal value to obtain a desirable urban form since these plans only indicated the location of community facilities and land uses.
- The Plan had an objective to develop self-contained District Centres for "best possible location of employment centres and housing facilities and to make employee housing accessible to such centres." The development of these District Centres as envisaged in the Plan could not be achieved. Even 14 years after the conception of the 1962 Master Plan and out of the 15 District Centres proposed, barely part development of the three had taken place. Even in these, no provision had been made for govt offices, flatted factories or community facilities. Inadequate area for commercial activities had resulted in unauthorised and disorganised development of shops, offices and other work centres in residential areas. This also led to high rents and land prices in commercial areas.
- Location of the District Centres: The DUAC pointed out that the locations allotted to the District Centres proposed in the

Master Plan were unsatisfactory. The Master Plan objective was 'to ensure the location of employment centres which are in places accessible to needed facilities and services.' But in reality, while finalising the Master Plan these District Centres were not properly integrated with the transport system. None of them had railway facility. In some even adequate road capacity-accessibility was not taken into account to cater to the magnitude of traffic generated by such Centres. Chaotic traffic conditions that prevailed around Nehru Place and Rajendra Place even when these Centres had not been fully developed were cited as examples.

- Commercial development: The Plan proposed to provide for increased space requirement in existing and planned work centres and District Centres to meet the increase in demand within the urbanised area. The proposed building regulations such as FAR, site coverage, etc. however, do not correlate with this intention.
- The present dispersal of commercial areas in the city ignores traffic and journey-distance consideration. As a result, wherever commercial activity is concentrated the traffic conditions is chaotic. Moreover, bulk of the poor to middle-class workers have to travel long distances to reach their work places.
- It was noted that for proper implementation of the plans of residential areas, detailed plans were required to be prepared based on urban form studies. This exercise was not carried out.
- The Master Plan had recommended that a major part of industrial units should be shifted in areas earmarked for flatted factories, service, light and extensive industries. There were 8,000 industrial units in 1961 in non-conforming areas, which were to be shifted. However, according to a study conducted by DDA in the 1980s the number of such units had increased to 24,000. Out of 23 sites earmarked for flatted factories, not one area had been fully developed. Consequently, non-implementation of this recommendation led to development of industries in non-conforming areas.

MPD 2001 – The Experience

The comprehensive Plan update should have been ready by 1982, but instead, Delhi was geared to host the completely unplanned Asiad Games in 1982[6]. Huge stadiums, roads, hotels, flyovers, offices, apartments and colonies were constructed to cater to the needs of the Games and the anticipated commercial spillover. This brought in its trail fresh wave of migration of about 10 lakh construction workers who swelled the number of squatter settlements. All these were outside the Master Plan. The Master Plan update 2001 was not notified until August 1990, nine years after the perspective period of MPD 81. The MPD 62 prepared for a period of 20 years thus had its operation valid till 1990 when its validity was updated up to 2001. Accordingly, another MPD update is presently under preparation up to 2021.

Based on the experience of MPD 62 and to cater to the increasing population and changing requirements of the city upto 2001, modifications were made to MPD 62 and the MPD 2001 was prepared by in-house professionals of DDA. In 1985, the first comprehensive draft of the MPD 2001 was published for comments. The draft came in for severe criticism from the government itself as being 'conceptually defective' and DUAC was asked to prepare another plan. DUAC took a close look at the failures of the MPD 62 to formulate its Plan. But the plan prepared by them was in conflict with DDA proposals. The task of carrying out civic surveys to gauge the socio-economic needs of the people was not undertaken by DDA and instead of preparing a new plan document the second plan was just called a Revised Version of the MPD-62. The modified plan, MPD-2001, was approved by the GoI and promulgated in 1990.[7] There is no provision in the Delhi Development Act, 1957 to prepare a second, third or subsequent plans – the provisions imply that until the perspective periods are updated, the Plan as now in force would prevail. Thus, MPD 2001 and the approved changes are currently in force until these are comprehensively updated and approved for the period 2021 i.e. through 2021.

---

6. Chakrabarti, P.G. Dhar. "Delhi's ongoing Debate on Informal Settlements and Work Places – Issues of Environmental Jurisprudence". Accessed online at http://www.naervs.net/sat/workshops/2001/papers/chakrabarti.rtf on 20 February 2004.
7. Roy, Dunu. 2004. "From home to estate". *Seminar*, 533: 68. Accessed online at http://www.india-seminar.com/2004/533/533dunuroy.htm on 20 February 2004.

- MPD 2001 faulted the MPD 62 for not proposing a monitoring system to register the changing socio-economic profile of the community and the physical structure of the city. The absence of such a framework had led to unintended growth, in the form of unauthorised colonies, squatter settlements, the informal sector and the non-conforming industry, all of which needed to be monitored.[8]
- The MPD 62 did not propose integration of the informal sector leading to their exponential growth that outstripped infrastructural facilities.[9] Then MPD-2001 marked out provisions for informal sector. *These provisions were not implemented and hawkers still hawk on the roadside.*
- Uniform standards of FAR, density and site coverage have been laid down for group housing. It is felt that different standards should be evolved for different categories of people to meet their respective demands.[10]

There were large-scale violations of the Plan with regard to the land use provisions. The number of mixed land use streets had increased illegally, i.e. against the Plan provisions. One of the reasons could be that even DDA had not developed all the land that had been earmarked for commercial use in the Plan itself. A look at the accomplishments of DDA as against a few of the targets mentioned in the Master Plan clears the picture:

Type of Commercial Centre	*Target in the MPD*	*Developed*	*Work-in-progress*
District Centre	29	7	3
Community Centre	124	27	7
Local Shopping Centre	-*	125	6
Convenience Shopping Centre	-*	429	6

Source: MPD 2001 and DDA Annual Plan 2003 (*: not mentioned)

Documents obtained from the DDA point to the unfeasibility of prosecuting property owners for putting residential premises to

8. Accessed online at http://www.ddadelhi.com/planning/mpd_1962_lessons.htm on 18 February 2004.
9. Accessed online at http://www.ddadelhi.com/planning/mpd_1962_lessons.htm on 18 February 2004.
10. Government of India. 1986. *Conceptual Plan: Delhi 2001*. Delhi Urban Arts Commission.

commercial use in contravention of the Master Plan, because of their own admission of shortage of commercial space in the city.[11]

This, in light of the fact that the population of Delhi is fast increasing as also the commercial needs of the populace, explains the spur in the commercial use of residential space.

MPD 2021 – Making of the Plan

DDA is currently engaged in modification of the Master Plan of Delhi 2001 for a perspective up to 2021 to cater to the increasing population and the changing requirements of the city.

To facilitate the implementation of the Plan, public land was placed at DDA's disposal under a policy of socialisation of land through large-scale public acquisition. DDA, according to this Plan, became the sole developer for the entire future extension of Delhi. The guidelines for MPD 2021 spell out the shortcomings of this policy. The policy of large-scale acquisition of the land has, contrary to the intentions of the policy, resulted in the creation of large number of unauthorised colonies and JJ clusters. Under the policy, the farmers could only get the price of compulsory acquisition. As a result, they have resisted acquisition and, in many cases, sold their lands for unauthorised colonisation through the intermediation of colonisers and land mafia. When the farmers could not escape acquisition they felt deprived of their share in the value addition that occurs upon conversion of agricultural land to urban land.[12]

Another drawback in the approach arose from the substantial time gap between acquisition, development and disposal of land, during which period it remained an invitation to encroachment. Consequently, a large number of unauthorised colonies and JJ clusters have come up which characterise a substantial part of Delhi today.

DDA, responsible for implementation of the MPD provisions, has often been criticised for the non-implementation of the Plan provisions. A World Bank report quoted it as the "most corrupt institution in the country" and a senior official of DDA has mentioned

---

11. Government of India. 1992. *Guidelines on Land Management*. Vol 1. Lands Department, Delhi Development Authority.
12. Government of India. 2003. *Delhi Master Plan—2021: Guidelines*. Delhi Development Authority.

that it has "emerged as the largest real estate agency in the world, with over 50,000 acres of prime metropolitan land at its disposal."[13]

- A prominent planner pointed out that the problems of squalor in Delhi are rooted entirely in non-implementation of 'non-profitable' Plan provisions. The Plan anticipated and earmarked space for integrating 0.45 million poor families in residential development across the city. These provisions were not implemented and Census has found about 0.4 million poor families in slums. The Plan anticipated and earmarked suitably dispersed space for about 0.1 million industrial units. These provisions were not implemented and about 0.1 million units function in places not meant for them in ways problematic for themselves and others. The Plan anticipated and apparently earmarked space in line with natural propensities to accommodate 0.3 to 0.4 million hawkers in a planned way. These provisions were not implemented and hawkers hawk on roadsides.[14]
- Implementation failures have grown from slow pace of development to priorities in favour of remunerative uses to veritable abandonment of the Plan through use of powers for Plan modification in pursuit of unplanned development for what effectively amounts to profiteering on public land. The skew in favour of up-market development is confirmed by an independent survey conducted by Dunu Roy's, Hazards Centre. The survey found that while the planned housing targets set for the rich were achieved more than three times over, the poor occupied only 40 per cent of the low-end Janata flats. Also, that the middle-income and rich groups owned 81 per cent of low income group (LIG) houses. Despite 23,000 applicants waiting for housing allotment in November 2002–some 22,000 of these for Janata and LIG flats–the DDA announced that it would take up schemes only for high-income group (HIG) flats and that Janata flats would not be constructed anymore. The one-room Janata flats cost a

13. Accessed online at http://www.frontlineonnet.com/fl2010/stories/20030523002104500.htm on 28 February 2004.

14. Verma, Gita Dewan. 2002. "An entitlements' perspective of the Master Plan and its revision". Accessed on 1 March 2004 at http://www.architexturez.net/FILES/archive/document.archive/e/www.delhiscienceforum.org/dmp2021/demystif.htm

minimum of Rs. 2 lakh, while a two-bedroom flat would cost anywhere between Rs. 9 lakh and Rs. 16 lakh.[15]

- At a conservative estimate, over 5,000 hectares of public land in Delhi, nearly a tenth of the area under the Plan has been denied outright to 'down-market' uses that it was planned for in order to be 'spared' for unplanned up-market development.
- While on the one hand DDA has failed to provide housing to a majority of Delhi's population, the growth of unauthorised colonies has been unchecked, because people find their own ways to fulfil basic needs that civic authorities are unable to provide. In 1961 the Delhi Development Authority (DDA) was handed over 19,190 hectares of land, but 38 years later the DDA has still not been able to build houses on half of this land.[16] The MCD's affidavit said that 93 per cent of encroachment by slums had taken place on land owned by the DDA and other agencies.[17] The post of Engineer Member and the engineering responsibilities of the DDA under the DD Act, 57 is to process land assembly and not housing. *Unfortunately over the years, housing has become their major involvement through a huge in-house professional team.* This makes it difficult for the DDA to return to its prescribed mandate.

  Over the past 20 years, the DDA has built only a third of the homes that it estimated would be needed to house the growing population, according to an analysis of DDA statistics by Sajha Manch, a federation of organisations working for the urban poor. Of the "low-income housing" that the DDA did build, 80 per cent was bought by middle and higher-income groups because it was too costly for the poor. Over the same 20 years, Delhi's migrant labour force has erected more than 1,000 slum colonies on public land, and the population of Delhi's slums has grown from half a million to 3.2 million.

---

15. Verma, Gita Dewan. 2002. "An entitlements' perspective of the Master Plan and its revision" [article online]. Accessed on 1 March 2004 at http://www.architexturez.net/FILES/archive/document.archive/e/www.delhiscienceforum.org/dmp2021/demystif.htm
16. Accessed online at http://www.humanscapeindia.net/humanscape/hs0799/hs7994t.htm on 1 March 2004.
17. Overdorf, Jason. 2000. "Start door-to-door garbage collection-Housing : Delhi's War on the Poor". *Hindustan Times*. Accessed on 1 March 2004 at http://www.fsa.ulaval.ca/personnel/vernag/EH/F/cause/lectures/HOUSING.htm

- Because of the lack of adequate developed land at affordable prices to different categories of residents, various types of unplanned settlements have come up in Delhi. According to an estimate, the population residing in different types of settlements in 2000 was as under:

Type of Settlement & Population in NCTD

Type of Settlement	*Approx. Population in lakh (2000)*
J.J. Clusters	20.72
Slum Designated Areas	26.64
Unauthorised Colonies	7.40
Resettlement Colonies	17.76
Rural Villages	7.40
Regularised-Unauthorised Colonies	17.76
Urban Villages	8.88
Planned Colonies	33.08

Source: DUEIIP-2021 (Economic Survey Of Delhi, 2001-2002)

- Employment, and with that, the sating of hunger, are prioritised over housing of any kind by slum dwellers. Anthropologist Joop W. De Wit's research has shown that slum-dwellers faced with resettlement protest the move most bitterly because they will be far removed from their existing jobs. Too far removed to commute on expensive or non-existent public-transport routes, they see no prospects for new jobs in the wildernesses to which they are typically banished. This is why many of them are prepared to sell off their new homes and return to live near their old neighbourhoods in housing quality that is worse than before – perhaps even on the pavements.
- Over 30 lakh Delhi residents stay in colonies that are labelled unauthorised because they are not part of the Master Plan. There are 68 projects of over a thousand crores each which have been proposed or are currently under construction (for instance, the Rs. 40,000-crore Metro railway), but which have no place in the Master Plan.[18]

18. Accessed online at http://www.humanscapeindia.net/humanscape/hs0799/hs7994t.htm on 1 March 2004.

- In view of the enormous response from the public for the allotment of a flat or plot in Delhi and the limited availability of land, there has been a long waiting period before the applicants have got the allotment. Prolonged delay in allotment of flats leads to certain inherent problems and has generated many representations for out-of-turn allotments and complaints. Similarly, a number of registrants also died during the endless wait, making it necessary for their registrations to be transferred to their legal heirs which is not being done at present.[19]
- Senior officials admit that the organisation is not very clean. There are a lot of irregularities in flat allotment. Quality is compromised by the use of inferior building materials. This is possible as construction officials and junior engineers choose to ignore construction standards. In its offices, no file would move without bribe. Those who refused to pay up found their documents rejected on the flimsiest of grounds or learnt that their files had been 'misplaced'.[20]
- The failure in making available adequate developed land for physical infrastructure and public utilities to the concerned agencies in time on the one hand and the lack of adequate developed land at affordable rates to the public for housing on the other hand, led to the further non-implementation of the Plan.

Much of the administration of land in Delhi formally restricts the conversion of land use for different purposes except the mixed land use provisions which allow that to a degree. These restrictions help perpetuate the enormous gap between plans and actual practice. The effectiveness of this administration is poor and allows the illegal conversion of agricultural land. Conversion is encouraged by the shortage of housing which is a result of this situation. Besides, the administrative bodies have compulsory stipulations and financial constraints that make the execution of large-scale and ambitious land-use projects a problematic affair.

---

19. Accessed online at http://www.hindu.com/thehindu/2001/10/12/stories/14122186.htm on 1 March 2004.

20. Joshi, Sandhya. 2000. "DDA corrupt, says vice-chairman". Accessed online at http://www.indiareacts.com/archivespecialreports/nat2.asp?recno=5&ctg=community on 1 March 2004.

Another influence of the government results from a complicated interaction among the multiplicity of government agencies and local private actors. Many government institutions implicitly represent conflicting interests. The alphabet soup will convey the confusion involved: MCD, NDMC, DCB, GNCTD, DDA, NCRPB and others.

What has been berated apart from the poor planning and implementation has been the immigration rates of about 5 lakh a year for Delhi. If the land in and around Delhi i.e. the National Capital Region, were allowed to be developed, the much flogged migration could become a strength for the opportunities of economic development that would follow. Immigration to Delhi (NCTD) is because the union government, public sector enterprises, industries and the distribution trade compete for a location in Delhi despite the NCR plan.

A little mentioned fact is the involvement of people in the planning processes. The Master Plan offers little knowledge and comfort to the layman who is interested at most in how his residence and residential area are affected. These nitty-gritties are only chalked out in the Zonal Development Plans which come out much later. For example, the Zonal Development Plan of MPD 2001 for the F-zone (South Delhi-1) was authenticated only on 5 June 1998 and by 2001, plans were already underway for preparing the MPD 2021! There have also been repeated complaints about the nature of notifications which are neither well publicised nor easily intelligible to the affected.

A word about the process of acquisition of land by the DDA would put the suggested reforms in the right perspective. The DDA notifies land for acquisition on the basis of the Land Acquisition Act, 1894. This Act is the most powerful legal tool used by the government to acquire land in the name of public purpose. The government then proceeds to acquire it on the basis of the doctrine of Eminent Domain. This taking of land is immaterial of the property rights of the title-holders who are mostly farmers in this case and hence, subject to deprivation of their livelihood. This acquisition of land by the government is seldom questioned either on the basis of the "coercive" mechanisms through which they are supposed to submit their land or on the basis of the violation of the property rights of the title-holders. The public purpose of the land is assumed to be paramount even in the face of the complex problems that the Act has engendered. The compensations are usually dis-satisfactory and often, enough time is not provided to vacate the notified land. No wonder that these disputes on land count among the greatest backlog of cases in the courts of India.

In fact, our intensive research efforts on land issues in Delhi could not shed any light on the following questions:

1. How much land does DDA own and what per cent is it of the total land in Delhi?
2. How much land do they own which can be developed for residential purpose but still has not yet been developed? Ditto for commercial development.
3. What per cent of DDA's undeveloped land is under encroachment?
4. What has been their exact achievement of the physical targets for 2001 mentioned in the MPD 2001?
5. Are there any studies or surveys that DDA has carried out before going in for the preparation of the MPD 2021? If so, where are they and are they accessible to the public? For that matter, any studies prepared by DDA since its existence. Unfortunately the Right to information Act in its present form is inapplicable for DDA.
6. Any evaluation or monitoring reports that have been prepared by DDA.

How DDA's policies could affect a person's livelihood can be brought home by a particular incident. A vehicle repair-shop owner near the Sainik Farm precincts wanted to avail a loan from a bank to expand his business by putting up the ownership of the shop's land as collateral. In this, he ran into a dead end. Most banks would not offer loan based on the power of attorney authority that he had despite that most dealings of land in Delhi occurred on the basis of transfer of the power of attorney. What gave rise to this huge reliance on the power of attorney? Apparently the high transaction costs that needed to be paid to the DDA in case of a transfer of ownership detered actual legal transfer and land ownership was usually transferred on a power of attorney basis and became a normal practice.

High transaction costs invariably discourage legal business activity. There is no reason why land ownership transfer should be as simple and with little transaction costs as in the case of transfer of shares!

A Note on Planners and Plans

It is often implicitly assumed that in case of a problem, the government will act in the public interest, but the government is not a single entity with public-spirited motivations. Rather, it is a group of individuals or groups who undoubtedly want to further the public interest but also want to take care of their own interests. People who work in government are no better or worse than people who work in the private sector. Everyone, whether in the public or private sector, wants to further the public interest, but also want to look out for themselves. Thus, any analysis of the policy-making process must take into account the incentives facing policymakers and not naively assume that they will further the public interest—especially when the public interest conflicts with their own personal interests. This is to draw attention to the fact that the plans are often supposed to be good or at least supposed to have possessed good intentions on part of the planners, but ineffective implementation is cited as the cause of failure. A plan without "implementation compatibility" is not worth the ideals that it stands for. Plans that do not take into account the incentives of the implementation authorities or the incentives facing the citizens are bound to end with failure.

The N-AERUS (Network-Association of European Researchers on Urbanisation in the South) has an interesting comment to make in this regard. "City planners plan cities, they do not make them. Cities have their own organic logic of growth. Unless the planners fully comprehend the dynamics of this growth, they are likely to end up planning a system, which will not work. This sums up the urban planning experience of Delhi. If the city creates opportunities of growth, it is bound to attract people, especially when it has a large hinterland of poverty. If a growing city embarks on a wholesale acquisition of land, as Delhi did, without converting them to gainful uses, it is bound to encourage squatter settlement on public land. And when the city has an abundance of cheap labour and a good infrastructure it is bound to encourage trade and industry. This cycle shall have its own spin off effect, which will create more opportunities of employment and therefore more migration. Over a period of time this will change the character of the city. When the poor will create demands for low priced goods and services that can be produced in a decentralised and unorganised manner which in turn will help a strong informal sector to emerge. Slowly the informal sector will upgrade its skill and competitiveness and create a market for itself. This is what has happened in the past few decades in Delhi. The growth of the informal sector has taken place spontaneously without the intervention of any planning or development machinery and on the whole their contribution to the economy has been very positive and desirable. Today, it is estimated that as much as 62.97 per cent of urban Delhi's total employment is in the informal sector, yet the planning process does not recognise it as a necessary component of urban economy. It restricts the growth of this sector by land use regulations. It neither provides land to the sector nor allows them to operate at places where they have created a niche for themselves. Similarly, it may be highly desirable to shift the polluting industries out of the residential areas, but a blanket order to shift all small scale and household industries from the non-conforming areas unleashes an avoidable catastrophe for millions of poor workers whose very existence and livelihood will be lost." [21]

Understanding the Lessons

The Delhi Development Act, 1957 and the Delhi Development Authority are the basic Act and institutions respectively based on which urban development has been modelled in most other parts of India and hence it would be beneficial to understand the lessons that a critique of them throws up.

1. Land management plans framed by a static body in a dynamic situation invariably fail to respond appropriately to the continuous changes. By the time they can respond they find that the measures are inadequate to deal with the situation at hand. When the government has failed in every other sphere of production it is difficult to fathom how it can successfully produce good plans and regulations. Regulations are passed on the abstract concern of enhancing public welfare without subjecting them to a thorough analysis of costs and benefits.
2. Implementation of land management plans is in the hands of authorities who are supposed to follow the public interest but are subject to their personal agenda. The distorted incentives result in poor implementation of plans, and vested interest of officials not to generate or display information crucial to the citizens for making informed judgements. If unconvinced, try finding out the studies performed by DDA on land in Delhi!

---

21. Chakrabarti, P.G. Dhar. "Delhi's ongoing Debate on Informal settlements and work Places – Issues of Environmental Jurisprudence". Accessed online at http:/www.naervs.net/sat/workshops/2001/papers/chakrabarti.rtf on 20 February 2004.

3. Illegality and conflicts with respect to land are rampant which are further enhanced in the face of bureaucratic arbitrariness and political interests not reflective of citizens' concerns.
4. We have a government body which takes land from one section of the populace in utter disregard of their property rights (when property rights are fundamental to economic development) which often affects their livelihood severely and then proceeds to use the land in a manner that it further negatively affects other people's livelihood opportunities. And to top it all, the government body's revenue is often seen as an index of success even in the face of continued failure of performance.
5. The land-use plans when framed do not reflect the interests of the tax-payers. The tax-payer may not want the sidewalk to be completely occupied by hawkers but neither would he want to be completely deprived of the advantages of affordability and access that they provide. She/he may want shops near to his/her residence for convenience of access and may not want to travel too far for reasons of poor transport facilities. Take another example: cycle rickshaws. Planning and implementation authorities build roads of certain width with particular objectives in mind. However, a societal demand for cycle rickshaws leads to their proliferation. Now the premise of the road not being large enough to accommodate this particular mode of transport is never questioned. And the consequent congestion is blamed on excess cycle rickshaws, but never cars or buses.

   Hence, regulations step in to limit their number, and more and more unintended consequences follow, all of which impinge on the cycle rickshaw puller's livelihood and many others who wish to enter this low-skill profession, not to forget the consumers of these services.
6. The plans severely underestimate how markets (in other words, societal demands and supplies) work and its attendant consequences. Examples include the informal sector and housing for the poor.
7. There is a continued erroneous perception and presumption that present situation has been mainly because of the government and the failure has been because of the market. So, slum housing is seen as an outcome of encroachment by greedy and

poor people and attention is not paid to the fact that it is actually an outcome of poor policies pursued by the government that depress the supply of affordable housing for the poor either through monopoly of providing housing or through regulations that encumber rental housing like the Delhi Rent Control Act.

As the problem unfolds itself, it becomes clear that there are inherent epistemological limitations regarding the planning for a complex urban environment. The plans are not able to account for the choices of people, which may even change over time given contemporary scenarios. It is not planning per se that is being criticised but the question of who should plan. It would be worthwhile to concentrate on the processes rather than plans. A government planning and or implementation institution has three irresolvable difficulties facing it. First, It cannot hope to capture all the knowledge required to plan for the present and future. This knowledge is widely dispersed over society and individuals have different motivations to utilise this knowledge, it would be impossible to keep all these actions according to a plan. Second, to correct any errors in decisions, continuous feedback is required. Government institutions usually fall low on this count due to the lack of interest and also because they do not have any direct stake in the success or failure of the plans. Third, government enforcement institutions have weak incentives to carry out implementation effectively.

Reforms

Community-oriented Approach to Planning

Planning tools think of the community as a static concept, which is why it is presumed that the future can be determined reliably and controlled by local and regional governments. This stunts the community's ability to adapt and grow as per the changing needs and preferences of the time. A city development plan should envisage what the community should look like after a period of time. But, the zonal plans prepared at the local levels and also land-use regulations don't integrate development as a fundamental element of the plan or planning process. The kind of government mandated central planning that we have encountered exemplifies planning by a static body in a dynamic situation which is unable to respond appropriately to demands of reality. (Holcombe, 1995)

The main aim of land use regulations was to preserve residential areas from urban expansion. It was based on the premise that these regulations provide a mechanism for protecting individuals from bearing the cost of others' activities. But problems arise when land use decisions of some individuals become harmful for others. But then again the decision to deal with them by imposing land use regulations is also fraught with problems. Foremost among them is political control – that is, who has more political clout in the ultimate analysis. Ironically, land use regulations are amended ad hoc despite the fact that variances are often legally permissible only under very restrictive conditions.

The other potential problem is desirable land use. While some people prefer to live in a bustling neighbourhood with lots of urban amenities nearby, there are others who prefer living in the suburbs with single-family homes even if they have to drive long distance to reach their workplaces. Since the city plan is a centralised unit, some people are able to put political pressure to put forth *their* views about desirable development.

Since land use decisions have a large impact on the quality of life, it is but natural for some to try and influence decisions rather than allow individuals to do what they want with their land. However, two factors should prove deterrents: first, market incentives can help property owners develop their property efficiently without government interference and harm to others; second, when government land use planning is examined, decisions made under the name of planned development could more likely hinder than help the development process.

Therefore, urban planning and land-use regulations need to view communities as constantly evolving. This enhances the quality of goods and services and thereby the quality of life. In cases where the property rights and responsibilities of all affected property owners are considered, markets maximise public welfare because ultimately land development is by nature speculative. Investments in land and property are based on expectations that buyers will be willing to purchase property in a desirable community.

Zoning ordinances do not make much difference in the process of land use planning. It could be a matter of concern that without land use regulations someone might decide to tear down the house next door and build a petrol pump. But petrol pumps are unlikely to come up on residential streets because they have relatively little traffic, and petrol pumps thrive in areas with lots of traffic. Thus, petrol pumps and large retail stores will be located on major thoroughfares with heavy traffic regardless of land use restrictions.

On the other hand, people may like to shop at convenient locations on well-travelled roads, but want to live on quiet streets without much traffic. These natural economic factors segregate commercial and residential users of land.

Law of Nuisance

The law of nuisance provides additional ways to promote efficiency in land use decisions without government planning. If someone's use of property becomes a nuisance for others, then the well-established doctrine of nuisance can be used as a remedy. But regulating land use has reduced the reliance on this law. For instance, if someone wants to build a retail store in a residential area, the issue will be taken up as a matter of land use violation. But without land use regulations, the issue would be whether *that* property would constitute a nuisance to its neighbours. The law of nuisance, if based on property rights and not regulations, says it is illegal to use property in such a way as to create a nuisance for others. But it is for the courts to decide what actually constitutes a nuisance. The law of nuisance also provides a legal, but non-regulatory, remedy for environmental harm. For this, the harmed party must sue the party causing the damage. This could be a tedious process, because the firms causing environmental harm have only to meet the standards set by regulatory organisations. Once these standards are met they can always argue that what they are doing is perfectly legitimate. Such firms have been judged as being in compliance with the law because they met the standards, whereas under the law of nuisance, a more general standard applies, which is that individuals are not allowed to harm the property rights of others, rather than that individuals must merely meet regulatory standards. If there were fewer regulatory standards, there would be better-defined common law standards for determining when the activities of individuals are causing environmental harm. It might also have everyone suing everyone else in the absence of regulation, but, as in other areas of law, once the courts define the law, people follow it to avoid lawsuits.

Ironically, government regulation has served to weaken the law of nuisance. Through zoning and other regulations people obtain government permits to use property in whatever way they want. This permit becomes their defense if and when a 'nuisance' complaint is registered against them.

It is a misconception that government regulation offers better protection than the law of nuisance. Government decisions are subject to political pressure and implementations are subject to vested influences and corruption. So those with political pull are able to get government approval to create nuisance, leaving the victims with little recourse. Resources are more efficiently allocated when property rights are clearly defined and legally protected. Thus a well established law of nuisance could play a bigger role if government mandates did not provide protection for those creating nuisances. If the solution was to merely eliminate government involvement, it would have been simpler. Here the issue is to get the government, which plays an important role, to do the right thing.

Restrictive Covenants

The other legality could be the restrictive covenant. A developer of a residential block could assure the buyers that a petrol pump will not be built next door by placing a restrictive covenant on all the lots in the block to residential use. Covenants are often much more restrictive than land use regulations. They may stipulate the floor space, the lot size, also that before any additions or exterior changes are made, approval must be sought from a subdivisional architectural board.

Thus, restrictive covenants can replace land use regulations and preserve the residential character of neighbourhoods. Here too there is a catch. Restrictive covenants can be altered with the approval of those property owners who are covered by them. Thus, owners retain control of land use decisions over their property. If ever an urban development board wishes to make a residential area more profitable by converting it into a shopping centre, it will be upto the property owners to decide whether or not they wish to do so.

In Houston, Texas, where there is no zoning, a network of land use covenants has matured into an efficient and relatively sophisticated system. Imposed either by subdivision developers before sale or by agreement of an association of neighbors, covenants affect single-family homes, townhouses, and industrial parks in about one-quarter of Houston's total area. Most provide for the agreement to run 25 or 30 years, with automatic extension unless a majority of the participating owners vote to terminate or amend the covenant at the end of the initial period or any following 10-year period. In this way, change can come if a majority desires it—but the requirement to wait until the covenant expires protects minority owners' interests as well. Obviously, the authority of private covenants extends only to those who participate; this means that the resulting diversity of land use restriction found in the community provides many avenues of choice to the property purchaser, without sacrificing his sense of security in the character of the immediate neighborhood he finally chooses. Private covenants deliver what government zoning and regulation cannot even promise: security and flexibility.

Ward Based Management for Utilisation of Public Space

Can we incorporate these approaches into our present set-up? Can we envision a model that integrates these principles to reduce the conflict over public and private space which is at the root of problems concerning land-use and consequently, livelihood. All powers of utilisation of public space except the major thoroughfares can be transferred to the Ward Committee. (Since the ward is the present lowest functional unit of urban governance and has even been accepted by the government through the 74th Constitutional Amendment as the unit to devolve powers.[22] It would be even better

22. *Dossier of Background Documents on the 74th Constitution Amendment Act*. 2002. Bangalore: CIVIC Bangalore.

to have the unit of governance an area and populace smaller than that of the present ward). Let them figure the best way to use or, in fact, not use the space. Decentralisation of powers always yields better results for it puts powers in the hands of those who would be most suited to influence outcomes or suffer the effect of a wrong decision and correct it. Hence, stepping down from the State machinery to the ward institutions is a step forward in this decentralisation of power akin to States having greater powers than the Centre in consonance with the Principle of Subsidiarity.[23]

Common Law for Resolving Disputes of Private Nuisance

Conflicts can be resolved through the common-law doctrines of trespass and nuisance. In general, a nuisance is defined as something that interferes with another person's right to use his own property in a reasonable manner. See box on page 175 for more information on the common-law. The advantage of this common-law approach is that it allows flexibility in determining what constitutes a nuisance. However, government regulations have crowded out the usage of the common-law approach.

A common-law approach to land-use disputes (through arbitration and not always local courts) would be superior to government planned land-use in that it focuses on the effects of a particular land use, rather than the use itself. For example, rather than imposing an outright ban on businesses in residential areas, the common law would focus on whether the business caused extra traffic, destroyed the natural beauty, or disrupted the family atmosphere of a neighbourhood. Instead of deciding which land uses to exclude, people could focus their energies on how to achieve the maximum freedom while mitigating any nuisances that might be caused.

Among other issues, the elected members of the Ward Committee would also envisage provisions for hawkers – whether they are needed, and what kind of hawkers would be needed. The

23. The "principle of subsidiarity" demarcates the proper arenas for civil and political society, and for local, state, and central government within the political society. The principle suggests that the state should undertake those tasks that people cannot undertake for themselves through voluntary associations of civil society. The functions thus assigned to the state must be entrusted first to local governments. The functions that local governments cannot perform should be given to state governments and only those that state governments are unable to undertake should be delegated to the central government.

same would hold true for shops or enterprises where the community is best placed to assess the consequences and take action. Ditto for cycle rickshaws. They have been expounded upon in the respective chapters. In case of the public space in wards used for transit purposes the Ward Committee can concur with the state transport authorities for the use of thoroughfares, thus allowing for better and focused negotiations. The power need not be relegated only to use of public space but may extend to other items of governance like electricity and water where they have the power to choose the best service provider among a host of service-providers. The premise that runs through these suggestions is the same: resident bodies who can use market mechanisms to fulfil their needs – best perform localised governance. Indeed, it would be short-sighted to underestimate the ingenuity and ability hidden in communities to respond to their demands through the market. (Osborne and Gaebler, 1993) Needless to add, the amount of learning that would happen through the different approaches of the Ward Committees would only entail better outcomes by each of the wards. All of this would not require a major shift in governance for Delhi but only latching on to the present scheme of "Bhagidari" governance.

The ward level model would definitely work better than the present mode of governance but it is not as if it is not ridden with its share of problems. The element of politicking and hence arbitrary discretion of power that pervades any collective ownership of resources also has its presence here. Also, this ward level model would entail on part of the government to set up a separate ministry/department and all the attendant bureaucracy for purposes of ward level management which will generate its own processes detrimental to the interests of the populace. These problems can be better solved if we go further down the ladder to the individual and empower him. It is only logical that if decentralisation of power for property rights works better through the ward model, at the individual level it would work that much better. *Property rights are truly prosperity rights!* Respect for ownership of private property allows the greatest freedom for its economic value to be maximised with consequent economic development for all. But can a matrix of property rights deliver and ensure good governance? A slight suspension of disbelief may well help to drive the point home.

Privatising Urban Governance Delivery

Imagine an Alternative Delhi where all the land was vested in numerous private property holders and there was no central land developing agency. A private developer wishing to build and establish a mini-city would acquire the required land, through voluntary exchange and satisfactory compensation to the title-holders. A developer knows that by selling governance opportunities, they are satisfying a profound consumer demand. To attract customers he would offer, apart from residences, shops and commercial establishments (apples to zippers) catering to all requirements and income categories, services and service professionals (banks to barbers, creches etc.), educational institutions, community centres, recreational centres (parks, gyms, theatres etc.), security personnel (who would also check for the maids working there), round the clock electricity-water and drainage-sewerage facilities, walkways for pedestrians, petrol pumps, religious premises, hospitals, parking space, railway booking office, libraries etc.

These are the obvious ones. Some of the not-so-obvious ones are:

- Safe streets.
- Clean environment (no pollution or garbage).
- Transport facilities (could be taxis/cycle rickshaws within and good roads).

People's choices often differ. Some might like to live near their workplace or at least, one that does not take too long a transit time: others might sacrifice shorter transit time for a good school or simply a clean environment. Accordingly, private developers have incentives to offer a "office park" where various offices are present. Assuming that there are different private property developers vying to attract these office workers, there would be competition among them to offer the best facilities at the most reasonable prices. There would be different types of residences depending on incomes and other suitable conditions. Some may like a bustling market nearby, others may not. In fact, some developers may have clauses like no parking for visitors' vehicles; others may make provisions for them to be parked. A variety of options give the customer a choice to seek the residence that answers his requirements the most.

Usually, people would not prefer to live close to industries. Again, those who develop industrial estates would try to locate them faraway from prime residential localities so as to decrease costs of acquiring land and also to avoid costs of litigation from affected people. Hence, there would be more and more congregation of industrial estates. As time changes, and if residences are affected, the common law of nuisance can be applied on a case-by-case basis. The private developers may even arbitrate among themselves for a mutually satisfactory settlement. The private developers may have restrictive covenants within the estate stating explicitly that such and such industry would not be allowed. Another private developer may only allow particular types of industries with the standards and the scale mentioned thereby making it possible for residents to know about it beforehand through the stipulated conditions in the contract.

Private Community Associations and Urban Livelihoods

Consider street hawkers. A private property developer would know the niche appeal of the hawkers and make space for them accordingly. Example: if he constructs a temple, he would know the importance of flower-sellers and seek to place them in the vicinity. A private road developer in one of the steps to recover his investment might seek to place hawkers on the roadside, leave enough space for pedestrians to walk and build enough road-space for road-users to defuse congestion. For too much of congestion might keep away customers. All in the attempt to attract more people to avail of his product. To take care of the quality concerns of food-hawkers he might even ask for a guarantee of quality about the food prepared. Private greed does public good!

That streets can be developed and owned privately is not too far-fetched an idea.[24] There are already numerous real world examples of private streets, which function highly effectively. Like the private streets of St. Louis, the streets to shopping malls and shopping centres (even the aisles of groceries and department stores may be considered), gated communities or townships world-wide, and the rural roads owned by associations of property owners in Finland and

24. It is indeed surprising how many of us consider a road to be a fixed parameter and envisage policies keeping the capacity of the road fixed. Private entrepreneurs would have every incentive to build required road space if the government does not crowd them out in urban cities, where returns can be impressive.

Sweden. There are said to be about 40,000 private roads in England and Wales.[25] Many are residential; some are roads on industrial estates or within large institutions such as hospitals. Contrast the private streets in most townships with the public streets in cities: the former are safe for passersby, while the latter have often been the location of murders and rapes.

In a scenario where the pedestrians spill onto the streets, (assuming that the owner of the pavement and the street is not the same in which case the issue gets simplified), both would seek to negotiate to their benefit what works in favour of the users. Street ownership induces the incentive to allow for optimally smooth passage of traffic, which can be harnessed effectively. (Roth, 1996).

Shop-establishment has primarily two grouses. First, they may be in an undesirable place, especially for the neighbours. Second, quality of the offered product. Right now, licensing does not achieve any of the above, though neighbours get inconvenienced and quality-inspection achieves only a fraction of the objective, even discounting the harassment. Private developers under competition are cognizant of these, hence they would seek to clearly earmark the areas and also define rules beforehand to seek compensation for any breach of contract. They also have an incentive to go into the nitty-gritties of the issue like availability of parking space. However, the measures would still leave room for feedback and improvement, something which is sought by private developers, for on it depend their profits in a sphere of unlimited competition, where residents can switch between private developers. There would be independent agencies that would provide certification of the quality of product or service and the developers would insist on these certifications not for themselves but for their customers. What about a first-timer? He would have to provide some kind of satisfactory guarantee to the developer. If developers set up only shops catering to the rich, another developer would perceive the lacuna in the market and set up low-cost shops and profit.

Property developers or private communities might offer to have slaughter-houses if given suitable compensation and built to well-defined standards. There are examples of communities who have accepted usage of a part of their land for landfill since the revenue they gained went into community development.

25. Accessed online at http://www.privateroads.co.uk on 18 February 2004

What about auto rickshaws and cycle rickshaws? The developers cognizant of the demands of low-cost transport would allow these vehicles to ply subject to their obeying certain standards, which may differ from one developer to another. Probably, the many unions of these vehicles would act as contractors and supply services to these mini-cities. A newcomer might even offer to undercut others and accept lower charges. On the private roads, a developer perceiving the demand for low-cost transport might offer separate lanes for these vehicles and allow the optimal number so as to achieve both profits and decongestion. Alternatively, to combat congestion, the developer might resort to a user fee-based approach on the principle of using pricing as a rationing mechanism which is far more equitable than the present system of broad-based taxes.

The point here is that we are already paying taxes for the provision and use of roads. And look at their state! A user-fee would be more equitable than allowing the general taxpayers' money to be funneled through political machinations. It would also address the bizarre situation of VIPs, political honchos or even World Bank delegations obtaining unfair use of the roads in terms of smooth passage at the cost of time and money to the others. In the light of trends of private provision of roads and sophisticated payment mechanisms that have evolved and are also under study, must we still stick to the beaten path?

In order for communities to live peacefully, there would be provision of private arbitration, fire extinguishing contracts for dealing with fires would be given to credible service-providers of this category. There would even be private prisons established for the offenders. Insurance agencies would take over many of the functions of inspection in accordance with the provisions that they cover, which would also extend to safety of housing. Extend the same to other functions of government we are so used to, that we stop looking for better possibilities, for instance postal delivery by a private service provider, burial/cremation facilities by another private service provider. Communities or associations like orphanages could also provide their functions on a purely voluntary basis. None of them can establish a monopolistic status for the users can always switch to another provider. Push the price of car-usage on roads too high and users would find it better to use buses. Make housing too costly and soon one will find the developer being disadvantaged by other competing developers.

The public services that are enjoyed in common are actually territorial goods in the sense that these service are supplied to sites rather than to individuals and most individuals gain access to them through the occupancy of these sites. Thus, owners of land, when they lease or sell sites, are the market purveyors of public services. Only thus can such services be distributed, as other goods and services are through the conventions of the market place. Only through property in land can they be freely and equitably administered by contract. It is not implausible for developers to go to the next step and produce as well as distribute these services. Their reward would be more market power and higher incomes from enhanced land values.

Ultimately, all governance would be voluntary and contractual. All taxation and burdensome licensing, regulation and other restrictions on enterprise will belong to the past. "Shadow governments" or the private institutions such as covenant committees, neighborhood associations, and development corporations would provide most of the functions we traditionally associate with government – from infrastructure to policing. Ultimate power in a purely voluntary city would be completely decentralised, down to the individual household and family. Its governance structure would be bottoms-up with power ultimately based on sovereign individuals. The distinction between the government and private sectors would disappear, as voluntary governance would be based on contracts among private members and property owners. Proprietary community associations will dominate the future of human settlement, replacing political administration. (Foldvary, 1994).

A recent trend in the United States of America has been the development of metropolitan enclaves that exist outside of any municipal government.[26] A few of them are Paradise, Nevada Casas, Adobes near Tucson, the Woodlands near Houston, Highlands Ranch near Denver and Spring Valley and Sunrise Manor near the city of Las Vegas. About 2,000 of such enclaves are governed by the strict bylaws of homeowners' associations. They establish covenants that regulate the appearance and lifestyle of the new subdivision. They collect homeowners' dues to pay for private roads, landscaping, lighting and

---

26. "Some big U.S. places find paradise in not being cities". Accessed online at http://experts.uli.org/Content/ResFellows/Mcavey/McAvey_Clips_12.htm on 18 February 2004

sometimes trash pickup. Fifteen per cent of American housing is located within these private neighbourhood governance jurisdictions and the trend looks set to continue.[27]

In the set-up delineated, there is incentive for the private entity to invest, get feedback and make suitable changes according to the change in the situation. Advances in technology have already made possible the unthinkable, like charges for using roads. Unleashing the spirit of free enterprise would make it possible to achieve the maximum value from scarce resources.

Just as private enterprises offer bread in various differentials of price and quality to render them affordable to different income groups, so too shall private developers offer housing in an array of costs and features that would cater to even the poor. In every product from clothes to computers the market offers a variety of options which the poor stand to benefit from and hence there is no reason to suspect that the same would not happen in the case of housing. In an age where individuals choose nations or cities or localities for the services and related benefits (territorial collective goods), developers would have every incentive to allow different schemes for different income brackets.

Now, imagine a network of mini-cities catering to different kinds of land-use: residential, commercial, industrial and even mixed land-use. Private road developers/associations would arise to network these mini-cities: users may be charged or the developers may contribute to maintain it for part of connecting to other mini-cities. There would be contracts between developers to seek road development by private road developers and pay the requisite fees.

In one sense, privatising governance is like attempting to unscramble an egg; it is very, very complicated, because what we are trying to do in effect is to bring about a situation today, which would have ensued had governance always been private. Our goal is to determine how this market would have functioned in the past, and then to set up a situation, now, as close to what would have been, in this imaginary condition.

The problem is that this is essentially an entrepreneurial not an economic task. It is impossible to anticipate the market. Suppose, for

27. Webster C.J. 2001. "Gated Cities of Tomorrow". *Town Planning Review* 72(2), 149-169

example, that the shoe industry had always been run under government supervision, and that we were now contemplating moving it from government-run to private enterprise. A whole host of questions would quickly arise, the answers to which would lie outside the realm of economics. For example, how many shoe firms would there be? What colour would be the footwear? What proportion would there be between black, brown, white, tan and other colour shoes? Between shoes, runners, sneakers, slippers? How many lace holes would there be in a shoe? How many shoe stores would be located on each block? Would there be one in every mall? How would the poor afford shoes?

In like manner, it is difficult in the extreme to know, at this late date, the precise configurations of private governance, had one been allowed to be fully developed from day one. On the other hand, we need not be too pessimistic about this either. An imperfect privatisation will be far preferable to none at all. Government streets are an administrative and safety nightmare. It is inconceivable that free enterprise initiatives could do worse than present models of governance.

Central planning in the context of governments has its limitations with respect to vision and enforcement. It is not planning per se that is under criticism. It doesn't hurt to have some people thinking of a neighbourhood as a whole. But those people needn't be city planners—they could be large landlords, neighbourhood association heads, or other sorts of voluntary organisations. Property rights and its trade enable people to achieve ends that are valued most by themselves and others.

The order present in a well-functioning urban area emerges as the result of human action but not human design. It arises from a myriad of individuals – each pursuing his own interest and carrying out his own plans, within a framework of rules that encourages peaceful cooperation over violent aggression.

But what of the poor, especially those who cannot afford much? That is why the emphasis is on livelihood opportunities. Denial of livelihood is denial of life. In an unfettered market with sound institutions of law and respect for property rights, there would be equal opportunity to pursue their ends, and mobility across economic barriers would happen as a consequence of human action, not of human design.

Conclusion

So, what reform lessons does this chapter hold for us?

1. The land agencies should stop further acquisition of land and reallocate existing undeveloped land to the original title holders at the original prices since it is unfair for the agency to even auction and benefit from what was not theirs in the first place.
2. Also most government agencies own land far in excess of their requirements and for reasons which do not hold much weight. Such excess land could be surveyed and sold to private parties for development. These private parties should not have any restrictions on land assembly.
3. Hold property rights sacrosanet. Reintroduce the Right to Poverty as a fundamental Right in the constitution.
4. Private parties should be free to develop land not only in Delhi but all over India to allow for a boom in economic development.
5. Land-use plans should not be subject to legislative processes. The DDA should cease to have a role in the issue of land. It must also be mentioned that the DDA is not only an enforcing agency of the Ministry of Urban Development but also subject to the influence of the Home Ministry, both of which are far removed from the people's participatory processes and subject to political vagaries.
6. Efforts should be focused to strengthen the judiciary for dispute resolution, contract enforcement and protection of property rights.
7. Repeal of the Rent Control Act for it is the most detrimental to the development of housing for the poor, since the poor's only recourse to housing is to rent and these regulations severely restrict the incentives to build housing and offer them on a rental basis to different income groups. According to the *India Today*, the Rent Control Act is responsible for over three lakh vacant houses in Delhi.[28] And the number is rising.

---

28. *India Today*. 2003. "How we live: Census India Household survey". 28 July.

Bibliography

Anderson, Terry L. and Huggins, Laura E. 2003. Property Rights: A Practical Guide to Freedom and Prosperity. Accessed online on 18 February 2004 at http://www-hoover.stanford.edu/publications/books/proprights.html

America's new Utopias: The growth of private communities. 2001. Accessed online on 18 February 2004 at http://www.economist.com/world/na/displayStory.cfm?Story_ID=760545

Block, Walter "Free Market Transportation: Denationalising the Roads," *Journal of Libertarian Studies: An Interdisciplinary Review*, Vol. III, No. 2, Summer 1979, pp. 209-238.

————. "Public Goods and Externalities: The Case of Roads," *Journal of Libertarian Studies: An Interdisciplinary Review*, Vol. VII, No. 1, Spring 1983, pp. 1-34.

————. Road Socialism, *International Journal of Value-Based Management*, 9 (1996): 195-207.

————. "Roads, Bridges, Sunlight and Private Property: Reply to Tullock," *Journal Des Economistes Et Des Etudes Humaines*, Vol. VIII, No. 2/3, June-September 1998, 315-326.

————. "Homesteading City Streets; An Exercise in Managerial Theory," *Planning and Markets*, Volume 5, Issue 2, October 2002

Brushett, Stephen. 2000. "Note on Study Tour undertaken to Sweden on Community Roads", Accessed online on 18 February 2004 at www.worldbank.org/transport/roads/ism_docs/annex3b.pdf

"Cabinet nod for conversion of properties in Delhi". 20 May 2003. *Businessline*.

Christy, Francis., Field, Barry., Leal, Don., Schlager, Edella., and De Alessi, Michael. "Common and Private Property Rights: A Roundtable Discussion". Accessed online on 18 February 2004 at http://www.privateconservation.org/pubs/roundtables/470common.pdf

Corkindale , John. "Fifty Years of the Town and Country Planning Acts, Time to Privatise Land Development Rights?" IEA Studies on the Environment No. 11. Accessed online on 18 February 2004 at www.iea.org.uk/files/upld-article13pdf?.pdf

Beito, David T., Gordon, D., Tabarrok, Alexander. 2002. *The Voluntary City: Choice, Community and Civil Society.* Ann Arbor: University of Michigan Press.

Foldvary, Fred. "Government and Governance," *The Freeman* 47, no. 1, January 1997: 33-37.

————. 1995. *Public Goods and Private Communities: The Market Provision of Social Services.* Aldershot: Edward Elgar, 1994. Reprint, Aldershot: Edward Elgar.

Friedman, David. 1973. *The Machinery of Freedom.* New York: Arlington House Publishers.

Flanagan, Gregory. "Free Market Roads" Accessed online on 18 February 2004 at http://www.libertocracy.com/roads.htm

Government of NCT of Delhi. 2002. *Economic Survey of Delhi: 2001-2002.* Planning Department.

Boudreaux, Donald and Holcombe, Randall. "Government by Contract," Public Finance Quarterly 17, July 1989.

" 'Guidelines' to substitute lawful Plan revision". Accessed online on 22 February 2004 at http://www.delhiscienceforum.org/dmp2021/documents/A_GL.htm

Government of India. 1992. *Guidelines on Land Management.* Volumes 1 and 2. Lands Department, Delhi Development Authority.

Holcombe, Randall G. 1995. *Public Policy and the Quality of Life: Market Incentives versus Government Planning.* Westport, Connecticut: Greenwood Press.

————. 2002. "The New Urbanism Versus the Market Process", Austrian Scholars Conference 8, Ludwig von Mises Institute. Accessed online on 22 February 2004 at http://www.mises.org/asc/2002/ASC8-Holcombe.pdf

Isotalo, Jukka and Heggie, Ian G. 1996. "Managing Undesignated Roads". Accessed online on 18 February 2004 at www.worldbank.org/transport/roads/ism_docs/annex3.pdf

John, Charles. "Zoning, Privatisation, and Liberty". Accessed online on 18 February 2004 at http://www.mackinac.org/article.asp?ID=1789

Jacobs, Jane. 1961. *The Life and Death of Great American Cities*. New York: Random House.

————. 1969. *The Economy of Cities*. New York: Random House.

Klein, Daniel, Adrian Moore, and Binyam Reja. 1997. *Curb Rights: A Foundation for Free Enterprise in Urban Transit.* Washington, D.C.: Brookings Institution Press.

Martin Ball. 1994. *Liberate the Roads! The Benefits That Will Come From Road Privatisation.*

Micklethwait, Brian. "The Private Ownership of Public Space: The new Age of Rationally Priced Road Use". Accessed online on 18 February 2004 at http://www.libertarian.co.uk/lapubs/econn/econn049.pdf

McPherson, Scott. "Is It Time for Private Roads?" Accessed online on 22 February 2004 at http://www.mindspring.com/~rob2d2/tal/commentary/scott_mcpherson/is_it_time_for_private_roads.htm

"New Master Plan for Delhi pardons all sins". 30 July 2003. Accessed online on 18 February 2004 at http://economictimes.indiatimes.com/articleshow/111874.cms

Nigam, Aditya. "Dislocating Delhi: A City in the 1990s". Accessed online on 18 February 2004 at www.sarai.net/journal/pdf/040-046%20(industry).pdf

Osborne, David and Ted Gaebler. 1993. *Reinventing Government: How the Entrepreneurial Spirit is Transforming the Public Sector.* New York: Penguin

Pennington, Mark. 2002. *Liberating the Land: The Case for Private Land-use Planning*. London: Institute of Economic Affairs.

Phillips, J. Brian. 1989. "Private Cities". Accessed online on 18 February 2004 at http://www.fee.org/vnews.php?nid=2043

————. 1990. Progressivism Comes to Houston. Accessed online on 18 February 2004 at http://www.fee.org/vnews.php?nid=2192

Roth, Gabriel. 1998. *Roads in a Market Economy.* Aldershot: Ashgate, 1996. Reprint, Aldershot: Ashgate.

Rothbard, Murray N. *For a New Liberty* (1994). The Public Sector, II: Streets and Roads. Accessed online on 18 February 2004 at http://www.mises.org/rothbard/newliberty10.asp

Roy, Dunu. 2002. "People and planning". *Seminar.* Accessed online on 18 February 2004 at http://www.india-seminar.com/2000/491/491%20comment.htm

Roy, Dunu and Batra, Lalit. 2003. *Dilli Kiski Hai.* New Delhi: Khatra Kendra.

Sahni, Ajai. (1998). "The 'privatisation' of public security". *Pioneer,* 12 December. Accessed online on 18 February 2004 at http://www.satp.org/satp.orgtp/ajaisahni/Pio121298.htm

Siegan, Bernard H. "Land use regulations should preserve only vital and pressing governmental interests". Accessed online on 18 February 2004 at http://www.cato.org/pubs/journal/cj10n1/cj10n1-8.pdf

Scarlett, Lynn and Staley, Samuel. 1997. *Market Oriented Planning: Principles and Tools.* Accessed at http://www.rppi.org/ps236.html

Shearmur, Jeremy. *Living with a Marsupial Mouse: Lessons from Celebration, Florida* Accessed online on 18 February 2004 at http://www.cis.org.au/policy/winter02/polwin02-4.htm

Siegan, Bernard. 1972. *Land Use Without Zoning*. Lexington, Mass.: Lexington Books.

Soto, Hernando de. 1989. *The Other Path: The Invisible Revolution in the Third World.* Translated by June Abott. New York: Harper & Row.

Saltzman, James D. "Houston Says No to Zoning". Accessible at www.libertyhaven.com/personalfreedomissues/freespeechorcivilliberties/ houstonzoning.html

Beito, David T. and Smith, Bruce "The Formation of Urban Infrastructure Through Non-Governmental Planning: The Private Places of St. Louis." Journal of Urban History 16 (May 1990): 263-303.

Tucker, William. 1991. *Zoning, Rent Control, and Affordable Housing*. Washington D. C.: Cato Institute.

Tiwari, G. 2003. "Transport and land-use policies in Delhi", *Bull World Health Organ, 81(6)*, 444-450.

Verma, Gita Dewan. 2002. *Slumming India: A Chronicle of Slums and Their Saviours*. India: Penguin Books.

Webster C.J. 2000. "Gates, Green-belts and Gemeinshaft: from public realm to club realm". Submitted to *Environment and Planning B*, special issue on Gated Communities, June 2000.

Winter, Bill. 1999. "Libertarianism's stealthy triumph". Accessed online on 18 February 2004 at http://www.lp.org/lpn/9901-triumph.html

Watt, P.A. 2003. "Voluntary Roads and Streets" *Economic Affairs*, June, pp. 3-10.

"We want to amend the Master Plan" *Frontline* Volume 17 - Issue 25, Dec. 9 - 22, 2000. Accessed online on 18 February 2004 at http://www.flonnet.com/fl1725/17250100.htm.

5

The Meat Market: Meeting Market Demand

Ever wondered how the meat-seller in your neighbourhood obtains the meat? By law a meat seller in Delhi cannot slaughter a goat or a buffalo by himself. As per Section 407 of the Delhi Municipal Corporation Act, no place other than a municipal slaughterhouse shall be used as a slaughterhouse. The municipal slaughterhouse in Delhi is at Idgah. Approximately 13,500 animals were slaughtered daily till 1994.[1] For this, the slaughterhouse functioned 24 hours a day in three shifts, taking breaks just for the cleaning up. Since the load placed on the abattoir was way over its built capacity, rules regarding sanitation were blatantly violated. In 1992, Maneka Gandhi filed a writ petition against the Idgah slaughterhouse regarding the inhuman and dirty conditions under which the animals were being slaughtered.[2] Following the petition, the Delhi High Court passed an order in March 1994 that only 2,500 animals[3] would be slaughtered each day; also, exporters were directed to make their own arrangements.[4]

Since people had to get their animals slaughtered at the Municipal Corporation of Delhi (MCD) abattoir, they would start queuing up at midnight while the abattoir was scheduled to open at 5 0'clock the next morning. The ones who were lucky enough to reach the abattoir early got as many animals slaughtered as they could and then sold the meat to actual shop owners. In fact, many persons who had an entry license often did not even have a shop for selling meat. As

---

1. Press Trust of India. 18 May 1994, Indian Court Sets up Team on Butcher's Strike.
2. Maneka Gandhi *vs.* Union Territory of Delhi, 1994 II AD (Delhi) 265 DB.
3. Actual built capacity specified as: buffaloes 500 (only *halal*); sheep and goats – *halal* 1500, *jhatka* 500.
4. Press Trust of India. 18 May 1994, Indian Court Sets up Team on Butcher's Strike.

per a MCD official in the buffalo section at Idgah, they made money by getting meat cut at the abattoir and then selling them to meat sellers.

Meanwhile, the case went up to the Supreme Court[5] and the Idgah Abattoir Committee was set up under Justice J.D. Jain. The Committee was formed to decide/identify the "conditions and additional facilities, infrastructure and services necessary to augment increase in the number of animals for slaughtering at Idgah and the establishment of a mechanised slaughterhouse of an adequate capacity to meet the requirements of consumers." These recommendations were then to be placed before the Delhi High Court.

One of the Committee's recommendations that was implemented was that no person should get more than two animals slaughtered. This implementation caused a lot of disorder at Idgah. The MCD authorities then decided, against the directions of the Jain Committee, to give coupons to the Meat-sellers Associations. Now, everyday the coupons are stamped with next day's date and given to the Associations by evening and the Association decides who to give the coupons to.

Imagine the chaos at the abattoir slaughtering 13,500 animals daily when its actual capacity is just 2,500. And now imagine the scenario if one fine day the supply is reduced by over 80 per cent. Was a majority of Delhi's meat eating population expected to become vegetarian overnight? Compared to the 2,500 animals being slaughtered daily at Idgah, the actual demand for meat including total number of goats, sheep and buffaloes in Delhi is estimated to be as high as:

- Saturday/Sunday/Wednesday: 12,000 - 15,000
- Monday/Thursday: 8,000 - 10,000
- Friday: 6,000 - 7,000

Illegal Slaughtering in Delhi

All this makes one wonder why it is so important for a meat shop owner to get their supply from Idgah alone. Once the animals are

5. Buffalo Traders Welfare Association v. Maneka Gandhi, 1994 Supp (3) SCC 448.

purchased from the auction centre outside Idgah, the meat shop owners have two options other than the legal one of getting them slaughtered at Idgah. The first one is to get them slaughtered by professionals near Idgah at Quasebura (there are many other such locations especially in the vicinity of Idgah). The second option is to get it slaughtered near the shop or home. Nevertheless, getting everything done at the MCD abattoir is more cost effective, because:

- Legal slaughtering is highly subsidised by the government. By providing land, water, electricity, medical and sanitation services and charging just Rs. 5-12 per animal, the MCD is incurring heavy losses.[6] If a person gets his animal slaughtered elsewhere, he is charged around Rs. 50 per animal. Other services such as skinning etc. are also provided at the MCD abattoir at cheap rates taking the total 'official cost' to the maximum of Rs. 50.
- At the MCD abattoir waste disposal is not the butchers' responsibility. However, in case of private slaughter, disposal of the biological wastes near the shops/homes results in medical problems, apart from the nauseating stink and the stray dogs crowding around to eat leftovers.
- Illegally slaughtered meat does not have the MCD stamp. Thus if caught by an MCD inspection team, a hefty fine has to be paid. The meat may also be confiscated.

The total monetary cost of illegal slaughtering combined with the fines can be as high as Rs. 2,200.[7] This explains why people prefer to get the coupons from the black market at rates of Rs. 50-150 per coupon. The rates vary according to the demand, and are higher during festivals.

Till date, there has been no further change in the situation at Idgah. Coupons are given to the Associations the night before and 2,500 animals are slaughtered daily. The Delhi populace is supposed to be satisfied by the supply of 2,500 animals per day, when the demand is at least four times the supply from the abattoir.

---

6. Official information from the slaughter house at Idgah.
7. Fine for selling unstamped meat (Rs. 2000), cost of slaughter (Rs. 50), other work done (Rs. 50), bribes paid (Rs. 20-100)

Modes of Killing: Jhatka and Halal

The *Jhatka* method is called so because the head of the animal is separated from the body in one stroke. The blood does not flow freely. Traders, though, do not prefer this meat apparently because it does not have a long shelf life. In the *Halal* method of killing, the animal is slowly bled to death by slitting its jugular vein in the neck.

Licensing of a Meat Shop

The next step in the meat market is 'selling' the meat once the carcass has been procured from the slaughterhouse. The MCD grants a license to meat shops called the Health Trade License. The procedure for getting this license has been detailed in the chapter on shop licensing. The Health Licensing Department of MCD dealt with this license till 2002, but now, there is a separate branch called the Veterinary Department that handles the licensing and inspection of the meat shops.

Running the Meat Shop

The entire process, from procuring the animals to selling the meat at the shop, is as follows:

Step 1: Every person who wishes to enter the MCD abattoir has to purchase an annual entry licence[8] costing Rs. 100. Coupons are available at the gate of each section (goat, sheep, and buffalo). The coupons cost Rs. 12 for a buffalo and Rs. 5 for a goat or a sheep. Each licensee is entitled to only two coupons.

Step 2: Each day, the meat seller has to bring 'healthy' animals to the MCD abattoir and get them slaughtered there. Usually the animals are purchased from the auctioning centre outside the Idgah abattoir.

Step 3: At the abattoir, the animals have to be taken to their respective sections for slaughter. There are three sections: one each for sheep, goats, and buffaloes.

Step 4: The meat now has to be stamped by MCD officials certifying that the animal has been slaughtered at the MCD abattoir.

---

8. No limit on number of licences.

9. Regulations a, b, c & d, sourced from http://pets.indiatimes.com/articleshow.cms?chname=pets&artID=1061592453 accessed on 20 January, 2004.

Step 5: The meat must then be transported to the licensed shop in a chilled van.

Step 6: At the shop, meat is supposed to be cut neatly and stored in refrigerators/iceboxes at below 4 degree Celsius.

Regulations that have to be followed during the process[9]

a. Every animal to be slaughtered must be certified healthy and free from disease by a municipal vet before it can be slaughtered.

b. No cattle below the age of 16 may be killed.

c. No animal shall be slaughtered in view of another animal.

d. Under the ISI, animals must be rested for 24 hours, given abundant water and rendered unconscious before slaughtering. All licensed butcher shops are required to follow the ISI code of health and hygiene standards.

e. Where a municipal slaughterhouse exists, it is illegal for animals to be killed anywhere else (Section 407, *Delhi Municipal Corporation Act*, 1957)

f. No pregnant animal may be slaughtered. (Technical Instructions, Butchers' Trade (8). Section 415, *Delhi Municipal Corporation Act*, 1957)

g. No person can in any public place or public street, carry meat exposed to public view. [Section 397 (1 iv), *Delhi Municipal Corporation Act*, 1957]

h. After the animals have been slaughtered, they have to be kept at temperatures below 4 degree Celsius.

The MCD lays down certain elaborate rules regarding the sanitation and hygiene to be observed by the meat shops. The technical conditions in the box on the next page showcase the detailing of input monitoring the MCD undertakes, at least on paper.[10] For an entire list of the rules to be followed by the meat shops, refer to the Appendix.

Therefore, every time a meat seller hangs a goat carcass at his shop to be prominently visible to the public, he is breaking the law. Also, every meat seller who does not use a refrigerator or an icebox to store the meat is again flouting the rules. None of the shops surveyed during the research were found to abide by these rules.

10. Delhi Municipal Corporation Act, 1957. Section 415. Technical Instructions, Meat Shop.

> *Rules to be Observed in the Meat Shops*
>
> - The premises shall be structurally sound.
> - The premises shall be completely fly-proof, perfectly with double doors, and the outer door will open outwards and will be fitted with springs to ensure they're self-closing.
> - Fly swats or flaps should be used to kill stray flies getting in the premises.
> - The implements and chopping block shall be washed with boiling water. The chopping block will be dried and salted every day at the close of business.
> - Workers shall maintain a high standard of personal hygiene at all times. No smoking, chewing pan, and snuff shall be allowed in the premises.
> - Clean wax paper polythene bags shall be used as packing material for the retail sale of meat. No carcass shall be kept in a manner so as to be visible to public view from outside.
> - Refrigerators/iceboxes of adequate size shall be provided for storage of meat and meat products.
>
> *Look around at any of the local meat shops in Delhi and you will begin to wonder what the MCD officials, responsible for enforcing these rules, are doing?*

Interestingly, one of the inspectors in-charge of enforcing these rules accepted that they were not too strict and would allow a person to go unpunished even if he used slabs of ice to store the meat. In essence, even the law-enforcers believe that some of the regulations are unfair and so they refuse to implement them.

Number of Meat Shops in Delhi

As per the official claims, the number of meat shops in Delhi as on July 1, 2002 is given in Table 1.[11] It is interesting to note that as per the Food and Agricultural Organisation (FAO) study of 'Food Marketing in Delhi', 1995 there were nearly 5,000 retail shops selling fresh raw meat in the city.[12]

---

11. According to the MCD, there were 1,646 unlicensed shops selling buffalo flesh, mutton, fish and chicken to 931 licensed ones in the capital, as on July 1 2002. Accessed online at http://www.dailyexcelsior.com/01july02/busi.htm on 20 January, 2004.
12. D.H. Dhankar, "Food-Marketing in Delhi—A Pre-Case Study", Sourced from <http://www.google.com/search?q=cache:RSgDd1bKqYQJ:www.fao.org/ag/ags/agsm/SADA DOCS/DOC EC3399E.DOC+%22meat+shops%22+delhi+statistics+number&hl=en &ie=UTF-8> (Accessed on January 10, 2004).

Table 1

	Licensed	*Unlicensed*	*Total*
Mutton	757	1236	1993
Buffalo	127	308	435
Total	884	1544	2428

The animal count of 2,000 mutton (sheep and goat) and 500 buffaloes distributed equally over the shops is given in Table 2.

Table 2

	Licensed	*All Shops*
Mutton	2.64	1.00
Buffalo	3.94	1.15

Assuming that there is no illegal slaughtering in Delhi and that the official figures are not an underestimation of the number of shops in Delhi, no meat shop would be selling more than 1.00/1.15 animals a day. (There are 2,428 shops in total in Delhi and the supply of meat is 2,500 animals a day.) This only implies that the meat sold in shops is being most likely obtained through illegal slaughtering.

Since government's intention behind formulating these rules is to maintain hygienic conditions at the meat shops, it is obvious to expect that the abattoir managed by the MCD authorities is kept in a completely sanitised condition. The expectations should build up even further given that the DMC Act prohibits slaughtering of animals at any place other than an MCD slaughterhouse.

Sanitation at the MCD Abattoir

A writ petition was filed in the Delhi High Court regarding the issue of unhygienic conditions at the abattoir. However, even after placing limits, the situation has not improved much, as observed by the researchers:

- The researchers had to wade through 1 inch of dung that covered the entire auctioning centre, and endure the stink. Most buffaloes were lying in that filth. There was also a dead calf on the ground. After the auction, the animals were walked into the abattoir, without being washed or cleaned.

- The sequence of killing is as follows. The animals are walked into the abattoir and made to lie on the ground. Using the *halal* method of slaughter, the animals are killed on the ground in the blood of previously killed animals.
- Workers walked among all this wearing normal sandals. They did not have any gloves or special clothing and worked with their bare hands.
- The animals were skinned, de-horned, and cut. all at the very place where they had been slaughtered, in the blood of other animals. The workers then carried the meat on their shoulders to rickshaw carts.
- All this time, stray dogs inside the abattoir were trying to get small pieces of meat lying around. Workers had to remain alert to prevent them from getting to the slaughtered body.
- The roof had around 50-60 crows on it. The researchers were witness to the spectacle of seeing 15-20 crows descend upon an unattended cart that was loaded with cut meat. When after a couple of minutes the workers noticed this, they ran up to shoo the birds away. The vehicle was then taken outside along with the other carts.
- Ideally, the meat should be kept in cold storage immediately after slaughter. However, what actually happens is that the body is dragged/carried by the workers and placed onto a rickshaw cart, which is then used to carry the meat outside the abattoir.

Medical Inspection of the Animals

The MCD veterinary officials are supposed to check the medical health of all the animals brought in the abattoir. One health official at the Idgah abattoir said that the veterinary officials posted at the gate looked for signs of ill health easily visible to the naked eye, such as hide, hair, walk etc. If they were suspicious, the animal was confiscated and medically examined. Another official said that the experience gained over the years enabled him to distinguish sick animals from the healthy ones in just a glance! Even as he said that, a butcher was dragging a goat into the abattoir because of some

▲
Work as usual — buffalo slaughter at Idgah

Blood on the "slaughter" floor
▼

▲ *Streams of blood*

Shall we talk about hygiene? ▼

▲

The buffalos' remains are heaped in the nearest garbage dump

Garbage dumps or fertiliser for your plants?

▼

Did the MCD get you this branding?

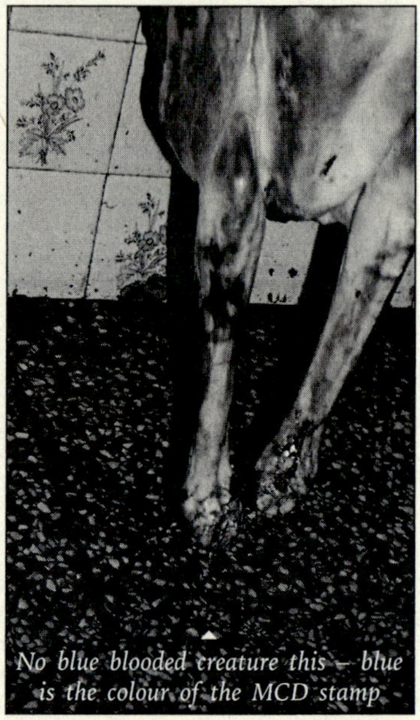

No blue blooded creature this – blue is the colour of the MCD stamp

Branding begets the rest

reason unknown to us, its legs were not able to support it. He was not stopped.

Though, to be fair to the officials, they did seem to have a difficult task set for them: they had to look for signs of ill health in up to 2,500 animals being pushed into the abattoir in droves of 5-20.

Transportation of Meat

The meat has to be transported from the slaughter house to the shop in boxes lined with zinc/aluminium/stainless steel, or wire gauze meat safes.[13] The vehicle used has to be a chilled van. A chilled van does not seem to be within the means of any shopkeeper. Of course, the way out is to get the animal slaughtered at a location wherein transportation becomes unnecessary, but this would entail breaking more rules. Meat sellers prefer to pay a bribe and reach the shop as fast as possible. An amount of Rs. 20 to 25 is usually adequate. The more the time spent on the streets arguing with the police, the more the chances of the meat becoming spoilt; there is also the urgency to open the shop as early as possible so as not to lose their customers.

Reforms

There are two prime issues of concern here: first, location and the quality of the abattoir; and second, the quality of meat sold at shops. It is evident that government regulations designed to control these have failed. Any measures to further government intervention to improve the situation would only lead to further deterioration due to lack of incentives in the right place.[14]

Allow for Private Slaughterhouses

In a scenario of private property rights of land and market competition that we propose, there would be abattoirs in places where they are not undesirable to their neighbours (worked out through contracts or compensation). Hence private abattoirs may be allowed to set up. But the model of only one abattoir for a city would not

---

13. Delhi Municipal Corporation Act, 1957. Section 415. Technical Instructions (21), Meat Shop.

14. The opposition to shift the slaughterhouse to Ghazipur is an outcome of these measures.

work because of a lack of competition. The process of competition between abattoirs would allow to up the quality of meat products and hygiene. The common law of nuisance would enable suitable protection of property rights. Restrictive Covenants could be applied to upcoming urban areas/townships.

Mechanisms of competition and private regulation/certification of abattoirs and their meat products would address concerns of quality, as consumers would want credentials of quality in a quality-sensitive environment. The assumption that government regulation is taking care has led to crowding out private regulators/certifiers and consequent absence of competition. Hence we don't have the same mechanisms that choice and competitions do in other spheres: drive down costs while enhancing quality. Instead of the government constructing and maintaining the slaughterhouse, private players could provide for the slaughtering facilities. There would be more than one player in the market for slaughterhouses. It will be difficult to argue that private slaughter-houses might be worse than government maintained slaughterhouses especially when there are private abattoirs that export meat abroad and have every incentive to maintain high standards of quality and hygiene to keep themselves competitive.

Location of the Slaughterhouse: Ward Committees

Ward Committees have user rights over all public space in the ward except the major throughfares. The Ward Committees, instead of the city government/municipality, would make the decision on where the slaughterhouse would be situated. In the present system, inhabitants of the locality where the abattoir is constructed bear the inconvenience without being compensated. In the system we propose, citizens of the ward would have the choice to allow or not allow the slaughterhouse to be built in the public space of their ward. In a scenario with more than one slaughterhouse in the city, the consumers would benefit by way of better quality and lower prices. Wards that allow for the slaughterhouse to be built would have to be compensated by the private player. The compensation could be in the form of monetary benefits that would accrue to the ward over a period of time or the ward may decide to provide the land at a premium price. The compensation would act as an incentive for the wards to allow the slaughterhouse in the ward. The revenue/compensation would be decided by negotiations between the wards and the private players and may be based on the standards of sanitation and waste disposal that the ward may desire in the abattoir. The ward may be concerned about the stench around the place, waste disposal (the manner in which the abattoir disposes the hides, bones and skins) and sanitation in general.

Thus, there might be prior contracts worked out between the ward and the abattoir company as regards the terms and conditions of maintenance of the abattoir. If the slaughterhouses were privately managed, either the private abattoir company could be responsible for the waste disposal or could even subcontract the function. There would be different models that would be worked out between various abattoirs and the wards. The private players would have to compete and provide greatest possible benefits to locate themselves. Since the decision to give the land to the private player to build an abattoir would be in the hands of ward, the private player would have to guarantee certain minimum hygiene conditions and a proper waste disposal mechanism that would be installed in the abattoir, ensuring that the inconvenience would be minimal. The abattoir companies may also branch into delivery of meat to homes and meat-shops akin to pizzas. Shops may find it profitable to have the meat delivered hygienically at their premises rather than undergo the present system of having to 'fight' for the meat every morning, bribe the officials and transport it in conditions unhygienic to the meat.

Quality Assurance

This can evolve through competition in the marketplace and branding of meat products. Readers would also be well advised to consult the chapter on shop licensing for reform measures relevant to quality of meat sold.

There would be various arrangements that develop once the market is allowed to function. Some abattoir companies might also extend business in packaging the meat slaughtered, there may also be companies that do not slaughter but restrict their activities to processing and packing the meat. The abattoirs may even provide transportation services, like refrigerated vans for the meat to be transported to the retail shops to get an edge over the other abattoirs. Or there may be other firms that may be specialising only in the transport of the slaughtered meat from the abattoir to the retail shops or to the packaging company (which may even devise its own transport system for the purpose). Brand names would evolve where a particular brand standardises the quality of the meat sold. The branding may happen either at the slaughter house level or for the meat products sold at the retail unit. The brand owning company would check the slaughtering activity, standardise packing and standards to be maintained at the shops selling the branded meat. To sell the product under the stamp of a particular brand, all of the component processes (slaughter, transportation, packaging, storage) must be either certified by the brand company or by certifying agencies.

With more than a single municipal abattoir in the city, the retail shops would then choose the private abattoir they consider the best (certifying agencies inform them). The abattoir would have the incentive to maintain sanitation standards set by the private certifiers, as their profits and ultimately even survival depends upon the maintenance of the sanitation and other standards.

Quality of the Meat Sold at the Shops:
Branding and Private Certification

There would be private certifiers who would monitor the quality of the meat sold at the shops. These certifiers would ensure that the meat is purchased from an abattoir that is maintained hygienically and is transported without causing damage to the meat (transportation in refrigerated vans). The certifiers would also ensure that the companies involved in packaging meat products maintain a certain level of sanitation at the premises (the certifiers may specify certain standards to be maintained by the packagers or there could be independent standard setting agencies) and also would certify the meat sold at the shops. Thus, the certifiers would keep a check on the entire process; and this would ensure that the meat sold at the shops is of the quality desired. The certifiers may even provide guarantee in case of damage caused on consumption of foul meat. Private firms may provide guidelines, standards, and other relevant criteria; render firm-specific recommendations; and perform inspections on the products that they certify.

The shops and consumers would have the option to opt out of private certification agency services. Thus, the private certification agencies would need to survive through reputation and efficient management. In such a scheme, consumers will have an option to choose between different levels of quality and safety they desire. If they would be consuming low grade meat, they would be doing so in full knowledge of the fact and not under the illusion of government ensuring quality, which is what happens now.

The use of brand names is one way that private firms can assure quality standards (example: ISI) for meat. A brand name enables consumers to identify a firm's meat product and choose it over competitors. Consumers may be willing to pay a premium for buying a branded product. Also, those consumers who are satisfied with a low quality product wouldn't have to pay for the higher standards. This model will avoid "one-size-fits-all" approach and generate more consumer satisfaction. Hence, a firm with an established brand name would have a strong financial incentive to adhere to quality standards. A company responsible for selling contaminated meat would be driven out by adverse publicity about its products.

It is true that meat may be contaminated even when it appears to be safe. If meat sellers have more information about quality than consumers do, can consumers look after their interests? Lack of information does not mean that sellers can sell unsafe meat. The sellers' interests protect consumers.

Tort Law

Torts are civil wrongs recognised by law as grounds for a lawsuit. These wrongs result in an injury or harm constituting the basis for a claim by the injured party. The primary aim of tort law is to provide relief for the damages incurred and deter others from committing the same harms. The injured person may sue for an injunction to prevent the continuation of the tortious conduct or for monetary damages. Among the types of damages the injured party may recover are: loss of earnings capacity, pain and suffering, and reasonable medical expenses. They include both present and future expected losses.

Products liability is derived mainly from Torts law. Products liability refers to the liability of any or all parties along the chain of manufacture of any product for damage caused by that product. This includes the manufacturer of component parts (at the top of the chain), an assembling manufacturer, the wholesaler, and the retail store owner (at the bottom of the chain). Products containing inherent defects that cause harm to a consumer of the product, or someone to whom the product was loaned, given, etc., are the subjects of products liability suits.

The common law of nuisance—also a form of tort—can be applied effectively in the case of one's inconvenience with regard to the location of a slaughter house. This allows for application of the law on a case by case basis rather than the blanket approach of a legislation.

TECHNICAL INSTRUCTIONS: MEAT MARKET

(As per Section 415, DMC Act, 1957)

Meat Shop

1. The premises shall be structurally sound.
2. The floor and walls upto a height of one meter shall be made of impervious concrete material and the corners will be rounded to facilitate smooth washing and cleaning of the premises.
3. The floor area shall not be less than 8 sq. m. and the height not less than 3 m.
4. The premises shall be drained into sewer, and where there is no sewer, into a surface drain to the satisfaction of health authorities.
5. The premises shall be well ventilated and adequately lighted.
6. Continuous supply of safe water shall be ensured in the premises. In case of intermittent water supply, adequate storage arrangements shall be made.
7. The premises shall be structurally sound.
8. A wash hand basin made of porcelain/stainless steel shall be provided alongwith soap and nail brush for thorough cleaning of hands.
9. The walls and ceiling shall be white/colour washed every 6 months and the wood work shall be painted every year. The premises shall be kept in a good state of repair at all times.
10. Sufficient number of fans shall be provided to keep the premises cool.
11. A waste bin with a pedal operated cover shall be provided in the premises for the collection of waste material. This will be emptied, and washed daily with a disinfectant.
12. All tables, racks, shelves, boards etc. shall have zinc/aluminium/ stainless steel/marble/sun-mica top to facilitate proper cleaning.
13. A sign board indicating the type of meat sold shall be displayed prominently. Nothing else but meat and raw meat products shall be sold at the premises.
14. The floor and skirted walls shall be washed with a disinfectant like phenyle at the close of day's business.
15. The premises shall be kept free from all insects by an insecticidal spray having knock-down effect at the close of day's business. No spraying shall be done during the conduct of business, but instead fly swats/ flaps shall be used to kill spray flies getting in the premises.
16. The premises shall not be used for residential purposes, nor it shall communicate with any residential quarter. No personal belonging like clothing, bedding, shoes etc. shall be kept in the premises.

17. No carcass shall be kept in a manner so as to be open to public view from outside. A small wire gauze show case shall be maintained for keeping pieces of meat ready for sale.
18. Only dressed carcass, meat and cleaned offal shall be stored at the premises. Hides, skins, hoofs, heads and uncleaned gut will not be allowed in the premises at any time. Refrigerator/Ice-box of adequate size shall be provided for storage of meat and meat products.
19. The implements and chopping block shall be washed with boiling water. The chopping block shall be dried and salted every day at the close of business.
20. All persons working in the premises shall be medically examined and immunised against cholera and enteric group of fevers at the time of issue/ renewal of license. The certificate of medical fitness and immunization shall be displayed prominently in the shop alongwith license.
21. A high standard of personal hygiene shall be maintained by workers at all times. No smoking, chewing pan and snuff shall be allowed in the premises.
22. Clean polythene bag shall be used as packing material for retail sale of meat.
23. The transportation of carcasses from the Slaughter House to the premises shall be done under hygienic conditions in boxes of adequate size lined with zinc/aluminium/stainless steel or wire gauze meat safes, which must be washed daily.
24. Wholesome meat obtained from authorised sources only shall be sold at the counter. Unstamped meat is liable to be confiscated and destroyed.
25. Failure to comply with any of these instructions may entail legal action against the defaulters, and even result in cancellation of license.

Butcher's Trade

1. No person below the age of 18 years or of unsound mind or suffering from any contagious, infectious or loathsome disease shall be given a license.
2. The license shall not be transferable.
3. The license shall be provided with metal token and an identity card. The token shall be worn by the licensee either on his left arm above the elbow or on the left side of his chest in such a way as to be conspicuous. He shall also keep the identity card with him without which admission to the Slaughter House shall be refused.
4. The licensee shall not create any nuisance at the Slaughter House premises.
5. The licensee shall be dressed in clean clothes while entering the Slaughter House.

6. The licensee shall properly wash his implements used for slaughtering.
7. The licensee shall not slaughter any animal in a premises which is not approved.
8. Only healthy and non-pregnant animals shall be slaughtered.
9. The licensee shall at once bring to the notice of the Supdt. Slaughter House/meat Inspector if he detects any evidence of the disease in a carcass and shall not alter, modify or obliterate the said evidence by any means.
10. The licensee shall observe the condition of this licence and all other lawful directions given by the Health Officer.
11. Licensee shall be immunised against Cholera and Typhoid and shall produce a certificate to that effect.
12. Licensee shall maintain a high standard of personal hygiene.

Markets for storage and sale of Meat, Fish, Poultry etc.

1. The premises shall be structurally sound.
2. The floor area shall not be less than 100 sq. m. and height not less than 3 m.
3. The floor and walls upto a height of one metre shall be smooth made of impervious concrete material and the corners will be rounded to facilitate thorough cleansing of the premises.
4. Premises shall be drained into sewer, and where there is no sewer, into a surface drain to the satisfaction of Health Authorities.
5. The premises shall be well-ventilated and adequately lighted.
6. Continuous supply of safe water shall be ensured in the premises. In case of intermittent water supply, adequate water storage arrangements shall be made.
7. The premises shall be completely fly proof, preferably double doors, with outer door opening outwards and fitted with springs to ensure self-closing.
8. Adequate number of wash hand-basins made of porcelain/stainless steel shall be provided alongwith soap and nail brush for thorough cleansing of hands.
9. The walls and ceiling shall be white/colour washed every 6 months and the wood work painted every year. The premises shall be kept in good state of repair at all times.
10. Sufficient number of fans (Propulsion & Exhaust) shall be provided to keep the premises cool.
11. Adequate no. of large waste-bins with pedal-operated lids shall be provided in the premises for depositing the waste material. These shall be emptied and washed daily with a disinfectant.

12. All tables, racks, shelves, boards etc, shall have zinc/aluminium/ stainless steel/marble or sunmica top to facilitate proper cleaning.
13. A sign board indicating type of flesh sold shall be displayed prominently. Nothing else but raw flesh and its products shall be sold at the premises.
14. The floor and skirted walls shall be washed with a disinfectant like phenyle or Cresol solution at the close of day's business.
15. No insecticidal spraying shall be carried out during the conduct of business, but instead fly swats/flaps shall be used to kill stray flies getting into the premises.
16. The premises shall not be used for residential purposes nor it shall communicate with any residential quarters. No personal belongings like clothing, bedding and shoes shall be kept in the premises.
17. Only dressed carcasses, fish, poultry etc., shall be stored at the premises. Hides, skins, offal etc. shall not be allowed to be stored at any time.
18. For carcasses, free hanging arrangement (preferably sliding hooks) shall be provided. For fish, raised/smooth impervious, sloping and suitably drained platforms shall be provided.
19. Adequate no. of sanitary public conveniences shall be provided inside the market by the owner.
20. The implements and chopping blocks shall be washed with boiling water. The chopping block shall be dried and salted every day at the close of business.
21. All persons working in the premises shall be medically examined and immunised against cholera and enteric group of fevers at the time of issue/renewal of license. The certificates of medical fitness and immunization shall be displayed prominently in the premises alongwith the trade license.
22. A high standard of personal hygiene shall be maintained by workers at all times. Smoking, chewing, snacks and snuff shall not be allowed in the premises.
23. Only wholesome meat, fish, poultry etc. shall be stored in the premises. In the case of meat it shall bear stamp of the authorised slaughter house.
24. Facilities shall be provided for storage of meat/fish/poultry etc. under cold conditions to improve keeping quality of product. In the case of poultry, feeding/water arrangements shall also be provided by the owner.
25. Failure to comply with any of these instructions may entail legal action against the defaulters, and may even result in cancellation of license.

6

Auto Rickshaw Permits: Limited Permits, Unpermitted Licences

The public transportation system in Delhi is characterised by high dependence and low availability. An increase in urbanisation and growth has further increased the dimensions of the crisis. A concrete example of this situation are the auto rickshaws in the city.

The auto rickshaws come under the category of Public Service Vehicle (PSV). A PSV is "...any motor vehicle used or any motor vehicle used or adapted to be used for the carriage of passengers for hire or reward..."[1] It comprises of all commercial passenger vehicles that do not ply on fixed routes, where the passenger for each trip specifies the destination. Delhi has about 86,185 auto rickshaws operating with official permits,[2] though newspaper reports use a much lower figure of 45,000 as the total number of TSRs (Three Wheeler Scooter Rickshaw) in Delhi.[3] Considering that most of these vehicles run on double shifts, the number of drivers operating them should be about 1.5 lakh.[4] Stifled by lengthy licensing procedure, endless paperwork, absurd regulations, *dalals* (touts) and palm greasing, the auto driver is subjected to enormous harassment and suffers from lack of information and awareness.

At no stage, by any authority, is he provided information or documentation regarding the regulatory requirements. He is required to wear a uniform while driving. With the negative societal attitude towards him, he finds the dress discriminatory and degrading and will

1. Section 2(35), Motor Vehicles Act, 1988.
2. *Road Accidents in Delhi 2001*, 2002, Delhi Traffic Police, New Delhi.
3. Roy, Shubhajit. 25 July 2002. "Police Go Soft on Autos", *Times News Network*.
4. Anand, Anvita and Rajendra Ravi. 2003. "Auto Rickshaw drivers in Delhi: Efficacy of dialogue with service providers" [article online] *Economic and Political Weekly*, accessed on 30 January 2004 at http://www.epw.org.in/showArticles.php?root=2003&leaf=08&filename=6179&filetype=html.

avoid being identified as an auto driver.[5] This paper aims at getting a better understanding of the perspective and the plight of the auto rickshaw drivers, emphasising primarily on the regulations affecting him.

Driving Licences

Entering into the profession of auto rickshaw driving means lengthy licensing procedures characterised by countless numbered forms, renewals, tests and checks. The first in line is the learner's license, which is a temporary license issued to learn driving of motor vehicles and is valid upto six months. A permanent license can be acquired after the expiry of one month and before six months from the date of issuing the learner's license. The woes of the auto drivers do not end here, as the permanent license needs to be renewed after every three years in case of commercial, passenger or goods vehicle (a private vehicle license is valid for 20 years).

Certificate of Fitness

The story does not end here. Apart from the above-mentioned lengthy licensing procedure the auto drivers have to go through a lot more paper work and consequently more trouble to obtain other documents that they need to keep as drivers of a public vehicle, i.e., documents for permit, fitness and badge.

Under the provisions of the Motor Vehicles Act, 1988 all auto rickshaws need to undergo a vehicle fitness test, the official cost for which is Rs. 200. The Certificate of Fitness (COF) is issued by the Chief Motor Vehicle Inspector of the Inspection Unit at the Burari Regional Transport Office for 2 years and subsequently requires an annual renewal. For fitness check of the vehicle, the driver has to submit an application (Form 20), Sales Certification (Form 21), valid insurance certificate, Letter of Intent from STA (State Transport Authority), (Form 22), road worthiness certificate from the manufacturers and pollution under control documents regarding temporary registration (if any) along with the prescribed fees.

---

5. Mohan, Dinesh and Dunu Roy, 2003, Operating on Three Wheels: Auto-Rickshaw Drivers of Delhi, *Economic and Political Weekly* Vol. XXXVIII, no. 3: 177-80.

For the renewal of COF (every year) you require the old COF, registration certificate, road tax clearance from account branch and prescribed fees. Under the provisions of Central Motor Vehicles Rules, 1989 everything from lights to exhaust emission to spark plug has to be checked by the inspector, but all that is checked is the chassis number and the engine number (See Table 2 - Appendix). If the inspector deems the vehicle unfit, the driver gets a 15-day period to do all the repairs and refurbishing required and take the test once again.

According to the drivers, it would cost them approximately Rs. 3000 to get all the work done. In fact, all the drivers surveyed said that even if the inspection was not there, they would still like their vehicles to be in a good condition as they believed that passengers were attracted towards a well-kept vehicle. Moreover, the vehicle was a source of prestige and not all of them would like to have a dirty or damaged vehicle.

However, spending Rs. 3000 doesn't ensure that the vehicle passes the fitness check. According to the drivers, unless the inspector is paid Rs. 200-500, the vehicle will fail the test even if it is brand new. On the other hand, a vehicle that does not meet any of the given criteria will still pass the test if the palms are greased. Thus, there is no correlation between vehicle fitness and passing of the fitness test. It all depends on whether the bribe has been given. Consequently, it is not surprising to learn that of the 17 factors given above, only the eighth one is checked – drivers said that the inspector verified only the chassis number and the engine number.[6]

Badge for Commercial Driving

After getting a license, the driver is required to obtain a badge for commercial driving. Earlier, the badge had lifetime validity, but now the driver has to get it renewed every year. The renewal process includes a 3-day training class (9 a.m.–4 p.m.) wherein the drivers are taught how to drive on the roads, hand signs, prominent locations in Delhi etc. After this, there is a test conducted to assess driving skills (something he has already got a license for!). Both the training class

6. Faruqui, Danish and Raghav Sud. "Auto-rickshaws in Delhi: Murder by Regulation". Accessed on 18 February 2004 at http://www.ccsindia.org/RP01_2.html

and the tests are conducted by the IDTR (Institute of Driving Training and Research). The test costs about Rs. 500 and if the driver is unable to clear the test, he has to retake the class and the test for Rs. 200. The drivers surveyed said that the classes were a waste of time since they already knew all that was being taught. All it resulted in was the loss of 3 days' earnings.

The next step after obtaining a license and badge is to acquire a vehicle to drive. The choices you have are either to drive your own vehicle, or to use another person's vehicle on a rental basis. For using a commercial vehicle, one needs to have a permit.

Permit for Driving Auto Rickshaw

Permit is an instrument issued by a State or Regional Transport Authority authorising the use of a motor vehicle as a transport vehicle and specifying the area in which the driver is allowed to ply his vehicle. Section 66 of the Motor Vehicles Act, (1988) mandates for the necessity of a permit for transport vehicles. In case of auto rickshaws such permits are issued by the Motor Licence Officer, (Auto Rickshaw Cell) Burari, for carrying passengers to various places within Delhi. The steps for obtaining the permit are as under:

1. Application for Letter of Intent (LoI)
2. Issue of LoI
3. Inspection of vehicle
4. Registration of vehicle
5. Issue of permit

Regulations state that the permit holder must be the one who drives the vehicle. If somebody else is permitted to drive the vehicle, it must be on a non-commercial basis; this licensed driver must have a 'Helper's Certificate' issued by the owner.[7] It is not clear as to how it is ensured that the arrangement is not commercial.

Permits are transferable among drivers but no new permits are being issued. Consequently, the transfer price of a permit ranges between Rs. 30,000 to Rs. 50,000. Further, since the transfer of permits takes up to 8 to 9 months, that is, if there are no touts involved (the costs start at Rs. 3000 though the official cost is

7. Sanjay Kaul, President of NGO People's Action.

Rs. 765), many sellers prefer not to go through the hassles of official transfer.

There is a lack of accountability, once the permits have changed hands. According to a government official, the addresses listed in the departments are either non-existent or the ownership has changed.[8] An interesting fact that came to light was that, *challans* are sent to the home address of the permit holder as he is supposed to be the owner-driver of the vehicle. But, since few of the addresses in the official records are correct and updated, the challans are returned back undelivered. According to a survey, out of the 33,439 notices issued, the transport department (STA) got back 16,300 notices. 35,049 complaints of customers were received till June 23, 2003 (for that year).[9] Another survey indicates that out of 32,719 *challans* issued, 22,444 (i.e. 65%) returned undelivered.[10]

After the auto strike of December 2002, the Transport Ministry of Delhi issued 5,000 new permits. The only conditions were that the driver had to be licensed, unemployed and would not sell the vehicle within five years of purchase. The "Helper's Certificate" rule would not be applicable for these new permits. The scheme was open from January to August 2003. The process is still underway as only around 2300 permits have been allotted. The files of the remaining applications are apparently still being scrutinised.

Purchase of New Vehicles

Once the allotment letter has been received, the driver can either go directly to the manufacturing company and get the vehicle by paying the full amount, or he can go to a financier (either the Delhi Financial Corporation or a private auto financier[11]) and pay the amount in instalments.

All the driver-owners surveyed said that they had purchased the vehicle under a financing scheme through private financiers. None of

8. Roy, Shubajit. 2004. "Autos: Government Signal to Fleet-owners". Express Online. 30 January.

9. Roy, Shubajit. 2003. "Autonomy Yes, Action No". Accessed on 20 January 2004 at http://timesofindia.indiatimes.com/articleshow/43530.cms.

10. From data given by Anil Sood of Chetna, an NGO involved in consumer rights and Three Wheeled Scooter Rickshaws (TSR) fares.

11. Chitra Gupta Road in Paharganj has around 15-20 private auto financiers. They also rent out autos.

them had purchased it from the Delhi Financial Corporation (DFC). The common grouse was that if one took the DFC route, it would take upto 8-9 months to finally obtain the vehicle to drive. The DFC would itself take around 6 months to process the papers, followed by another 2-week to 2-month wait for Bajaj to deliver the vehicle depending upon the stocks available. A private financier would give the vehicle within a fortnight, if not earlier. He would also get all the paperwork done, starting with the licence, down to the permit and the fitness check. All that he asked for was part of the money and a guarantor. The guarantor is one who is already a familiar auto rickshaw driver and gives an informal guarantee for the credibility of the person applying for the loan, to return the borrowed amount. In fact, even the requirement of a guarantor could be waived by paying a higher interest rate.

On further inquiry, it was found that if one went by the account books, purchase through the DFC was a better option. The amount had to be paid back in 3-5 years, and the interest rate was 12 per cent per annum. Yet, everybody preferred the private financier for his services – complete paperwork and giving the vehicle within 2-3 weeks. But there is a price for the additional services provided. The ex-showroom price of a TSR is Rs. 1.02 lakh.[12] After fixing the meter and other customised changes, the total cost of the vehicle comes to Rs. 1.20 lakh. However, if one purchases through a private financier, the total amount paid varies from Rs. 1.75 lakh to Rs. 2.25 lakh. The compound interest rate *(chakravarti byaj)* varied from 18 per cent to 26 per cent per annum.[13] Moreover, the amount has to be paid back in 2 years. Most auto drivers said that they assumed they would be able to repay the loan through daily earnings but were unable to do so. On defaulting the monthly payment twice, the vehicle was seized.

Interestingly, no auto driver dared to get away with the vehicle, or even complain to the police if he was manhandled or beaten up on defaulting the instalment payment (Incidentally, the driver has to pay charges for the goons who beat him up!). This is apparently because the financier gets the signatures of the driver on blank sheets of paper

---

12. Information obtained from Bagga Auto, Karol Bagh.
13. Confirmed in the Khullar report (para 34) that states that the interest rates start at 20 per cent per annum. Khullar report - Report of the 'Group of Experts' constituted by the Government of Delhi; chairperson Rahul Khullar, Commissioner, Sales Tax.

(usually 15-20 sheets). The Hire-Purchase agreement is also taken. Moreover, being a commercial vehicle, it cannot be taken out of Delhi. These factors ensure that the financier never suffers a loss, all at the cost of the poor auto driver.

Ending the contract and returning the auto to the financier before the loan period was over seems to be an easier way out. However, drivers surveyed said that, in such a case, most financiers did not return their money. Therefore, when a driver was unable to pay the instalments, he preferred to dump the vehicle in a convenient corner of the city rather than go back to the financier and be humiliated for being unable to pay back the loan.

Purchase of Second Hand Vehicles

Since buying a new vehicle seems to be a lengthy and cumbersome process, how about buying a second-hand auto? This is a much simpler process and is often completed within a day. The cost varies between Rs. 50,000 and Rs. 1,30,000.[14] All that you need to do is go to a private financier and 'show him the money', that is, convince him of your ability to repay the loan amount. The presence of a guarantor known to the financier and proof of residence are added advantages, but not necessary.

Renting of Vehicles

As is evident from the documents required for obtaining the licenses etc., it is not possible for a non-Delhi resident to obtain a permit for driving an auto. However, it is as knotty an issue for a Delhi resident because a newcomer (even if he has the licence and all other documents mentioned earlier) cannot get a new permit from the transport authorities. Nevertheless, he can buy a permit from any of the existing auto drivers who are willing to sell theirs. This would undoubtedly set him back by atleast Rs. 30,000. A permit is of no use without an auto, which again would cost atleast Rs. 50,000. The only option is to ply the vehicle on rent. The daily rent (*dehari*) paid varies from Rs. 250 to Rs. 350.[15]

---

14. Private financiers at Chitra Gupta Road, Paharganj.
15. The rent was increased after the fare hikes of February 2003. It is speculated that the fleet owners influenced this fare hike. The earlier rent was Rs. 150 to Rs. 200 per day.

According to the Khullar Committee report,[16] there are three categories of auto service suppliers in Delhi:

1. Autos run by owners cum drivers.
2. Small fleet owners, who owned autos, possessed permits but engaged auto drivers to ply the autos.
3. Financiers/fleet owners, who owned autos, possessed permits to ply and leased out autos on a monthly/daily basis to persons who plied them.

From 1998, all vehicles over 15 years old were prohibited from plying on Delhi roads. A replacement scheme was brought in wherein a person who had a permit for plying autos would have to get that exchanged for a new one subject to the condition that they would ply only CNG (Compressed Natural Gas) vehicles. If the permit holder did not exercise the option, the permit would simply lapse. The transition took place in the following manner:

1. Some of the owner-operators sold their permits in the grey market. A few of them wanted to continue to ply autos but lacked the capital required to switchover to CNG.
2. Some owner-operators exercised the option of switching over, procured a loan, purchased a CNG vehicle and continued operation.
3. Some were unable to pay back the loan taken (usually at exorbitant interest rates of loans from the informal credit market) and the loaner repossessed their vehicles. Then they started to rent out the auto.
4. Fleet owners decided to switch *en masse* to CNG. Most of them were able to augment the size of their fleets by acquiring permits sold in the grey market.

This transition has resulted in a shake-up of the auto service supplier market. Only a small percentage of autos plying in the city are now owner-operated. Fleet-owners and financiers own the bulk of the autos plying in the city. Estimates of auto drivers and auto financiers put the actual figure of autos on the streets at around 70 to 90 thousand, while the number of auto drivers is around 120 thousand. However, if one were to go by the official records, there

16. Paragraphs 6-12, Khullar Committee Report.

should be only 45 to 50 thousand autos[17] on the streets. The rest of the autos ply either without permits or use false or old permits - the government has no records for these.

Moreover, the police do not ask for the permit when checking the vehicle's papers. It is an open secret that most vehicles are probably taken on rent and thus if the driver (who may have an old/false permit) were to say that the auto owner has the permit, no one would suspect a lie. In addition, even if the police officers insisted, a little bit of palm greasing would be sufficient to quieten them up.

Violations[18]

In Delhi, there are two enforcement agencies for regulation, monitoring and enforcing of provisions of the Delhi Motor Vehicle (DMV) Rule 1993, CMVR 1999, and the MV Act 1988 and Rules framed therein:

a. Enforcement wing of the Transport Department.

b. Traffic Police.

According to the regulations, a driver is required to carry the driving license, registration book of vehicle, insurance certificate, pollution under control certificate, permits, certificate of fitness and road tax receipt, failing which the vehicle can be challaned. Violation of any of the traffic rules or regulations can also lead to a challan, which can be disposed off in two ways:

i. By Paying

This refers to the settlement between the enforcement agencies and the offender by which the challan is disposed off by paying the notified fee to the enforcement agency itself.

Traffic Police Challan: The challan can be paid on the spot itself by depositing the notified amount.

OR

Transport Department Challan: The challan is compounded at Transport Department Head Quarters at Under Hill Road.

---

17. 45,000 vary permit holders who switched over to CNG, plus 5000 new permits issued in the Jan 2003 scheme.

18. Accessed on 20 January 2004 at http://transport.delhigovt.nic.in

ii. Disposal of Challan in the Court

The driver has to appear in the court on the date and place mentioned in the *challan*, in case the driver wants to challenge the *challan*.

In case of a serious offence, the vehicle or its documents are impounded, i.e. retained by the enforcement agencies. It is released by paying the designated enforcement agency in case of a compounded challan, or from the court in other cases.

However, when we asked the auto drivers they said that in case the vehicle is impounded, they have to sign documents stating that the police will not be responsible for any theft or damage to the vehicle. Often the tyres and the battery of the vehicle are replaced by old ones. The only option left is to stay with the vehicle for three days, i.e. the time it would take to get the *challan* cleared. Paying the magistrate the notified fee takes less than a day, but handling the police is where the problem is. The drivers further added that at the end of three days the police would often ask for 'service charges'.

The table below provides estimates of the total inspections and the average number of inspections per month for 2002-2003. A closer look however reveals the abnormally high number of inspections in the month of November 2002. Sources revealed that this was due to a high ranking official in the Delhi Administration being fleeced by a auto-driver and hence the high number of inspection drives that particular month.

Table 1

Year	*Month*	*Total Inspections*
2002	May	321
	June	886
	July	0
	August	0
	September	0
	October	0
	November	4223
	December	0
2003	January	0
	February	0
	March	0
	April	0
	May	0
	June	0

Conclusion

Delhi's auto rickshaw regulatory framework provides a unique lens to view how the regulatory regime of a city can affect economic opportunity for the working poor. It is one of the most heavily regulated low-skilled businesses. In principle, the skills needed to ply an auto are minimal. Those with a thorough knowledge of their city, a good driving record, and an auto (which can also be hired) should be able to start. But regulation of the autos is such that, plying an auto in Delhi legally is an arduous task, if not impossible. Rather, the number of permits to be issued by the authorities is fixed, implying that no new entrant in the profession can legally ply an auto in Delhi. The cap on the number of permits implies that the demand exceeds the supply. This increases the price of the permits, as existing permits, which can now be sold to the drivers, command a premium.

However, these are in reality only artificial scarcities and translate themselves into illegality. An illegal market comes up, where the unlicensed entrepreneurs interact to meet the gap in consumer demand. A look into reality shows that one of three autos plying in Delhi is illegal. This fact just exemplifies the failure of the policy of fixing the number of the autos that can be plied in the city.

Reforms

Removal of Permit System

The permit system is redundant and the cap on the number of autos that can be plied in the city should be removed. Entry should be deregulated, with the transport authority acting only as a registering authority. The obvious criticism of this reform is the number of autos would then increase dramatically, causing congestion as well as environmental problems. However, a simple demand – supply analysis would prove this critique wrong. The number of autos in the city after deregulation would be a reflection of the demand for the services. The number would not dramatically increase or decrease from the present number; but deregulating entry and exit would make the supply responsive to the actual demand of the passengers and stem the illegality and economic insecurity of the auto drivers.

The market for auto permits should be freed. This could be on the lines of the medallion system prevalent with cabs in New York where the drivers are allowed to trade medallions (these are licenses to ply taxis, which are fixed in number). This would not only give a freer hand to the drivers but also reduce unnecessary government interference. Also, we should free the market for the machines themselves so that the auto-rickshaw driver can sell his vehicle to anyone, anywhere. He could thus obtain a competitive price for his vehicle and not necessarily sell it as scrap to the government.

A possible step to reduce congestion on the roads would be to introduce pricing for plying, as a rationing mechanism. This would imply leveraging technology to price entry on busy thoroughfares at peak timings.

Allowing Branding to Evolve

Another step in the direction of reforms would be to recognise the auto cartels that give out autos on rent. This would allow cartels to compete with each other as a brand, by allowing them to form independent companies. This would encourage the companies to build and maintain the brand identity and reputation, and benefit from the brand value that the customers will start identifying with them. This would also ensure that the autos are maintained in proper condition and that traffic rules are followed. In case of violations, the company would be held responsible and they would have the incentive to discipline the drivers they hire.

Minimising Pollution

The 'polluter pays' principle should be introduced, instituting an enforceable system of monetary penalties. One way of doing this would be to have an 'emissions tax' for the vehicles; a flat rate for the first, say five years of the vehicles' life and an increase in the rate thereafter depending on the emissions, corresponding to the vehicles' age.

Appendix

S.No	*Item*	*Central Motor Vehicle Rules*	*Check*	*Type of test*
1.	Tyres	94,95	Cut, deformation, thread case wear	Visual, wheel tester
2.	Steering	98	Gear backlash, kingpin, stub axle, steering freeplay	Manual (check free)
3.	Engine	120	Noise level 85 dB, vibration, leakage, missing, performance.	Engine analyser/engine dynamo meter
4.	Suspension		Leafspring, position, clamping, shock absorber, center bolt, bushes, shackle	
5.	Horn		Electrical bulb, horn, pressure horn	Noise meter for decibel
6.	Brake	96, 97	Stopping distance at 30 kmph<13 meters, parking brake, brake oil leakage	Brake tester
7.	Lamp/ Signal		Headlamp, parking, turn signals, top lights, reflectors, stop lights	Visual/Lumino scope
8.	Embossing of chassis E/G	122	Chassis No., engine no., idento plate, manufacturing month and year	Visual
9.	Speedometer	117, 118	Speedometer functioning (speed governor in the stage carriage)	Visual
10.	Painting	1	As per act and rule, N.P., N.P. local, stage carriage, school, AITP	
11.	Wiper	119	Wiper fitment/functioning	Visual
12.	Body	93	Seating, mudguard, emergency gate, window size,	Visual
13.	Electricals	101-110	Insulations, switches, starter, accessories, doom light, spark arrester	
14.	Finishing		Riveting, welding bonnet, crank case cover etc.	
15.	Road test	99	Clutch, transmission, differential axles and performance	
16.	Others		As per notification and permit condition	
17.	Pollution	115	Pollution level of vehicle	Smoke meter, gas analyser

Source: http://transport.delhigovt.nic.in

7

Cycle Rickshaw Licencing: Cycles of Poverty

Kanam Ram, aged 35, came to Delhi in 1989 from Zila Katihar in Bihar in the hope of getting a good job and earning some money. He worked as a carpenter for 11 years but it did not generate enough income to support his family—wife and five children—back in the village. He left the job and started pulling a rickshaw in Lajpat Nagar for a *thekedar* (contractor) some two years back. He thought this will provide him financial security and he could gradually move on to a better job. But that still remains a distant dream. On an average, he earns Rs. 150 daily, out of which he has to pay Rs. 20 to the *thekedar* as daily rent, leaving an income of about Rs. 130.

To top it all, the police authorities and the Municipal Corporation of Delhi (MCD) officials harass him. He is beaten up and his vehicle has been impounded several times ostensibly for not following the traffic rules. He has to pay hefty fines to the *babus* and the police *wallahs* for which no receipts are issued. Notwithstanding the free rides he has to give to the police officials and other influential people and the humiliation he has to suffer at their hands.

This just goes to show that even getting into an entry-level profession like pulling a rickshaw is not a cakewalk. This is the story of not one but all cycle rickshaw pullers for whom the license – quota *raj* has made their pursuit of livelihood very difficult.

Cycle rickshaws are an important mode of public transport in many cities in India. They first came into existence in India in the early 1940s and were a technological advancement over the traditional hand-pulled, wooden-wheeled rickshaws. In most parts of the country their operations are governed by the Cycle Rickshaw Bye-laws.

Background of the Licencing Regime for Cycle Rickshaws

The rickshaw licensing policy was first formalised in 1960 with the introduction of special Bye-laws for this sector. The first phase lasted till 1975. Under this, the Municipal Corporation of Delhi (MCD) had initially decided on a quota of 600 rickshaws. Despite all attempts at controlling the number of rickshaws, they kept registering a steady increase. Thus, the MCD has had to review and hike the sanctioned quota upwards every few years. In 1998, the quota of sanctioned rickshaws was 99,000. As of now, there are 73,072 licensed cycle rickshaws in the city. The MCD licenses for cycle rickshaws are issued under Section 489 of the MCD Act and the bye-laws framed therein.

Restriction on the Number of Rickshaws in the City

Article 15 of the Bye-laws states that, "The number of cycle rickshaw licenses to be granted in a year shall be fixed by the Corporation in the beginning of each year, having regard to the desirability of eliminating cycle rickshaws plying for hire ultimately."[1] To this effect, the MCD doesn't issue licenses all through the year. It invites applications for licenses once in a while through notifications in the newspapers.

But the illiterate rickshaw pullers hardly get to know about it. Those who manage to get the information allege that the officials at the licensing office are extremely reluctant to give licenses to individual applicants (discussed later in the paper). Also, by the time they reach the office, the licenses are already 'sold' in bulk to the contractors.

According to the MCD, the reason behind controlling the number of rickshaws is the growing congestion and pollution due to traffic on Delhi roads. While the authorised strength of licensed cycle rickshaws remains around 99,000, the actual number of cycle-rickshaws (authorised and unauthorised) in Delhi has been estimated to be much higher. According to the Traffic Police estimate, and studies conducted by the Bureau of Police Research and Development (BPR&D) the figure ranged from 2 lakh to 5 lakh in the early 90s.[2] Currently, the

1. Delhi Municipal Corporation Cycle Rickshaw Bye-Laws, 1960.
2. Pereira, Maxwell. "How cycle rickshaws multiplied". Accessed online at http://www.delhitrafficpolice.nic.in/art22.htm, on 1 February 2004.

number of cycle rickshaws plying on Delhi roads is as high as 10 lakhs, though more conservative estimates put the figure at 7 lakhs.

Quantitative Limits on the Ownership of Rickshaw Cycles

Apart from attempting to restrict the total number of rickshaws on Delhi roads, government regulations also extend to who can get a license and the number of rickshaws a person can own. Article 3 (1) of these Bye-Laws stipulates that, "No person shall keep or ply for hire, a cycle rickshaw in Delhi unless he himself is the owner thereof and holds a license granted in that behalf by the Commissioner, on payment of the fee that may, from time to time, be fixed under the sub-section (2) of Section 430." It further goes on to state that "no person will be granted more than one such license". Moreover, the license is non-transferable. A person who lets out his rickshaw on hire is treated as a legal offender. If a person gives his rickshaw on hire or allows his brother, son or any other relative to ply it, the law allows the municipality to seize and confiscate his vehicle.

Contractors

Despite laws that mandate that licenses will only be issued to owners who pull their own rickshaws,[3] very few rickshaw pullers own their vehicles in Delhi. Majority of them is owned by contractors (also called *thekedars*) who own anywhere between 10 and 200 rickshaws, a few even own in thousands. The bye-laws, which were meant to outlaw the contractors, have outlawed the owner-puller.

These contractors bribe the MCD officials and get hold of licenses in bulk, issued in the name of real or imaginary pullers. However, paying hefty bribes does not ensure that all the rickshaws will get the licenses. Out of, say, hundred rickshaws owned by a contractor, only half will have licenses—rest of them are illegal. The contractor has to pay a certain agreed-upon amount to the MCD as well as the police as "protection money" (also called *suvidha shulk* by some). This also does not rule out the possibility of confiscation by the MCD and the police, which may require palm greasing. Thus the rickshaw owners are caught in a web of illegality, whereby the police and the MCD hold them hostage for extortion.

3. The law makes an exception for widows and handicapped persons who may be granted more than one license subject to the maximum of five licences.

According to the contractors, they have to pay Rs. 50–100 per month to the MCD as well as the police for every rickshaw they own (licensed or unlicensed) in order to operate on the city roads. For easy recognition by the officials, the rickshaws have the name of the contractor as well as a number displayed on them. Thus, the MCD officials can recognise and seize the rickshaw of the errant contractor (one who has not paid his due). Moreover, the license has to be renewed every year, the official fee for which is Rs. 50. However, according to the contractors, after including under-the-table payments, the cost of each renewal works out to be Rs. 250–300.

Licences

For pullers who don't own the rickshaw, getting the license is so difficult (since officially, no fresh licences are being issued) that most pullers ply their vehicles without the owner-puller's license. So they are dubbed as illegal, thus inviting confiscation of the vehicle. Even with a bribe, MCD officials are extremely reluctant to give licences to individual pullers. They are far more inclined to give them to contractors for obvious reasons. This explains why very few rickshaws in Delhi are owned by the actual pullers.

The reluctance to give licenses to individual pullers can best be understood by recognising the logistics of bribe collection. The MCD and police officials find it much easier to collect bribes from contractors who rent a fleet of rickshaws because they have to operate from a fixed location. By contrast, collection from six lakh individual pullers is a daunting task.

Given the fact that it is virtually impossible to get a private license made, majority of rickshaws are owned by the contractors who let them out to pullers on a daily rent ranging from Rs. 18 to Rs. 25. The monthly hire charge of Rs. 600 that a rickshaw puller pays to the contractor represents nearly one-sixth the cost of a new vehicle (around Rs. 3500) or half the price of a second-hand vehicle (around Rs. 1500).

Most rickshaw pullers are seasonal migrants from Bihar, Uttar Pradesh, West Bengal and Haryana. Their families are still living in the villages. Most of them own small pieces of agricultural land and go back to their villages during harvest time. This is one of the primary reasons why they prefer to ply the rickshaw on rent. Also, it is impossible to deal with the officials individually, leave alone getting hold of the license.

Traffic Regulations

Paying the contractor does not save the rickshaw puller from the harassment and extortion by the police. Under the ostensible intention of decongesting the Delhi roads, the Lieutenant Governor of the city has empowered the traffic police to seize the rickshaws without the involvement of MCD. This exposes the rickshaw pullers to further hardship, as a large number of rickshaws reach the police stations for the offence of entering 'No Entry' areas. Getting the rickshaw released from the police station is far more difficult and involves higher pay-offs. A licensed rickshaw driven by a licensed puller can be legally released only by paying a minimum fine of Rs. 325 (Rs. 300 as the fine amount + Rs. 25 as storage charges per day). The irrationality of the law becomes obvious when you calculate that the fine amounts to 10 per cent of the price of a new rickshaw (which costs around Rs. 3500) and more than 20 per cent of the price of a second hand rickshaw (which costs around Rs. 1500). The fines would amount to several lakh if applied at the same rate to motor cars.

Penalties

According to the bye-laws, any cycle rickshaw found plying for hire without a license or found driven by a person not having proper license, shall be liable to be seized and disposed off by public auction after dismantling.[4] This gives ample opportunity to the MCD officials and police to exploit the rickshaw *wallahs* who enter into an unofficial agreement whereby the rickshaw is released after an illegal payment of Rs. 200-300 by the owner.

When the MCD authorities impound a rickshaw, it should be retrieved in 15 days time. The authorities do not keep the rickshaw after 15 days. They dismantle it and auction the scrap. "Any cycle rickshaw found plying for hire without a licence or found driven by a person not having proper licence as provided under bye-law 2(1) and (2) shall be liable to be seized by the Commissioner or a person duly authorised by him in this behalf" states a notification of Delhi

---

4. Article 17(1), Delhi Municipal Corporation Cycle Rickshaw Bye-Laws, 1960.

Municipal Corporation (rickshaw bye-laws, 1960) issued on 22 June 1994 by the Department of Urban Development. The notification further states that "The cycle rickshaw, so seized shall be disposed off by public auction after dismantling, deformation by such process including smashing it into a scrap after a reasonable time as may be decided by the Commissioner from time to time. The sale proceeds of the public auction after deducting the expenses of the auction and other departmental charges/dues shall be distributed equally amongst owners of the seized cycle rickshaws put to auction, who come forward within 30 days of public auction. In case no owner comes forward for claiming the amount, then the sale proceeds of public auction shall be deemed to be the municipal funds and the same shall be deposited in the municipal treasury".

An apparent reason under which these rickshaws are seized is that of causing congestion of the roads. However, upon payment of Rs. 200-300 by the owner, a majority of the seized rickshaws are released before they reach the municipal yards. Those, which are entered into the records, involve a minimum payment of Rs. 325 plus the cost of affidavits and other paper work. This is in addition to the opportunity cost of the working days lost by the puller on which the rickshaw did not ply (approximately Rs. 100 per day). Thus, in effect, the total cost of getting a rickshaw released comes to around Rs. 500-600.

Even if the seizure turns out to be illegal or *mala fide* according to MCD rules and provisions, then too the *babus* are not held accountable and the vehicle seized is entered into the records as *lawaris* (ownerless). In 2000-2001, 23,000 vehicles were shown as being destroyed in municipal records. In addition, 33,000 rickshaws were recorded as seized and released after paying fines. However, people in this trade allege that at least 50,000–60,000 rickshaws per year are not returned to the owners.[5] The contractors surveyed revealed that many a time the MCD officials surreptitiously sell the seized rickshaws for a meagre payment of Rs. 500.

A subtle example of the nexus between the contractors and the traffic police is the Central Market area of Lajpat Nagar where cycle

5. Kishwar, Madhu. "License-Quota-Raid Raj – Economic Warfare against Rickshaw Owners and Pullers", sourced from http://free.freespeech.org/manushi/125/license.html accessed on 4 February 2004.

These will be now crushed and sold as scrap

Confiscated rickshaws at the MCD store

rickshaws are not allowed to ply, as they tend to cause traffic jams. But a visit there any day will reveal a different picture – rickshaws ply on the roads without any restrictions and form an important mode of commuting. On inquiring, one was told that the contractors who have already paid the protection money to the MCD as well as the police, own a majority of rickshaws.

Individuals owning single rickshaws are the ones who are worst affected, as they have to deal with the officials individually. The owner-pullers surveyed said that they paid MCD Rs. 100 per month as "road tax" (also called *mahina*), for which no receipt was issued. Also some of them had either lost their license papers or had not bothered to get the license renewed. Clearly, this unofficial payment (protection money) takes care of all the problems they might face in carrying on their business.

The rickshaw pullers alleged that their rickshaws were seized several times by the police for plying in the prohibited areas. They also alleged that the police officials beat them up, punctured the tyres and also dismantled the rickshaw. They often had to pay Rs. 400-500 to get the rickshaw released, though no receipt was issued for the same.

Violations

Apart from this, the MCD can fine a license-holding rickshaw for any number of violations which include not wearing the uniform and the badge, not having a bell or a reflector or a light or proper mud guards.[6] Despite the fines for all these violations, virtually no rickshaw on the Delhi roads seems to be having these safety accessories because checking them is merely a pretext for harassment by the officials.

Prime Minister's New Policy for Rickshaw Pullers in Delhi

Media articles based on *Manushi*'s study, and facts that emerged through the *Lok Sunwayi* (Public Hearing) of street vendors and rickshaw operators organised by it urged the Prime Minister to look into the matter. The Prime Minister's Office (PMO) recognised that the restrictive licensing system enables rents to be collected by the

6. These norms are detailed in the Cycle Rickshaw Bye-laws of 1960 framed under Section 481 of the Delhi Municipal Corporation Act 1957, which had been repealed but have been brought back into practice again.

officials who process, issue, and enforce licenses. The "Prime Minister's New Policy for Street Hawkers and Rickshaw Pullers in Delhi"[7] (1991) mentioned that since no specific Supreme Court ruling is available for rickshaws, they may be interpreted as street hawkers providing a transportation service, (rather than a tangible commodity), and accordingly covered by the Supreme Court's, Saudam Singh vs NDMC decision (relating to the fundamental right to livelihood subject only to minimal regulation).

The policy suggested an alternative regulatory regime for cycle rickshaws with the following basic contents:

- Scrapping the licensing system with quantitative limits.
- Dividing the metropolis into "green", "amber", and "red" zones, signifying free access, fee-based access, and prohibited access, respectively. It stated such zoning must be both formally notified, and prominent street signs put up to indicate their boundaries and timings, and must be made with the formal consultation of residents' associations and the area's elected representatives.
- Other general restrictions on cycle rickshaws may be specified in minimal terms and strictly consistent with the general convenience of the public, including health and security considerations, e.g., avoidance between midnight and 5 a.m., no stopping on carriageway, no obstructions at traffic lights or bus stops.
- There must be an absolute prohibition on municipal and police authorities from impounding, or destruction, or seizure of goods and equipment, except when permitted under other laws (e.g. excise laws).
- Entry into the profession should be by way of a simple registration process on payment of a nominal fee and production of identification proof. Upon registration, which should be done on the spot, the person would have unrestricted access to all "green" areas. Penalties for non-registration must be restricted to a surcharge on the fee, but impounding, destruction, or seizure of the goods and equipment by any authority must be

7. "Reforming the Licensing Regime: Prime Minister's New Policy for Street Hawkers and Rickshaw Pullers in Delhi", accessed online at http://free.freespeech.org/manushi/125/reforming.html on 18 February 2004.

absolutely prohibited. It clearly specified that registration is not a permit to ply the trade and that no such permits shall be needed, right to livelihood being a fundamental right. Also that there must be no numerical limits on registrations.

- Plying in an "amber" zone would be upon payment of a fee, but there would be no numerical restrictions. As the numbers of cycle rickshaws may instead be regulated by adjustment of the amount of fee periodically (this fee need not be nominal, but may serve to limit numbers to a level at which significant congestion does not occur).

The task of translating the policy into a legal framework and implementation of those laws was left to the municipal authorities.

Following a letter from the Prime Minister to the Lieutenant Governor to end the harassment brought about by the licensing system for cycle-rickshaws in Delhi, the MCD passed a resolution on 10 September 2001. Under it, the cycle-rickshaw pullers will no longer need to get licenses from the MCD (the Hackneyed Carriage Department, MCD handles all matters relating to cycle-rickshaws in Delhi), but the cycle-rickshaw will still need to be registered.

Also, a new scheme was brought out by the MCD (in collaboration with the Traffic Police) to divide Delhi into three zones — green, amber and red. According to it, there will be no restriction on operating cycle-rickshaws in the green zone, a fee will have to be paid for operation in the amber zone and no cycle-rickshaws will operate in the red zone.

According to the MCD officials, the resolution remains on paper and the Delhi Municipal Corporation Cycle Rickshaw Bye-Laws, 1960 (as in the MCD Act) hold true even today. The rickshaw puller is still required to carry the cycle-rickshaw license (on his person) along with the ownership papers of the rickshaw and the renewal of licenses is still going on.

Moreover, the PMO's policy draft had directed that "the metropolis may be divided into "green," "amber," and "red zones," signifying free access, fee based access and prohibited access for rickshaws. The notification issued by the Traffic Police has effectively banned the entry of rickshaws not just in "red zones" but also in large parts of the city earmarked as "amber" zones, by notifying that rickshaws cannot operate in these areas between 8 a.m. and 10 p.m. This makes a mockery of the PM's directive and policy note which had envisaged free access for cycle rickshaws without numerical restrictions in "amber" zones under the pay and ply scheme. Nevertheless, some of the prescriptions of the PMO's policy draft defy the lessons of past experience. Would the earmarking of zones reflect the natural demand for cycle rickshaws? Would the pay and ply scheme not turn into another extortion cycle?

Conclusion

Contrary to the perception of the general populace, the unlicensed cycle rickshaw puller has to pay costs of illegality to the municipal and police authorities and is not using the public place for free.

The government by limiting the number of rickshaws has created scope for renting out the rickshaws by the contractors. Regulations restricting the number of rickshaws a person can own, stifles the incentive of the owner to invest his savings to expand by buying more rickshaws for renting them out. This means that working under the present laws, a rickshaw puller would be earning almost the same income throughout his life, as all the legal alternatives to expand his trade and increase income have been sabotaged. In Saharanpur (a district in Uttar Pradesh) unlike Delhi's' case, the rickshaw-owner and the rickshaw-puller may be different. This is legally permitted. This has led to a definite improvement in the pursuit of livelihood for the cycle rickshaw pullers there.

It also reflects in the meagre technological advances that have been seen in this area. In the late 1970s, a motorised version of the rickshaw was introduced which never really caught on, as the rickshaw pullers became worried about getting a licence as well as maintaining the motor.[8] Technology upgradation requires investment. The quantitative licensing system enables the enforcer to extract the entire rents of the activities, leaving almost no savings (and thus no investment) for the rickshaw pullers.

Reforms

- Removal of quantitative quotas
- Removal of licensing and allowing only registration, and making sure that this is implemented

8. Menon, Sindhu. "The relentless struggle of rickshaw pullers," accessed online at http://www.labourfile.org/Richshaw/Report.htm, on 1 February 2004.

- Ward-level decision making.

The existing licensing system with quantitative limits had been abolished by the government but is still prevalent in practice owing to absence of clear guidelines. And now, the licensing system will be back into practice again.[9] Concerns about the possible social costs of this are centered on street congestion. The number of rickshaws is inherently limited by market demand.

The demand for cycle rickshaw services varies by locality, time of day, day of week, and in each of these, over a period of time. Depending on the density of streets and built-up areas, without licensing or other regulation, street congestion may not occur in particular areas at all, in some areas almost all the time, and in others, at particular times (of day, day of week, etc). The decision on whether the rickshaws would be allowed to ply in a particular area or not would be made by the Ward Committee. If the citizens of a particular ward want the rickshaws to ply in their ward they would allow for that and vice *versa*. The Ward Committees, the cycle rickshaw unions and the transport authorities of the city can negotiate or arbitrate contracts, probably involving monetary payments, for smooth passage of rickshaws between wards.

Each rickshaw puller/contractor would have to pay a certain registration fee to be able to operate in the ward. The puller would have to pay the registration fee and a parking fee that would be reflective of the actual costs incurred in the maintenance of the parking space for the rickshaws in the ward. The Ward Committee could vary the prices to limit or increase the number of cycle rickshaws. Either way the rickshaws would be "driven" where they are valued the most. Other aspects like the area and time of operation, fees, etc. would be subject to negotiations between the ward and the rickshaw pullers' union.

An unfettered market for cycle rickshaws would allow sophisticated and probably powered versions to enter the business and would be helpful for those who are willing to pay for them. Better technology upgrading may also help reduce street congestion (by increasing mobility). Since technology upgrading requires investment, if the policy environment is conducive to investment, suppliers of improved technologies will enter the market which has hitherto not happened.

9. Parashar, Vikas, 2004, Spoke in the wheel, Down to Earth, 15 April, Volume 12, Number 22: 16.

Delhi Municipal Corporation Cycle-Rickshaw Bye-Laws, 1960

3. (1) No person shall keep or ply for hire a cycle rickshaw in Delhi unless he himself is the owner thereof and holds a licence granted in that behalf by the Commissioner on payment of the fee that may, from time to time, be fixed under sub-section (2) of Section 430.

Provided that no person will be granted more than one such licence.

[Provided further that the Commissioner may grant more than one licence to a widow or a handicapped, subject to the maximum of five licences.]

[(2) No person shall drive a cycle rickshaw for hire unless he holds a driving licence granted in that behalf by the Commissioner or payment of the fee that may, from time to time be fixed under sub-section (2) of Section 430.

Provided that the licences granted to the pullers shall be valid only for a period of three years.]

4. Conditions of licence—No licence shall be issued unless the following conditions are fulfilled:

(1) The cycle rickshaw shall conform to the following specifications:

(a) Width over-all	3 ft. 9 inch
(b) Length	8 ft.
(c) Height of rickshaw on wheels excluding the over head shade (head)	36 inches.
(d) Width of seat	[Not less than 29 inches provided that this requirement shall not apply to old cycle rickshaws already existing before the commencement of the Cycle Rickshaw (Amendment) Bye-laws 1993.]
(e) Leg room for passengers	1 ft. 9 inches.

(2) The cycle rickshaw shall be in good order and repair in all parts.

[The Cycle Rickshaw shall be painted, marked or otherwise made identifiable in such manner and of such pattern as may be decided by the Commissioner from time to time in this behalf. Each licencee of the cycle rickshaw shall be liable to pay such charges as may be determined by the Commissioner from time to time or by an officer designated by him in this behalf which shall generally be the actual cost incurred on such exercise. The impression or marking, which is affixed thereon by the Commissioner or by an authorised officer, shall not be removed, altered, defaced or obliterated. If the number becomes defaced or obliterated, the cycle rickshaw, in question shall be brought before the Commissioner or its authorised officer, who may order the mark/impression or number to be re-painted or remarked by paying such charges again.]

(4) The cycle rickshaw shall be brought for inspection to the place set apart for the purpose whenever so required by the Commissioner.

(5) The cycle rickshaw shall be painted with a serial number on payment of 25 p. in such manner and of such pattern as the Commissioner may decide in any particular year. The number which is affixed on the cycle rickshaw shall not be removed, altered, defaced or obliterated. If the number becomes defaced or obliterated, the cycle rickshaw in question shall be brought before the Commissioner who may order the number to be repainted on payment of painting charges at 00.25 p.

(6) A licence granted under these bye-laws shall expire on the 31st October next following the date of issue.

(7) The driver of a cycle rickshaw shall attend in person when so ordered by the Commissioner.

(8) The driver of a cycle rickshaw shall produce his licence and the list of fares whenever so required by the Commissioner, Municipal Magistrate, Police Officer or any person hiring or intending to hire the cycle-rickshaw.

[(9) Any licence to be granted to any person under these Bye-laws shall be a licence with photograph affixed thereon and expenses incurred thereon shall be borne by the licencee. These charges shall be on acutal cost basis as determined by the Commissioner from time to time.]

5. Conditions of Licence of driver—

(a) Every person applying for propelling a cycle rickshaw shall be required to satisfy the Commissioner and undertake that:

(1) he is well trained in driving a cycle rickshaw;

(2) he is acquainted with principal streets and offices in Delhi;

(3) he knows the rules of the road and signals used by the drivers of other vehicles or by the traffic police and drive with all care and attention, and observes all the rules of the road;

(4) he possesses a good physique, is in good health and is not less than 21 year of age and has not been convicted of any offence involving moral degradation;

(5) he shall not when propelling a cycle rickshaw pass a terminal tax barrier without stopping and reporting himself on the clerk-in-charge there and shall not move the cycle rickshaw from the said barrier unless the clerk-in-charge has had opportunity to assess and collect terminal tax on goods if any carried by it;

(6) he shall not disobey any direction of any police officer for the regulation of traffic or the control of cycle rickshaw on rickshaw stand;

(7) he shall keep the lamp properly lighted during the hours of lighting time;

(8) he shall not propel a cycle-rickshaw while intoxicated or make use of insulting, abusive or obscene language or willfully obstruct or hinder the puller or propeller of any other vehicle in taking up or setting down any person or wrongfully prevent or endeavour to prevent the puller or propeller of any other vehicle from being hired.

(b) The uniform of the person propelling a cycle-rickshaw shall be clean and he shall wear a *khaki* coloured uniform consisting of a coat or shirt or both and trousers and a cap only.

(c) There shall be attached to each licence of a cycle-rickshaw driver, in such manner as the Commissioner may prescribe, a photograph, and the left thumb mark of the driver shall also be affixed thereon. A duplicate copy of the photograph of person propelling the cycle rickshaw shall be attached to the application for a licence.

6. Obligation as to hiring of Cycle Rickshaw—

(1) No driver shall refuse to let his licenced cycle rickshaw on hire when it is not bona fide engaged.

(2) No driver shall, when hired for fixed tune, desert from the hiring before discharging his hirer.

7. Parking of Cycle Rickshaw—No licenced cycle rickshaw shall be parked anywhere except in places set apart for the purpose.

8. Demand of Fares—The driver of a licenced cycle rickshaw shall not demand more than the maximum fare permissible.

9. Maximum number of persons and weight to be carried in cycle Rickshaw—

(1) Not more than 2 persons shall be carried in a licensed cycle rickshaw. Two children under 12 year of age shall be counted as one person, but children below 3 years shall not be counted.

(2) The maximum weight of the load which may be carried on a licensed cycle rickshaw shall be as follows:

(a) When carrying two persons — 20 seers.

(b) When carrying one person — 2 maunds.

(c) When no passenger is carried — 3/2 maunds.

10. Schedule—A printed schedule of fares permissible shall be exhibited at a conspicuous place on every licenced rickshaw.

11. Badge of Drivers—

(1) Every driver of a licensed cycle rickshaw shall wear on his arm the metal badge inscribed with the number of his license issued to him by the Commissioner with his license.

(2) Every driver of a licensed cycle rickshaw shall return his metal badge to the Commissioner on termination, suspension or revocation of his licence.

12. Prohibition of transfer of licence or Metal Badge—No licence or metal badge granted to driver of a cycle rickshaw shall be transferable.

13. Deposit of lost property—Property left in a licensed cycle rickshaw shall at once be deposited by the driver at the nearest Police Station.

14. Removal of Cycle Rickshaw—The Commissioner, or any person duly authorised by him in this behalf may remove the cycle rickshaw found plying on hire.

(i) if the licence issued in respect of it has been suspended or revoked under sub-section (3) of Section 430;

(ii) if it is being plied by an unlicensed driver.

15. Number of Cycle Rickshaws to be licenced in a particular year—The number of cycle rickshaw licences to be granted in a year shall be fixed by the Corporation in the beginning of each year, having regard to the desirability of eliminating cycle rickshaw plying for hire ultimately.

16. Licence not to be transferred—A licence granted under these bye-laws shall not be transferable.

17. Penalty—Whoever contravenes any provision of any of the bye-laws 3, 5, 6, 7, 8, 10, 11 or 13 shall be punishable:

(a) With fine which may extend to fifty rupees; or

(b) With fine which may extend to fifty rupees and in the case of a continuing contravention with an additional fine which may extend to five rupees for every day during which such contravention continues after conviction for the first such contravention.

[17-A. Any cycle rickshaw found plying for hire without a licence or found driven by a person not having proper licence as provided under bye-law 3(1) and (2) shall be liable to be seized by the Commissioner or a person duly authorised by him in his behalf. The cycle rickshaw, so seized shall be disposed off by public auction after dismantling, deformation of such process including smashing it into a scrap after a reasonable time as may be decided by the Commissioner from time to time. The sale proceeds of the public auction after deducting the expenses of the auction and after departmental charges/dues, shall be distributed equally amongst the owners of the seized cycle rickshaws put to auction, who come forward within 30 days of the public auction. In case no owner comes forward for claiming amount then the sale proceeds to public auction shall be deemed to be the municipal funds and the same shall be deposited in the municipal treasury.

Provided that if the licenced cycle rickshaw driven by an unlicenced puller is seized and the owner of the licenced cycle rickshaw applies for the release of the seized licenced cycle rickshaw with 48 hours of its seizure, the same shall be released after levying a penalty and recovering all the departmental charges/expenses incurred by the Corporation for the seizure of the vehicle and storage etc. at the rates as may be determined by the Commissioner from time to time which shall not be less than Rs. 100 plus Rs. 3 as storage charges per day per cycle rickshaw.]

8

Licencing of the Railway Porters: Burden of the Badge

Contrary to popular misconception, the porters who have been serving train passengers ever since the inception of the Indian Railways are not employees of the Indian Railways. They are merely authorised by the Railways to provide porter services within the station premises. While the Railways does not put a tab on their earning potential, it does fix an official rate for their services.

The Railways' primary objective while creating this class of workers was to ensure that luggage transportation facilities are available to the train passengers at all times and at reasonable rates. To achieve this objective, the Railways decided to authorise a certain number of people to provide *coolie** services at various stations, and to revise this number periodically in accordance with growing passenger traffic over time.

If you thought becoming a porter was a simple thing, you can think again. Given the regulation *raj** that our government follows, everything from the number of new licenses to the selection procedure is decided by the Railway authorities. And even this one requires political connections and palm greasing!

This study was initially aimed at understanding the procedure followed for licensing of railway porters by the Delhi Division of Northern Railway. However, as we went along we discovered a variety of other interesting issues like the permanent validity of a porter's license; the huge premium commanded by a porter's license; the strange rules regarding transfer of licenses; and the illegal practices that are an unintended consequence of these rules and regulations.

We attempt to showcase and make the reader aware of these issues, which need to be tackled urgently.

---

* The Hindi words *coolie* and *raj* translate to porter and regime, respectively in English.

The Good, the Bad and the Ugly of Being a Coolie

As already clarified, the licensed railway porter is not an employee of the Indian Railway. He is licensed by the Railways to earn a livelihood by offering his services to railway passengers for transport of their luggage. He is required to follow certain rules and regulations, failing which his license can be suspended or cancelled. Licensed porters are also not governed by the Labour Laws or any other Act.

Although the Railways is in no way obliged to provide monetary or other benefits to licensed porters, they are offered some facilities purely as a goodwill gesture. In fact, the strong unionisation of porters in the past few years has helped them obtain these privileges from the Railways.

Licensed porters do not enjoy facilities like pension, gratuity and insurance. Also, they are not entitled to any compensation by the Railways in case of injury, disablement or death while performing their duty at the place of work. Licensed porters do not have the provision of taking voluntary retirement and passing on the license while they are still fit. The only social security they have is the provision to pass on their licence to a close relative who promises to bear their expenses once they are unable to work.

The benefits that accrue to a porter are as follows:[1]

1. Complimentary travel pass for self in second/sleeper class from station of work to any station in India, and back (granted annually).
2. One set of Privilege Ticket Order (PTO) in second/sleeper class for self and spouse from station of work to any station in India, and back (granted annually). A PTO enables the porter to travel at one-third of the normal fare.
3. Facilities for medical treatment of self, spouse and dependent children at a Railway hospital, in case such exists at his station.
4. To have their children admitted in Railway schools wherever these exist, subject to availability of seats in these institutions, preference being given to wards of Railway employees.

1. As listed in "Terms and Conditions of Working of Licensed Porters Directly Licensed by the Railways".

5. Two sets of summer uniform or one summer and one winter uniform (alternate).
6. Casual leave in a year as may be allowed by the Station Master.
7. Free use of Railway's light trolleys and hand barrows for carriage of luggage.
8. Free use of waiting halls, latrines, canteens provided at stations and, in some cases, rest houses (aka coolie shelters).

Ever since the porters' unions have strengthened and become more influential, they have constantly been demanding more and more privileges. Some of their most recently met demands include the extension of medical facilities to the porter's family members in 1995 and provision of the PTO in 1998. However, there are a few demands put forward by various porter unions, which are still unfulfilled. Some of these are: inclusion of indoor treatment at Railway hospitals under medical facilities to porters, provision of voluntary retirement after 20 years of service (i.e. authority to transfer license while being fit) and inclusion of porters under Workmen's Compensation Act.

Though licensed porters do not enjoy any housing facilities provided by the Railways, there is a provision for a Coolie Rest House or Coolie Shelter at most large stations. However, these shelters have the capacity to accommodate only a few of the large porter strength at the station. While this set of porters make the rest house their home, others rent cheap accommodation where they chip in and stay together. Mostly, Coolie Shelters are shabby and cluttered with beds and clotheslines in the same premises.

On the other hand, the good part about being a licensed porter is that you are your own boss. These men are the fortunate few who can enjoy the luxury of taking an afternoon nap while at work! One is free to choose his hours of work and can put in anything ranging from two hours to 16 hours a day. The duration of time a porter puts in broadly depends on his capacity to work and his urge to earn more. Putting in eight hours of work each day, a licensed porter can earn about Rs. 7,500 per month.

I Still Love The Profession—How Do I Enter?

As we have already warned you, obtaining a porter's license is as knotty as most other government licenses! Quite unaware of this fact when we started off, yours truly actually dressed up appropriately and reached the station, all set to apply for a license and experience the process first-hand! While we presumed it would be a short and simple procedure, we soon learnt how painstakingly complicated and lengthy the process was. We describe the process in detail for your enlightenment.

First and foremost, it is not very often that the Railways comes out with openings for licensed porters. Although it is required that the demand for porters at various stations be assessed on a regular basis, the system in practice is quite ad-hoc. The average time span between fresh recruitments for the Delhi Division is 3-4 years, with the last batch of new entrants recruited in 1998. The process for recruitment of porters was initiated again in December 2002, but was still underway and unfinished at the time of research in May 2003.

Arriving at Vacancies

The prime factor that governs the demand for porter services is the passenger traffic at a given station. Since the number of long-distance trains (originating, terminating and passing through a station) has a very high correlation with passenger traffic at that station, it is used as the best indicator for porter demand. It is true that the *Rajdhani Express* would carry more porter-requiring passengers and hence produce more demand than the *Magadh Express,* which is bound for economically backward states. In addition, the quantum of wheeled suitcases and other easily portable luggage affects the demand for porter services. However, the Railways does not go into much detail regarding the analysis and is concerned only with the number of trains. In case a review takes place, all station managers are required to assess the situation at their respective stations and submit a report stating their requirements.

The Divisional Railway Manager (DRM) is the competent authority with regard to recruitment of licensed porters. After a proposal for additional requirement of licensed porters is approved by the DRM, the following process is initiated:

Publishing openings: The Commercial Department, Delhi Division, Northern Railway publishes openings by way of a "Vacancy" advertisement in leading national dailies giving details of the number of vacancies at various stations, eligibility criterion, required documents and the application deadline.

Interestingly, the latest opening published in December 2002 in the *Times of India* appeared on Page 14, the sports page and the advertisement measured a mere 28 square centimeters in size, which is about one-fortieth the size of a newspaper page! A high level of ambiguity regarding the documentation required is also evident in the advertisement.

Receiving applications: The Railways received applications from aspiring coolies through registered post. An estimate of the vacancies to applicant ratio is 1:100.[2]

Given the level of ambiguity in the 2002 advertisement, the Railways received a wide variety of documents accompanying the applicants' bio-data. These documents ranged from ration cards to college degrees to SC/ST certificates. Even though there is no requirement for any educational qualifications, a majority of applicants had completed their school education.

Scrutiny of applications: The applications are scrutinised by the Commercial Department. All applicants who have been able to provide the required documents along with their application are then sent interview letters.

The interview letter mentions the date and venue of the interview. Besides, it gives a list of the documents that the interviewee has to produce on the day of the interview. These are:

a) Valid proof of Date of Birth

b) Certificate showing verification of character and antecedents from the police station where applicant resides

c) Three copies of applicant's recent passport size photograph

d) Interview letter.

Screening: The Screening Committee is appointed by the Railways. It screens all eligible applicants over a time span of two months. The Committee comprises of three members. They are:

a) Railway Officer: He/She is usually a gazetted officer of Northern Railway and can be the Divisional Commercial Manager (DCM), or Divisional Traffic Manager (DTM) or Assistant Commercial Manager (ACM). This officer is nominated from within the Railways by the DRM.

---

2. *Source*: Official of the Delhi Division.

b) Employment Officer: He/She is a senior scale officer nominated by the District Employment Office.

c) Education Officer: He/She is nominated by the Education Department and is usually the principal of a government school.

The DRM is the approving authority for the Screening Committee.

The interview process focuses on medical fitness and physique of the applicant. The primary concern of the Committee is to ensure that those selected for the job have adequate load-carrying capacity. In order to assess this, all applicants are required to lift and carry sand filled sacks weighing about forty kilos, which is the average weight that passengers normally carry. It is ensured that they can lift these weights in one go and without too much effort or difficulty.

Final list: Names of those selected for the job are submitted to the DRM. A list of selected candidates is put up at the DRM's office. The DRM's office then issues appointment letters and the porter is made to sign an agreement.

On appointment, a licensed porter is provided the following:

a) Badge with license number inscribed

b) Two pairs of uniforms for summer and winter seasons respectively.

Licensed porters are required to pay an amount of Rs. 10 as one time security deposit (refundable) and a monthly license fee depending on the kind of station they operate on.

For A-class stations, with over 150 porters: Rs. 10 per month

For B-class stations, with 50-150 porters: Rs. 5 per month

The Golden Arm-Badge

Since licensed porters are not entitled to any kind of old-age pension or retirement benefits, the Railways have made a provision for them to live comfortably through their grey years by allowing them to transfer their licence to an inheritor, against the promise that he will take care of their financial and other requirements in their last years.

According to the Railway Board Policy, a licensed porter's badge may be transferred to his son or, if he has no son or his son is not alive, to his near relative in the event of his death or when he becomes old, infirm or very sick and is not able to carry out his duties properly. Near relatives here include the porter's brother, his brother's son (nephew) and his wife's brother.

The transfer of badges takes place at the station itself. A gazetted officer such as the Station Manager, Station Master or Area Officer is the competent authority to accept such transfers.

The following documents are required in case of a transfer:[3]

1. Medical certificate by a Railway doctor, certifying the retiring porter (applicant) as medically unfit for work.
2. Fitness certificate of transferee, issued by a Railway doctor.
3. Affidavit indicating that the applicant is the sole earning member of his family thus proving their dependence on him; and that the transferee is his nearest relative.
4. Affidavit indicating that the transferee will bear the expenses of the applicant post-retirement, or of the widow of the deceased licensed porter.
5. No Objection Certificate for transfer of badge from both transferee and transferor (or his widow, in case of death).
6. Police verification report of transferee.
7. Proof of residential address from *sarpanch*.*

The transferee should not have worked as a licensed porter for Indian Railways in the past. Also, it has to be established that the transferee does not have any other source of income and is in dire need of work. The competent authority is supposed to personally scrutinise each case and to further verify the doubtful cases. In case of a bogus affidavit, the badge is cancelled and an FIR[4] registered.

Transfer of Licences

While the system of transfer of licenses was initiated with a noble cause, it did not take too long for people to start misusing it. Being a long-term investment with flexible work-schedule and fair returns, a porter's licence was soon in demand attracting a high premium. Touts and agents would get bogus affidavits prepared and people paid

3. As per Policy Letter issued by Railway Board in 1995.
4. Stands for First Information Report, which is lodged at the police station to report a crime.
* *Sarpanch* translates to Village Head in English.

huge sums of money to obtain these licences second-hand. Moreover, these premiums have been increasing over time at a rapid rate.

Premium on a Porter's Licence (in Rupees)

Railway Station	*1994*	*2003*
Nizammudin	60,000	4,00,000
New Delhi	1,00,000	3,00,000
Old Delhi	80,000	1,80,000

Source: Head *Coolie*, New Delhi Railway Station.

Why would a poor man pay so much for a porter's job? After some running around and speaking to a substantial number of people (including loads of porters!), we reached the conclusion that a porter's situation is not as pathetic as it seems on the face. Agreed that they put in a lot of hard physical labour, but they do have a fairly high earning potential. Though the figures stated below are their average earnings, licensed porters can earn substantially more by putting in extra hours of work.

A Porter's Average Income (in Rupees)[5]

Railway Station	*Daily Income*	*Monthly Income*	*Yearly Income*
Nizammudin	250	7,500	90,000
New Delhi	220	6,600	79,200
Old Delhi	100	3,000	36,000

Second, a porter's job comes with the flexibility of choosing his own work hours and the amount of work he desires to put in. It leaves them with a lot of freedom and very few restrictions as compared to other low-paid jobs.

Third, since a porter's licence can be passed on from one generation to the next, it becomes a long-term secure investment whereby one can recover his money over a period of time.

Due to extensive misuse of the transfer facility, it was withdrawn for a few years before 1988, until the late Rajiv Gandhi ordered its restoration. Ever since, the apparent misuse has continued with the policy, giving rise to a racket of fake transfers.

5. As revealed by substantial number of porters at the three railway stations.

The *modus operandi* for these fake transfers is fairly simple. In most cases, a fake medical certificate establishing illness of the license holder and a bogus affidavit certifying the transferee and transferor's relationship is obtained by way of bribe. Concurrently, any officer in charge of verification is also bribed to ensure that documents move smoothly. Since the relationship of a brother-in-law is the easiest to fake and most difficult to verify, in most bogus cases the transferee is the brother-in-law *(sala)*.

Transfers to Various Relatives at New Delhi Railway Station[6]

Year	*Transfer of license to*				*Salas as % of total transfers*
	Son	*Brother*	*Nephew*	*Sala*	
1999	7	Nil	1	12	60%
2001	6	2	1	24	72%

There have been cases where bachelors (Numbers 1028 and 1317 at Delhi) have transferred their license for money, producing bogus affidavits declaring the transferee as their brother-in-law!

Most porters claim that the agents for such malpractice are some porter union leaders who charge a high commission. It is strange that while some union leaders are the flag-bearers in such practices, others are strongly against it and complain regularly in this regard to the authorities. The National Federation of Railway Porters, Vendors and Bearers has been continuously writing letters to the DRM's Office, informing them of this 'bogus affidavit' racket. One of their pleas was to ban transfer of license to brother-in-laws, since most fake cases happen through that method.

After repeated complaints, an inquiry was set up in 2001 to look into the matter. The Assistant Commercial Manager was deputed to personally visit few villages and verify the genuineness of the verifying authorities! Three cases picked up at random were found genuine and were consequently cleared.

Arranging Themselves to Get Work

It is interesting to note how porters arrange themselves with regard to division of business. For departing passengers (who are

6. Figures from Northern Railway's data on transfer cases.

bound for another city and require luggage to be ported from the station entrance to their respective platform) the licensed porters follow a queue system and get customers turn by turn.

The case of serving passengers arriving from other stations is slightly different. Porters begin to assemble at the station a few minutes before the arrival of the train. Along the platform there are demarcations that divide the entire platform into a number of parts (called *hadh*) and each of these parts extends up to about 50 meters (approximately the length of a train bogie). There is a common understanding that a first-come-first serve system will be followed in each *hadh*. Within each of these areas, a maximum of 4-5 porters assemble initially. On arrival of the train, they approach passengers and get customers in the same order as they assembled. Unless the first porter leaves a passenger of his own will, the others do not come and undercut him with regard to the charges.

While this system is to the advantage of the porter community, it often goes against the railway passengers who are not left with too many alternatives. This arrangement is a direct fallout of the porters' cartel which has come into existence due to the licensing system of porters. Since the existing porters face no threat of external competition (as entry into the business is regulated), they have unionised and arranged themselves to gain maximum benefit as a group.

The Business of Rate-fixing and Overcharging

While initiating the system of licensed porters, a main concern of the Railways was that these porter services should be available at reasonable prices, being affordable to the average traveller. Since a market-determined rate was a highly unreliable option for our planners and policy makers, a rate regime determined by the Railways was imposed on the licensed porters. This rate, called the official rate for porter services, has to be reviewed every two years. The rate is not uniform for all stations though it might be the same for a group of stations under a particular division of the Indian Railways. For instance, all stations under the Delhi Division follow a uniform rate, which has been revised rather infrequently and by amounts having no relevance with increase in prices.

The Railways does its best to keep passengers informed about the official rates for porter services. There are repeated announcements and appeals on the public address system to follow the official rate and complain in case of overcharging. However, a majority of the people shell out the amount they arrive at after haggling, which usually exceeds the official rate. This amount is mutually agreed upon by the passenger and the porter and so is essentially market determined.

Porter Charges for Stations under Delhi Division (in Rupees)[7]

Year	*Up to 40 kilos (head load)*	*Up to 200 kilos (trolley)*	*Over 200 kilos (trolley)*
1989	3.50	7.00	11.50
1995	7.00	12.00	20.00
1998	9.00	15.00	25.00

The current rate for head load, at Rs 9 per 40 kilos, is without question insufficient for survival given today's ever-increasing price levels. And most authorities do admit to this fact. However, when asked as to why the official rate remains so low, pat comes the reply, "Given an official rate of Rs. 9, the porters normally charge Rs. 30–35. Had the official rate been Rs. 30, they would be charging Rs. 100!"

Since the rate is demand and supply driven, we feel, this system of fixing rates for porter services does not make sense and must be scrapped. The official rates exist only in the rulebooks. The current initiative to hike the rate for head load from Rs. 9 to Rs. 15 is again a futile exercise and will not cease the problem of overcharging. Its implementation is clearly a waste of time and resources.

Numbers, for a Clearer Picture[8]

	Old Delhi	*New Delhi*	*Nizammudin*
Long Distance Trains[9]	100	170	95
Platforms	18	12	5
Sanctioned Licensed Porters	1,034	1,478	281
Working Licensed Porters	1,001	1,453	281
Licensed Porter Inspectors	1	1	1
Licensed Porter Supervisors	12	4	Nil
Average Daily Income (in Rupees)	100	220	250

7. Data obtained from the following Northern Railway letters: GM/Commercial Letter No.43AC/O/P.Charges/95 dated: 28.04.98 DRM NDLS Letter No.23-AC/406/7 dated 31.01.89.

8. All figures correspond to July 2003.

9. Estimate as given by Public Relations Officer of Northern Railway.

Misconduct, Supervision and Suspension

As per Clause 8 of "Terms and conditions of working of licensed porters directly licensed by the Railway," the licence of a porter may be suspended for a period not exceeding 15 days at a time or may be cancelled by the Station Manager/Station Master for any misconduct, like:

1. Catching or alighting a train in motion.
2. Cornering of train seats.
3. Discourteous behaviour towards passengers and/or causing damage to their luggage.
4. Charging a rate in excess of the official rate for porter services fixed by the Railway administration.
5. Rough handling of Railway luggage.
6. Disobedience of orders of authorities like Platform Inspector/ Supervisor.
7. Unauthorised absence from work.
8. Conviction in a court of law for any offence.
9. Any other misconduct causing annoyance or harassment to passengers.

To make sure that these instructions are strictly followed and not violated, a policing mechanism has been set in place. The following is the list of officials who have been appointed by the Railways to deal with licensed railway porters, in decreasing order of seniority:

1. Licensed Porter Inspector (LPI)
2. Assistant Licensed Porter Inspector (ALPI)
3. Licensed Porter Supervisor (LPS)
4. Licensed Porter *Jamadar* (LPJ)

While the LPI remains at the top of the hierarchy, the other three categories have more or less merged and are required to perform almost the same functions. All these officers are either Class III or Class IV salaried employees of the Indian Railways and enjoy all benefits that accrue to Railway employees, including post-retirement benefits.

It is interesting to note that the lowest rung officers – i.e. the LPJs – are selected from amongst the licensed porters, by a committee of two officers. These LPJs can then further seek promotion and move up the ladder as they become more and more experienced.

While most LPJs claim that their main job is to ensure that no passenger is overcharged, they are quite aware of the fact that almost nobody pays the official rate. They agree that the official rate for porter services is a measly amount and is not enough for a 'decent' living. Hence, the LPJ normally interferes only when the passenger lodges a complaint of overcharging. As long as the passenger is paying an amount higher than the official rate of his own will, the LPJ is okay by it. However, some people claim that it is because the Jamadars share the booty equally with porters, and not on sympathetic grounds, that they do not interfere. Another reason for the ineffectiveness of Jamadars is that they themselves being ex-coolies do not command much respect from the licensed porters.

Given the fall in the number of LPJs year after year with current LPJs retiring and no new recruitment, it is humanly impossible to keep a check on the coolies. For instance, the New Delhi Railway Station is now left with only 4 LPJs to keep a check on the 1,478 porters who operate there. That leaves us with 1 supervisor per 370 coolies! Even worse is the case of Nizammudin station, where the LPJ species is altogether extinct. In fact, the Licensed Porter Inspector (LPI) controls the 281-strong porter population single-handedly.

Overall, this whole system of licensing and state control over porter services needs to be re-assessed. Since one drawback leads to another, the problem at hand is even more critical and complex. We attempt to highlight the urgency of the situation, so as to rouse the authorities from their state of hibernation and initiate the process of change.

Reforms

The process of licensing seeks to ensure that the luggage transportation services are available to the passengers and to establish a modicum of guarantee of the luggage security for a passenger in case of a loss.

The reforms here can be two sided. One which aims at changing the manner the porters supply their services, and the other which aims at changing the system of their employment.

Deregulate the licensing system for entry and institute a registration process: The licensing system should be removed and a registration system should be put in its place. The authorities can start off by contracting the porter-work to any number of interested entities. The private entities can do a better job of verifying the applicant's origin and credentials. This is how most security firms deal with in providing security personnel for residences. As in the case of security bureaus, a porter bureau would ensure efficient and dependable services. To further ensure efficiency an insurance company would give a certificate to the porter/union that any loss by a particular porter would be compensated for by the insurance firm to the passenger. This would make the entire procedure more credible. Alternatively, the porters' union can stand for by the loss. There could be any number of porter unions at work. There only has to be a display of the porter's number and affiliation on his self.

With entry unrestricted, porters' fares would fall to optimal levels, there would be no premiums of huge sums of money to be paid for the job and livelihood options would open up for many more.

Privatisation of railway management and its beneficial effect on porters and other professions on the station premises: On the other hand reforms need to be brought about in the railway management itself. The platforms and the networks if privatised would ensure benefits for both the passengers and the porters. In such a scenario, when two private players will interact, the negotiations will be based on only one principle: higher gains. And higher gains can accrue only through better service. Thus, it would be in the interest of both the porter bureaus and the railway owners/agencies to have contracts that are price efficient and service efficient. Also, competition in such a case would drive prices downwards till they reach a stable and optimal level.

In a system where the railway networks and stations are entirely privatised with competitive mechanisms in place, porters and passengers would undoubtedly benefit. A railway station if privatised, stands to benefit passengers and livelihoods through the provision of diverse services including porter services. There would be provisions for different kinds of hawkers and goods with a mechanism of regulation of food stepping in due to the incentives for credibility of the service-provider.

References

"Terms and Conditions of Working of Licensed Porters Directly Licensed by the Railway" obtained from Commercial Department, Delhi Division, Northern Railway.

Vacancy advertisement (Number 3583/2002) issued by Northern Railway.

9

Opening a School in Delhi: A Learning Experience

The educational sphere (before the University level) consists of primary stage (Class 1–5), middle stage (Class 6–8), secondary stage (Class 9–10) and higher secondary stage (Class 11–12). The schools are classified as government schools, government-aided schools and private (actually called 'Public') schools. While in government-aided schools, the government only provides financial aid to the school, the government schools are run by the government directly. Private schools are run by a society from its own funds.

The Directorate of Education (DoE) of National Capital Territory (NCT) of Delhi is responsible for regulating the education system in Delhi, keeping the Delhi School Education Act and Rules, 1973 in the backdrop. The agencies involved in the process of setting up schools are local municipal authorities (Municipal Corporation of Delhi, New Delhi Municipal Corporation), land owning authority (Delhi Development Authority) and authorities conducting public exams of the students (CBSE, ICSE), besides Directorate of Education (DoE) of Government of NCT, Delhi.

This chapter focusses on the working of private schools emphasising on the licensing procedure to open them. It examines the restrictions imposed on opening a private, unaided school in Delhi. As it turns out, opening a private school is a mind-numbing task; it involves a colossal amount of paperwork. An applicant faces many agencies, making the procedure financially expensive and time-consuming. The chapter also takes a look at two practical case-studies of schools to illustrate the process.

The first step for anyone who wishes to open a school (up to any level) is to get an association or group of individuals registered as a Society under the Societies Registration Act, 1860 or alternatively as a Trust under the law in force. If the drafting of memorandum of association to registration is not enough to dampen one's enthusiasm, then the procedures and routines for opening and running the school involving lots of time and money will suffice to do so.

According to information obtained from the Directorate of Education:

- The primary schools are established with recognition from the local municipal authority, MCD or NDMC, as the case may be.
- Schools having class 6 and onwards need to have the Essentiality Certificate (elaborated later) from DoE and then, after establishment of the school, recognition is to be obtained from the same office.
- Additionally, schools offering classes 10th and 12th have to be affiliated to CBSE or 'ICSE' in order for the students to be able to appear for public exams.
- The Society shall ensure that the percentage of freeship from the tuition fee as laid down under rules by the Delhi Administration from time to time is strictly complied with. They will ensure admission to the students belonging to weaker sections to the extent of 25 per cent and grant freeship to them, in case public lands have been allotted on concessional rate/free of cost by DDA for the school.
- For setting up a school, the DoE brings out notifications in the newspapers, after which the interested parties apply for the Essentiality Certificate and the process starts.

Opening of Primary School in MCD Area

An application for requirement of land has to be filed with the Delhi Development Authority if one seeks to obtain land from DDA towards opening a primary school. However, no application has to be filed in DDA if the school is opened on self-owned or leased land. After land has been acquired, the school building has to be established. Then recognition has to be obtained from the Municipal Corporation of Delhi (MCD), which has divided its area into 12 zones. Depending upon the location in which the school has to be opened, application for recognition of primary school has to be filed, under that respective zone.

The application can be made at any time of the year, by paying a sum of Rs. 1,000 as processing fee to MCD with the following documents:

- Building Safety Certificate
- Health Certificate

Other conditions that must be fulfilled for the grant of recognition include:

1. Total land area of the school must be 1800 sq. ft.
2. There must be a playground on 720 sq. ft. of open, non-constructed area.
3. The school must have Classes 1 and 2, each with two sections, and at least one more section of another class.
4. Each section must have at least 25 students.
5. Maximum number of students allowed per section for:
   (a) Classes 1 and 2: 53 students
   (b) Classes 3, 4 and 5: 56 students.
6. The total number of classrooms should be equal to the total number of sections in the school with space left for additional three rooms for the Head Master, staff-room and a library for at least 1,000 books.
7. Each classroom must be 150 sq. ft. in area.
8. The school has to follow the books prescribed by the National Council for Educational Research and Training.
9. The process for grant of recognition takes about a year.

After the school has been set up, the respective zones handle all the matters regarding it. The zonal inspectors of MCD have to make annual inspections[1] of primary schools. According to an official, the breakup of inspectors is:

General Inspectors	66
Physical Inspectors	24
Nursery Inspectors	12
Science Inspectors	17
Total Inspectors	**119**

1. Section 24(1), The Delhi School Education Act, 1973.

As per official sources, the number of primary schools are:

MCD schools	1833
Private schools recognised by MCD (Unaided)	548
Private schools recognised by MCD (Aided)	44
Total schools (Primary)	**2425**

Opening of Middle, Secondary or Higher Secondary School

Any individual, association of individuals, society or trust, desiring to establish a new school, not being a minority school, shall before establishing such new school, give an intimation in writing to the administrator of his or their intention to establish such school.[2] An application form for obtaining an Essentiality Certificate (EC) has to be submitted. The EC is a document certifying the requirement of a school in the particular zone, on the basis of which land is allotted to the society for building a new school. An EC is stipulated to avoid proliferation of schools, which could make existing schools redundant.

The status of ECs is as shown in the following Table.[3]

S. No.	*Name of the District*	*No. of ECs to be granted in the first year commencing from year 2003*	*No. of ECs to be granted in each subsequent year till 6th year i.e. 2004 to 2008*	*No. of ECs already granted from February, 2003 to 31.12.2003*	*No. of ECs to be granted in the year 2004*
1	*2*	*3*	*4*	*5*	*6 (3-5+4)*
1	North West-A	72	14	19	67
2	North West-B	72	15	39	48
3	North East	74	15	10	79
4	East	34	07	07	34
5	Central	—	—	—	—
6	New Delhi	—	—	—	—
7	North	—	—	—	—
8	South	132	26	11	147
9	South West-A	36	07	07	36
10	South West-B	36	07	36	07
11	West-A	27	06	—	33
12	West-B	27	06	08	21

2. Rule 44, The Delhi School Education Rules, 1973.

3. Accessed on 18 April 2004 at http://www.edudel.nic.in/Circularregarding number of Essentiality Certificates issued in different districts (10th Jan 2004).doc

The government ostensibly assesses the need of new schools in Delhi over the next 10 years and accordingly frames the number of ECs to be granted in various districts. This system effectively amounts to the license-permit *raj* once prevalent in the industry.

While applying for grant of Essentiality Certificate, the following documents are required to be submitted along with the application for Essentiality Certificate (See Appendix–A for EC Application Form)[4]:

1. Processing fee of Rs. 500/- (Rupees five hundred only) in the form of DD drawn in favour of Director Education, Government of National Capital Territory of Delhi.
2. Memorandum of Association of the Society/Trust.
3. Affidavit as to the relationship of the members of the Society/Trust.
4. Registration certificate of the Society/Trust.
5. Copy of FDR in the joint name of the Society and the concerned Deputy Director of Education for Rs. 2.00 lakhs valid for three years.
6. Affidavit that the Society/Trust will run the school under the provisions of the Delhi School Act, 1973 and the Rules framed there under.
7. Undertaking regarding fees and other charges.
8. Complete list of the members of the Society/Trust along with full particulars (educational qualification, occupation, residential and occupational address) and signature of the members.
9. Details of land and building with supporting documents, if any.
10. Project report of the proposed school.
11. Experience of the members of the Society/Trust in the field of education.
12. List of other facilities proposed to be provided for the students of the proposed new school.

---

4. Directorate of Education [official website]. Accessed on 15 February 2004 at http://edudel.nic.in/forms.htm.

13. An undertaking to the effect that if the Society/Trust is granted Essentiality Certificate for a period of 05 (five) years, the Society/Trust will not apply for extension of Essentiality Certificate beyond 05 (five) years.

After the Deputy Director is satisfied with the non-proprietary nature of the Society/Trust, the EC is issued. Now the school can be established on any type of land i.e. own land, lease land (lease should be for a period of minimum 30 years) or allotted by DDA. If the Society/Trust neither has its own land for the purpose of the school nor has it taken land on lease for the same, then it has to obtain land from the land-owning agency DDA at subsidised rates. For land to be allotted to the Society/Trust, the Society needs to obtain a "letter of sponsorship" from DoE.

Once the land has been acquired and the school is established, the Society/Trust needs to apply for recognition at the district office of DoE. The application form for grant of recognition has to be supported by the following documents (See Appendix–B for Recognition Application Form)[5]:

1. Copy of the registration certificate of the Society.
2. Copy of the certificate of EC/MCD.
3. Copy of the scheme of the management.
4. List of managing committee members along with an affidavit regarding relationship.
5. Copy of legal documents regarding ownership of the land allotted to the school.
6. Undertaking in a form of affidavit that the society has obtained a land in a proper way and there is no violation of the master plan in the land used.
7. Copy of the registered rent agreement for a period of 30 years, as the case may be.
8. Site plan of the building.
9. Building fitness certificate issued by MCD or registered architect – mentioning full particulars of the building.
10. Health certificate issued by the local body.

---

5. Directorate of Education [official website]. Accessed on 15 February 2004 at http://edudel.nic.in/forms.htm.

11. Undertaking regarding availability of potable water with proper testing and certificate from the local authorities.
12. Copy of the auditor's statement of account for the past three years.
13. Copy of fixed deposit valid for atleast three years.
14. No loan certificate against fixed deposit issued by the bank.
15. Staff statement as per the proforma.
16. Rates of Fee and other fund charges (class-wise).
17. Enrolment of students (class-wise).

Recognition of Schools

Recognition for primary and middle schools is granted after inspections, as provided for in the Delhi School Education Act, 1973, have been made. For recognition of secondary and higher secondary schools, an application for grant of upgradation to the requisite stage has to be filed, but this can be made only after a minimum of two years of the previous application for recognition or upgradation, as the case may be. The following documents have to be submitted with the application form for upgradation (See Appendix–B for Upgradation Application Form)[6]:

1. Copy of the Registration Certificate of the Society.
2. Copy of the Essentiality Certificate (EC).
3. Copy of the Recognition letter.
4. Copy of upgradation letter in case of application for upgradation upto Senior Secondary level.
5. Copy of the Scheme of Management.
6. List of managing committee members alongwith an affidavit regarding relationship.
7. Copy of legal documents regarding ownership of the land allotted to the school.
8. Undertaking in form of affidavit that the society has obtained a land in a proper way and there is no violation of the Master Plan in the land used.

---

6. Directorate of Education [official website]. Accessed on 15 February 2004 at http://edudel.nic.in/forms.htm.

9. Copy of the registered rent agreement for a period of 30 years, as the case may be.
10. Site plan of the building duly certified by Regd. Architect.
11. Building fitness certificate issued by MCD or Regd. Architect mentioning full particulars of the building.
12. Health certificate issued by the local body.
13. Undertaking regarding availability of potable water with proper testing and certificates from the local authorities.
14. Copy of auditor's statement of account for the past three years.
15. Copy of the fixed deposit valid for atleast three years in the joint name of the manager of the school and Deputy Director of Education (DDE) concerned.
16. No loan certificate against fixed deposit issued by the bank.
17. Staff statement as per the proforma.
18. Rates of fee and other fund charges (classwise).
19. Enrolment of students (classwise).
20. Copy of PF, Bonus statement.

The whole process for grant of recognition/upgradation takes about a year each (the stipulated time period), but the spate of forms etc. does not end here. Next, the school has to apply for grant of provisional affiliation on the prescribed Application Form in original for approval of Middle Class Syllabus/Provisional Affiliation to Secondary and Senior Secondary classes to CBSE, so as to enable the students to appear in public exams. The prescribed Application Forms are required to be submitted by 30th June of the year, preceding the year in which Class VII/IX/XI, as the case may be is proposed to be started. Before applying for affiliation, the school should fulfill the essential requirements of affiliation as are given in the Affiliation Bye-Laws of the Board. The major essential conditions are as follows (See Appendix–C for Application Form for Approval of Middle Class Syllabus/Provisional Affiliation to Secondary and Sr. Secondary)[7]:

---

7. CBSE (Central Board of Secondary Education) [official website]. Accessed on 15 February 2004 at http://cbseaffiliation.org/formalities.htm.

1. The schools seeking affiliation with the Board must have formal prior recognition of the State/UT government. The application should either be forwarded by the State Government or there should be an NOC that the State Government has no objection to the affiliation of the school with the Board.
2. The school must possess about two acre of land and a building constructed on a part of the land and proper playgrounds on the remaining land. In case of lease, it will be accepted if it is for at least 30 years and in favour of Society/School by registered deed.
3. In metropolitan cities with a population exceeding 25 lakh, the land should not be less than one acre with adequate building, and arrangements with other institution/organisation for physical and health education and games to the satisfaction of the Board.
4. There are detailed requirements for land area for the schools seeking affiliation in NCT, Delhi depending on the number of streams. The minimum requirements vary from 2000 sq. mts. to 4000 sq. mts.
5. The Society/Trust running the school should be registered under the Societies Registration Act, 1860, and its character should be non-proprietary.
6. The school should have a well-qualified staff as per the norms of the Board given in the Affiliation Bye-Laws.
7. The school must pay salaries and admissible allowances to the staff, not less than the corresponding categories of employees in the State Government schools or as per scales etc., prescribed by the Government of India.
8. Classes VIII and above should not be started without written permission by the Board. The Board will not be responsible for any consequences if these classes are started without prior affiliation etc. granted by the CBSE.
9. The school must have sufficient financial resources to guarantee its continued existence. It should have permanent source of income to meet with the running expenses of the school so as to maintain it on a reasonable standard of efficiency.

10. The school accounts should be audited and certified by a Registered Chartered Accountant and proper account statements are required to be prepared at the time of submission of application. The school is also required to enclose Statement of Accounts and Balance Sheet for the last two years.
11. The school affiliated with the Board is required to prepare candidates exclusively for the examinations conducted by the CBSE.
12. The requisite fees prescribed for submission of Application Forms is as follows:

Affiliation fee in respect of Independent schools

(a) Approval of middle class syllabus - Rs. 10,000

(b) Fresh Provisional Affiliation for Secondary Classes (Class X) - Rs. 10,000

(c) Upgradation to plus-two stage - Rs. 10,000

Case Studies

For reasons of confidentiality, the actual names of the schools have not been provided.

ABC School: ABC school is a private, unaided school located in Jungpura. It was established in 1956 and recognised by the DoE of Delhi in 1959 (till class 10th currently). Despite not conforming to regulatory norms, like having a certain area set aside for a playground, as required by the Directorate of Education and agencies like MCD, DDA, and CBSE, it has been functioning for the past 44 years. The school functions from a building in an area classified as "residential" in the files of DDA and MCD. The school easily gets *ad-hoc* affiliation to the CBSE on a year-to-year basis. Whenever withdrawal of affiliation or recognition is threatened, the management takes recourse to the courts. The zonal inspectors of DoE inspect the school once in 3-5 years as against the rule of annual inspections.[8]

XYZ School: XYZ school is a recently opened, private, unaided school located in IP Extension of Delhi. A member of the society of the school, revealed that after filing an application for EC, it took 6

8. Section 24(1), The Delhi School Education Act, 1973.

months for the school to obtain it. Moreover, the society had to pay Rs. 2 lakh as bribe to obtain the EC. Then, the application for obtaining land, filed in the DDA office took another 12 months. The DDA took another 6 months to approve the building plan. The next hurdle was to obtain recognition from DoE. One reason for denying recognition was regarding the salaries of employees[9]. According to the provision in the Act, the pay scale of government school teachers is between Rs. 9,000 to Rs. 13,000, but this school was paying Rs. 8,000. The society paid approximately Rs. 12 lakh as unofficial payment and managed to obtain recognition from DoE.

Conclusions

The requisite list of documents produce enough paperwork for schools to employ an additional person just to gratify the government authorities or devote time to their work. To top it all, the laws are ill-defined and manipulative. From the above-mentioned list, there are at least eight documents that have to be obtained from the MCD or the DDA. These departments are responsible for inflicting maximum damage. A case in point is the Health Certificate issued by the MCD; it is to check the safety and hygiene level within the campus of the school, but the price set by the inspection officer is approximately Rs. 1,000, thus destroying the purpose of the certificate.

According to school authorities, it requires Rs. 15 lakh to open a primary school, Rs. 25–30 lakh for a middle school, Rs. 60–70 lakh for a secondary school, and finally a whooping Rs. 1–1.2 crore for a higher secondary school. Without catering to the illegal demands of the *sarkari babus* (government officials), it is next to impossible to run a private school. In other words, operating through a purely legitimate route is wishful thinking on the part of an applicant.

Reforms

Allow for-profit Schools

At present, the law allows establishment of only not-for-profit schools though they are allowed to make a reasonable surplus for

---

9. Section 10, Delhi School Education Act, 1973. "The scales of pay & allowances, medical facilities, pension, gratuity, provident fund and other prescribed benefits of the employees of a recognised private school shall not be less than those of the employees of the corresponding status in school run by the appropriate authority."

running the school. It is left to the discretion of the authorities as to what constitutes a reasonable surplus. This creates a web of illegality due to schools seeking to bypass the stringent regulations that are framed to eliminate profits of schools. Why restrict private unaided schools only to societies/trusts with a non-profit motive? Why cannot an individual seek to run a school at a profit? Whether a school is worth the cost of the education that it provides, is a decision that is best left to its users.

Studies invariably point to low quality of schooling as one of the prime reasons for drop-out among the poor, notwithstanding the myth of children working and hence not attending school (Banerji, 2000). The low quality of schooling is primarily due to lack of free competition among schools which is in turn due to state-mandated regulations that lead to low returns of schooling for the poor and hence the drop-out.

Remove the Essentiality Certificate Requirement

The Essentially Certificate requirement is a killer recipe to strangulate good quality schooling. Artificial barriers to entry did not work in the industrial sector and there is no reason to suppose that it can work in any sector. Central planning to provide even cement has demonstrably failed in various countries and we are talking about education here, arguably much more complex than cement-making. It is the dangerous combination of arrogance and ignorance regarding dynamic social processes that leads a government department to base the future requirement of schools on the present limited understanding of demand. The requirement of schools such as location, type and other defining characteristics is an issue that is best left to the forces of the market, in other words, or the demands of people. For example, the number of ECs for the year 2003 in the South Zone was fixed as 132. On what basis was this number fixed? If it reflected the demand for schools, then how come less than one-fifth of 132 ECs were actually granted? Is there any cost-benefit analysis where the number of children who could not attend school due to this EC requirement was assessed? What about the low quality of schooling suffered by the pupils of a school which was insulated from competition? How many school-going children bore the cost of this policy measure?

The pressure on the government to license an activity rarely arises from the people. Often, on the contrary, the pressure invariably arises from the occupation itself on grounds of keeping the quality bar high and protecting the consumers' interests (Friedman, 1962). However, in reality, these policies only serve to limit the quality and supply of schools thereby hurting the consumers' interests the most. Hence a complete removal of entry barriers would serve the students' interests best for that would give more choice to them, as well as provide competition to the existing schools and help raise the quality bar of schooling.

Regulation and Inspection of
Schools – Barriers to Entry and Operation

A parent's prime concerns regarding education for his child are the quality and costs incurred. Both of these can only be achieved in a scenario where there is choice of schooling for parents, competition among schools for quality, and entrepreneurship for providing better schools. Various studies show that government regulation of schools achieves little in terms of desired outputs (PROBE, 1999; Kingdon, 1996) and only depresses the demand-side of good schooling. The license-permit *raj* may have disappeared for the industry but it continues to flourish in the field of education (Das, 2001). A cursory look at the form of inspection report in Appendix D will drive the point home.

Imagine an urban scenario where there are absolutely no regulations for schools. However, there might be different private regulatory bodies that set standards and provide certification depending on the school's performance. Schools, considering their long-term nature, would be interested in acquiring any credentials that might better their chances of attracting students. Private regulators and certification authorities would be cognizant of their credibility and seek to enforce or monitor standards rigorously. There would be a plethora of schools competing with each other to attract students through better quality and lower costs. In the existing situation where the supply-side of schools is limited by government regulations and procedures, it is not difficult to imagine who bears the brunt of the consequences. Inevitably, the limited numbers of private recognised schools charge high fees from the parents who lack choice. Competition in every other sphere has driven down prices and improved quality and it would not be irrational to expect the same in education. The importance of competition cannot be understated for it is competition that allows the weeding out of the ineffective schools from the arena thereby keeping the system of schooling healthy. The emergence and choice of 'budget private schools' for the poor, preferably in comparison to government schools is an indicator of the failure of government schooling and a precursor to the success of private initiatives in providing quality schooling.

Another entry barrier for the private-school entrepreneur is the mandatory provision of Transfer Certificate by the child in case of transfer between schools. This puts the schools unrecognised by the government at a significant disadvantage, for the Transfer Certificate from an unrecognised school would not be considered valid. If recognition's only aim is to provide a valid Transfer Certificate to the child, then this should be done away with. A school should be able to test the child's ability and/or look at the previous school's credentials and make an informed decision.

For a school, the structural safety and other health measures can be taken care of by insurance agencies which would add to a school's credibility. The pay scales of the staff can be left to the discretion of the school. Schools would offer a merit-based system in order to attract the best talent and not simply pay the best and mediocre teachers on equal terms.

The government would state myriad reasons against the removal of the license-permit *raj* in the intrests of the welfare of the students and parents. Of course, no government department would seek to give up authority by relinquishing control. But if parents can be trusted to vote for politicians, then they can as well be trusted for the patronage of the school of their choice without any interference from the government.

Decentralise Curricula and Examinations

Government-set curricula and examinations, often centrally planned, would not be reflective of actual demands and needs of parents and children. A decentralised market-based approach allowing schools to evolve or adopt curricula from the market will allow for innovations in the curricula of education. This freedom on part of schools regarding curricula would allow greater flexibility on part of private school entrepreneurs to offer better education services to the students. Only competitive markets, through the process of entrepreneurship allow for the discovery of improved or better services (Kirzner, 1998).

Land Subsidy

With the provision of land and recognition of schools vested in the hands of government, it is inevitable that there is a great deterrence to the emergence of private schools. There are more than 1500 unaided, recognised private schools in Delhi and more than 1200 of these schools have been allotted public land. The practice of the government holding land and then providing it at subsidised rates to schools should be done away with. This allows only the well-connected and the privileged to gain access to this land thereby disadvantaging the honest entrepreneur and misuse of taxpayer's resources. Another note worthy of of mention is the high costs of enforcement and monitoring required to implement the provision of freeship to students in exchange for land.

Education Vouchers for the Poor

A common complaint has been the absence of purchasing power on part of parent to access private schooling. In tune with the new paradigm of "provision and not production" in governance, the government need not run schools to provide education for the poor. They could provide financial assistance (a voucher as it is called) to the student and allow him to go the school of his choice. The advantages of this system are enormous. The locus of decision-making — the choice of school — is transferred from the government to the student. This reflects in "voting on his feet" if he finds a particular school unattuned to his needs. This makes the school accountable and compels it to provide competitive education. A voucher in the hands of the students would also incentivise entrepreneurs to set up schools and encash on the opportunity thus stimulating supply-response for providing schooling. The amount of the voucher could even be flexible to incentivise entrepreneurs to accommodate the marginalised groups like girl children and the physically handicapped.

Allow Private Boards for Affiliation Purposes

Why should only the government set up boards for the affiliation of schools? Any private player should be able to establish a board and schools may seek to obtain affiliation from this private board if parents value the board's credentials.

Reference

Banerji, Rukmini. 2000. "Urban Poverty and Primary Schooling: Field Studies from Mumbai and Delhi". In *Economic Reforms for the Poor*, edited by Shubhashis Gangopadhyay and Wilima Wadhwa. Delhi: Konark Publishers Private Limited.

Das, Gurcharan. 2001. "If India can, why can't we?" Accessed online on 18 February 2004 at http://timesofindia.indiatimes.com/articleshow/35348091.cms

Dixon, Pauline. 2003. "The Regulation of Private Schools Serving Low-Income Families in Andhra Pradesh, India: An Austrian Economic Approach". Accessed online on 18 February 2004 at http://it.stlawu.edu/sdae/dixon.doc

Friedman, Milton. 1962. *Capitalism and Freedom*, pp. 138-44. Chicago: University of Chicago Press.

Jain, Sunil. 2003. "Education: The Next Big Thing". Accessed online at http://www.business-standard.com/today/story.asp?Menu=26&story=30819 on 18 February 2003.

Kingdon, G. 1996. The Quality and Efficiency of Private and Public Education: A Case Study of Urban India, *Oxford Bulletin of Economics and Statistics*, 58(1): 83-118.

Kirzner, I. 1998. *How Markets Work: Disequilibrium, Entrepreneurship and Discovery*. New Delhi: Centre for Civil Society.

Mandava, Naveen. 2003. "Education: Fund Students not Schools". In *State of Governance: Delhi Citizen Handbook 2003*. New Delhi: Centre for Civil Society.

Shah, Parth J. 1998. "The Full Truth in Prof Sen's Half Truth," *Business Standard*, January 3.

———. 2000. "On the Role of Government and Civil Society in Education: Liberalisation, Accountability, and Empowerment," *New Economic Policies for a New India*, edited by Surjit S. Bhalla, Indian Council of Social Science Research. pp. 90-117.

———. 2002. "Liberalise the Education Sector" *Economic Times*, New Delhi, July 18.

Tooley, James, and P. Dixon. 2003. "Providing Education to the World's Poor: A case study of the private sector in India," *Handbook of Educational Leadership*. London: Pearsons.

Tooley, James. 2001. *The Enterprise of Education: Opportunities and Challenges for India* accessed on 18 February 2004 at http://www.libertyindia.org/pdfs/tooley_education.pdf

The PROBE Team. 1999. *Public Report on Basic Education*. New Delhi: Oxford University Press.

Circulars Regarding Essentiality Certificates

Government of National Capital Territory of Delhi

Directorate of Education
Old Secretariat, Delhi - 110 054

No.F.DE/Act/EC/2002-2003 Dated : 17.01.2003

CIRCULAR

On the basis of fresh assessment of the future requirement of Essentiality Certificates in various districts and to cater to the need of new schools in Delhi, the Essentiality Certificates are required to be granted during the next ten years in the following districts as per requirement indicated against each

Sl. No.	*Name of the District*	*No. of ECs to be Granted in the First Year Commencing from Year 2003*	*No. of ECs to be Granted in Each Subsequent Year till 6th year i.e. 2004 to 2008*
1.	North West-A	72	14
2.	North West-B	72	15
3.	North East	74	15
4.	East	34	07
5.	Central	—	—
6.	New Delhi	—	—
7.	North	—	—
8	South	132	26
9.	South West-A	36	7
10.	South West-B	36	7
11.	West-A	27	6
12.	West-B	27	6

A copy of the Guidelines along with Application Form for Essentiality Certificate is enclosed. A specimen copy for issuance of Essentiality Certificate to the Society/Trust (in case of grant of Essentiality Certificate) is also enclosed. Kindly note that an additional paragraph (No.6) has been inserted in the letter of issuance of EC. In case the Society/Trust requires land from DDA for running of the proposed school and indicates accordingly in his application form in Column No.16, the paragraph no.6 in letter of issuance of EC should be struck out.

Applications for issuance of the Essentiality Certificate from the desirous Society/Trust can now be accepted.

All the district DDEs are directed to maintain a register regarding receipt and disposal of applications for grant of EC w.e.f. year 2003 onwards till 2008. All such applications be examined and processed on merits and submitted to the Director Education for final decision within 45 days of receipt of application. **It may clearly be noted that the department will not issue ECs over and above the number of ECs mentioned in the above table.**

Any laxity in complying with the above directions will be viewed very seriously.

-SD/-

Director of Education

Encl. : As above

To

All Distt. DDEs

Copy to :

1. Secretary to the Minister of Education, Government of NCT of Delhi for information of the Minister of Education please.
2. PS to Secretary Education for information of Secretary Education please.
3. All Regional Directors for monitoring.
4. ADE (Capital Works).

Government of N.C.T. of Delhi
Directorate of Education
Old Secretariat, Delhi - 110054

No.F.DE/Act/EC/2003-2004/206-228 Dated : 10.01.2004

CIRCULAR

Vide circular no.F.DE/Act/EC/2002-2003/32647 dated 12.11.2003, the number of Essentiality Certificates issued in different districts as on 12.11.2003 was intimated. It was also intimated that while districts South West-B has already exhausted its quota of 36 ECs to be issued and hence further issuance of ECs in this district has been restricted during the year 2003, other district DDEs may carry forward the number of ECs, which have fallen short of the required number of ECs to be issued during the year 2003, to the next year i.e. during 2004.

The position with regard to ECs issued as on 31.12.2003 and the number of ECs to be issued during the year 2004, after carrying forward the number of ECs, which have fallen short of the required number of ECs to be issued during the year 2003, is as under :

S. No.	*Name of the District*	*No. of ECs to be granted in the first year commencing from year 2003*	*No. of ECs to be granted in each subsequent year till 6th year i.e. 2004 to 2008*	*No. of ECs already granted from February, 2003 to 31.12.2003*	*No. of ECs to be granted in the year 2004*
1	2	3	4	5	6 (3-5+4)
1.	North West-A	72	14	19	67
2.	North West-B	72	15	39	48
3.	North East	74	15	10	79
4.	East	34	07	07	34
5.	Central	—	—	—	—
6.	New Delhi	—	—	—	—
7.	North	—	—	—	—
8.	South	132	26	11	147
9.	South West-A	36	07	07	36
10.	South West-B	36	07	36	07
11.	West-A	27	06	—	33
12.	West-B	27	06	08	21

All the district DDEs are requested to cross check the above figures of ECs issued as on 31.12.2003 as per record maintained in my personal branch with that of register maintained in their respective district and in case of any deviation, the same be brought to the notice of the undersigned.

-SD/-

Director of Education

APPENDIX – A

Application Form for Essentiality Certificate

1. Name of the Individual/Society/Trust/Association of Individuals (with complete address), which intends to establish a new school.
2. Memorandum of Association, Rules and Regulation of the Society/ Trust.
3. Whether the Society/Trust is registered, and in case so, a copy of Registration Certificate be attached.
4. The Zone in which the new school is proposed to be established and the approximate number of students likely to be educated in such school.
5. The stage of education intended to be imparted.
6. The number of schools of the intended stage in existence in the Zone where the new school is proposed to be established and the population of such zone.
7. Whether the persons proposing to establish the new school have any alternative Zone in view; and if so, the particulars of such alternative Zone with respect to the matters specified in clauses (a) & (c) of Rule 44 of DSER, 1973.
8. The particulars including measurement of the building or other structure in which the school is proposed to be run.
9. Date, number and amount of F.D.R./Deposit Receipt in the joint name of the Society and the concerned Deputy Director of Education.
10. The financial resources from which the expenses for the establishment and running of the school are proposed to be met.
11. Whether the undertaking by School Management/Society/Trust in the form of an affidavit that they will run the school as per provisions of the DSER, 1973 is enclosed.
12. The proposed procedure until recognition under the Act for the selection of the Head of the new school and other teachers and non-teaching staff and the minimum qualification for their recruitment.
13. The proposed scale of pay for the Head of the School and other teaching/non-teaching staff until the school is recognised under the Act.
14. Admission fee, tuition fee and other charges (by whatever name called), which would be levied and collected from the students of the proposed new school until its recognition under the Act.
15. Any other facility which is proposed to be provided for the students of the proposed new school.
16. Whether the Society has its own land or it requires land from DDA for running of the proposed school.

APPENDIX – B

Application Form for Recognition/Upgradation

1. Name of the school
2. Name of the District and Zone in which it is situated
3. Date of first opening of the school
4. Special aims of the school
5. Stage up to which education facilities provided (Primary, Middle, Secondary)
6. Medium of instructions at various stages
7. Stage of education up to which recognition desired (Primary, Middle or Higher Sec.)
8. If recognition is desired up to Middle and Higher Secondary stage, subject in which recognition is desired.
9. Number and categories of recognised schools already functioning in that locality
10. Central desirability of the school with reference to the suitability and sufficiency of existing school in the locality and the probable effect on them
11. Whether the school is run on commercial basis for profit by any individual or group of individuals
12. Constituting of the Managing Committee of the school together with the names of members of committee and their occupation
13. (a) Is the society running the school registered under the Societies Regn. Act, 1860? If registered an attested copy of certificate of registration be attached
    (b) Name of the Manager of the school
    (c) Whether the school has duly approved scheme of management
14. Has the school its own building or house in a rented building?
15. Total area of the campus with total built up area
16. Accommodation provided in the school Bldg. (dimension to be indicated in all cases)
17. (a) Number of class rooms with seating capacity in each (detail).
    (b) Details of furniture and ventilation in each class room/ other rooms
    (c) School Library and reading room
    (d) Science Laboratories
    (e) School Halls
    (f) Staff Room
    (g) Room for head of school

(h) Office Room
(i) Store Room
(j) Refreshment room for students
(k) Bath rooms and lavatories for Day scholars
(l) Drinking water facilities.

18. Total area of playground and games played
19. Details of apparatus and equipments
    (a) Physics
    (b) Chemistry
    (c) Home Science
    (d) Physiology and Hygiene
    (e) Drawing and painting
    (f) Music
    (g) Biology
    (h) Agriculture
    (i) History
    (j) Geography
    (k) Cookery
    (l) Craft
    (m) Commerce
    (n) Technical subject
20. No. of books in Library
21. Is there a separate section of library for teachers? If so how many books are there in the section?
22. Amount spent on the purchase of books for library every year from the date the school started.
23. Financial position of school
    (a) Reserve Fund as fixed deposits
    (b) Average monthly Income
        i) From fees
        ii) Other sources
    (c) Total monthly income
    (d) Average Monthly expenditure and Disbursement of salaries
23. Number of students in each class specifying
    (a) Name of class
    (b) No. of Sec.
    (c) No. of students
    (d) Average attendance in each section

25. Whether admission in the school is made to all without any discrimination based on religion caste, race, and place of birth or any of them
26. Whether any religious instruction is imparted and if so, whether it is Compulsory
27. Details of curriculum syllabus followed in each class
28. Educational and vocational guidance facilities available
29. Whether management maintains a Provident Fund Scheme or any other Similar scheme for staff
30. Rates of fees and other funds charged classwise
31. Number of students residing with their parents/guardians and other arrangement made for their residence
32. Details of staff including head of the school
33. Details of facilities available for physical education and recreation
34. Medical facilities for students
35. Details of co-curricular cultural and other activities organised in the school
36. Any other information

APPENDIX – C

Application Form for Approval of Middle Class Syllabus/Provisional Affiliation to Secondary and Sr. Secondary

1. Affiliation code of the school
2. Name and address of the school
3. Phones/Fax/E-mail of the school
4. Dates of
   (a) Application for affiliation upto Sec. stage
   (a) Affiliation for Secondary stage granted on
   (b) Affiliation for Secondary stage granted upto
5. Dates of
   (a) Application for affiliation upto Sr. Sec. stage
   (a) Affiliation for Sr. Secondary stage granted on
   (b) Affiliation for Sr. Secondary stage granted upto
6. Date of Last inspection of the School
7. Building infrastructure of the school
   (a) Total area in acres
   (b) Built-up area
   (c) No. of office rooms/staff rooms
   (d) No. of laboratories

(e) No. of libraries/reading rooms

8. Particulars of the Principal
   (a) Name of Principal
   (b) Qualification
   (c) Teaching experience
   (d) Date of Appointment
   (e) Date of superannuation

9. Particulars of other teaching staff (each)
   (a) Name of staff
   (b) Date of Birth
   (c) Qualification
   (d) Date of Appointment
   (e) Date of Confirmation
   (f) Experience
   (g) Subjects

10. Classwise students strength
    (a) Class
    (b) No. of sections
    (c) No. of students
    (d) Student-section ratio

11. Results of Board Exams for the last three years of:
    (a) Secondary
    (b) Sr. Secondary

12. Details of Income of the school for last three years for all stages i.e. pre primary, primary, middle, secondary and sr. secondary
    (a) Annual - Admission fees, Security deposits, Annual charges, Corpus fund, PTA, Any Other
    (b) Quarterly/Monthly - Tuition fee, Development fund, S.U.P.W, Computer fee, Lab fee, Bus fee, Boarding fee, Any other
    (c) Other Income Sources – Donation, Canteen, Book Stall, Parking, Bank, Tailoring Shop, Funds transfer from society to school, Funds transfer from trust to school, Any other

13. Details of Fixed deposits, Bank balance, Budget provision of last three years

14. Details of Expenditure of the school for last three years
    (a) Capital Expenditure - Building/Land, Furniture/Furnishing/Fixtures, Any other
    (b) Non Capital – Salaries, Wages, Other allowances/perks, Contingency, Sports and cultural activities, in-service training programmes, Conveyance, Advances, Postages and Telephones, Electricity, Miscellaneous, Any Other

(c) Multimedia and IT – Computers, Printers, Media Items, Projectors, Internet, Softwares, Any Other

(d) Library/Labs/Workshop - Library books, Lab Equipments/ items, Workshop Equipments, Any Other.

(e) Annual Maintenance Contract – Building, Plantation, Security services, Transport, Computers, Lab Equipments, Any Other

APPENDIX – D

Form of Inspection Report

FORM V
[*See* Rule 192(3) and Rule 194]

PART A

1. (a) Name of the school.

   (b) Date of establishment.

   (c) Date of last recognition as: Primary/Middle '[Secondary/Senior Secondary School].

   (d) Subjects taught (group-wise/stream-wise).

   (e) Areas from where students come to the School.

   (f) Names of feeder schools.

   (g) Date of last inspection.

   (h) Date of present inspection.

2. Follow-up action taken by the school or Managing Committee on the last Inspection Report containing suggestions given; evidence of improvement; steps taken for improvement.

3. Staff statement-giving qualifications of the teaching staff :

   (a) Teaching staff – showing the name of the teacher, qualifications (showing subjects taken in B.A. and M.A.); Date of first appointment with grade; Date of posting at the school; present grade and pay and the date from which appointed; classes and subjects taught and number of periods per week.

   (b) Clerical and other Class IV staff – showing name; qualifications; date of first appointment in school with grade; present pay; date from which present post held; total number; teacher-pupil ratio; minimum, maximum and average periods per teacher per week; whether teaching staff is adequate; period for which posts lying vacant—category-wise; names of teachers transferred from the school during the year and last two years.

4. Scale of fees and contributions to Pupils' Fund, stage-wise:

   (a) Whether fees and funds charged are in accordance with the rates prescribed under rules; Whether any compulsory levy or other charges have been collected from students, if so, the details

(b) Pupils' Fund - Details of various funds; Whether accounts maintained properly.

5. Total amount spent out of Pupils' Fund and balance on the day of inspection.

6. Furniture – Requirements; Available in stock; Unserviceable.

7. Managing Committee - Names of members and address of the Managing Committee; Whether Committee formed according to the Rules; Number of meetings held in the past one year.

8. Finances - Source of income (Grant-in-aid; Fees contribution; Other charges and payments; Endowments; Donations; Gifts; Any other

9. The School Plant - Is the building adequate; Are playgrounds available, if not, how are games and other physical training programmes organised; No. of rooms required; Any repairs or other needs urgently to be attended to.

10. Service conditions of staff:

    (a) Whether the Managing Committee is following the specified rules of recruitment, promotion, confirmation, superannuation and agreement forms duly executed?

    (b) Whether payment of salaries is made regularly and in time. Indicate the dates on which salaries were paid during the last 12 months.

    (c) Whether provident fund accounts maintained and subscribed regularly?

11. Examination: Class - 1st year, 2nd year, 3rd year

    (a) Class-wise pass percentage for the last three years and No. of students remaining in the same class for more than a year.

    (b) What percentage of school funds is utilised in conducting - Periodical tests; Half-yearly and annual examinations.

12. Remedial teaching and other help given to weak students – Class; Subject; Number of students.

PART B

Supervision/Inspection of the Academic Work (Actual Teaching and its Different Aspects)

The Supervisor/Inspector whether alone or in a term shall thoroughly supervise the teaching of an individual teacher and the work done by students. Inspection shall be as objective and critical as possible. It shall be effective and aimed at bringing about improvements in the standards of teaching-learning situation.

Points to be observed and notes made on the following:

1. (a) How has the teacher planned his lesson?

(b) The types of lesson/notes written by the teacher and how far are they useful.

2. Whether the teacher has covered the specified course and syllabus for the term and has adhered to it in the programme of teaching?

3. Was the lesson taught on the day of inspection already scheduled and planned for the day?

4. (a) Were the questions put to the students thought-provoking and well-distributed?

   (b) How far the teacher encouraged the students to put questions to him on the subject?

5. What types of audio-visual aids were used by the teacher in the class and how far were they effectively used?

6. (a) Did the teacher write a proper blackboard summary?

   (b) How far was it a true synopsis of the lesson taught?

7. Are the assignments given by the teacher and if so, are they judicious and scientifically given?

8. (a) Does the teacher give the classwork to students regularly?

   (b) If so, is it regularly corrected and corrections followed up?

9. (a) How much homework does the teacher give?

   (b) Is it regularly corrected and followed up?

10. (a) How far is the assignment for classwork and homework assessed and evaluated?

    (b) Has any record of such assessment been kept by the teacher and if so, how?

11. (a) What methods were used by the teacher in teaching the lesson and how far were the methods effective?

    (b) How far did the teacher effectively teach the lesson?

    (c) How far did the students grasp the subject?

    (d) How far did the teacher achieve the objectives of the lesson?

12. (a) Are periodical tests held? If so, at what intervals?

    (b) What type of papers are given to the students?

    (c) How are they evaluated?

13. How are the tests and examinations in schools organised?

14. How far are modern techniques in setting and evaluation of papers used?

15. How is the record of tests and examinations kept in the school? Is it properly maintained?

16. (a) Are progress reports of students regularly sent to the parents?

    (b) Do the Class teacher and the Head of the Institution signs them?

(c) Are they kept in proper and safe custody?

17. (a) What remedial steps have been taken by the teacher to remove the weakness of students in different areas?

(b) Does he keep any record of such students and of the progress achieved by them?

18. (a) What efforts has the teacher made in helping the gifted children?

(b) Is there any record of their progress and achievement kept?

19. (a) What projects, if any, has the teacher taken up in the school?

(b) How far are the students and teacher involved in the project?

(c) How far have the objects of the project been achieved?

20. (a) Have any innovations and new experiments been made by the teacher?

(b) If so, with what results?

21. How does the teacher encourage love for the subject and love for reading amongst the students?

22. (a) What efforts has the teacher made in improving the handwriting of his students?

(b) How far has he succeeded in it?

23. (a) Does the teacher write his diary properly and regularly?

(b) How far does it help him and the authorities in assessment in his work?

24. (a) Did the teacher keep a class-library?

(b) If so, how is it organised and with what results?

25. (a) How does the teacher control his class?

(b) How are his relations with his students?

26. (a) Has the teacher participated in any seminars, refresher courses, summer-institutes or in-service training programmes?

(b) If so, give details.

27. (a) Has the teacher contributed any articles or published any textbook, etc.?

(b) If so, give particulars.

28. (a) Has the teacher (in the case of Primary School) been able to ensure optimum enrolment in his class and avoid dropouts by retaining those children who have joined the school?

(b) If so, indicate steps taken by him in this direction.

29. (a) Has the teacher received any recognition, award or prize from the School, community or the Government?

(b) If so, give particulars.

30. A critical and objective impression as a whole of the teaching learning situation observed by the Inspector may be recorded.

PART C

Library Facilities

1. Does the school have an adequate library, standard books and a reading room for students and teachers both?
2. What kinds of dailies, weeklies and educational and other journals are subscribed by the school?
3. How far are they used by the students and with what results?
4. How has the library service been organised in the school?
5. What is the system of issue of books, reference books and journals, *etc.*?
6. How far has the librarian succeeded in inculcating the habit of general reading amongst the students who go to the library?
7. (a) The librarian and the teacher are rendering what help to the students so far as reading of books and journals, etc. is concerned?
   (b) How far has it been effective?
8. (a) What is the system of purchase of books in the school?
   (b) Is it proper and helpful in building up a good library?
9. How does the Librarian display the books and new arrivals?
10. Are the seating arrangements in the Library and Reading Room adequate and proper?
11. Is there any library period in the school timetable? If so, who attends it?
12. The average number of books issued by the librarian daily to students.
13. (a) Is physical verification made every year?
    (b) Who makes it?
    (c) Has it been properly done?

PART D

Physical Activities, Games and Sports in the School

1. Does the school have adequate playgrounds?
2. If so, how are they maintained?
3. If no, how is the physical education programme including physical training exercises, gymnastics, games and sports organised by the school?
4. How does the school organise the games and sports? (If the playground is available)
5. Are games available to all the students or only to a few?
6. How does the school, propose to provide games for all?

7. (a) Are games and sports materials adequate in the school?
   (b) If not, give the deficiencies.
8. What percentages of the school-fund are utilised for:
   (a) Organisation of games and sports;
   (b) Purchase of games material and other equipment;
   (c) Participation in the tournaments and competitions;
   (d) Refreshment to the players?
9. What are the achievements of the school at: Zonal; District; State; National level competitions or tournaments?

PART E

Co-curricular Activities

1. What specific co-curricular programmes or activities does the school organise?
2. What is the percentage of the participation in each programme by the Students and Teachers?
3. On what system are the co-curricular activities organised (House system, class or prefect system)?
4. How do these activities fit within the school timetable?
5. How much time students and teachers devote on these activities: Within and outside school hours.
6. How does the school organise group activities?
7. How far do these programmes help individual talent to grow?
8. How and in what manner are these activities evaluated?
9. What record is kept of the participation: of students; of teachers along with names?
10. How far does it give the correct picture of the achievements of the students and the teachers?
11. Is any weightage given for achievement in this programme to the students for promotion to the next class?
12. What facilities, if any, have been provided for:
    (a) Work Experience Programme
    (b) Workshop Practice
    (c) Development of Hobbies
    (d) Dance, Drama and Music
    (e) Other activities, such as National Cadet Corps, Scouting, Girl Guides, etc.?
13. What percentage of the school funds is utilised for various activities under the co-curricular programme?

14. How does the school celebrate various functions and important days (e.g., United Nations Day, Independence Day, Republic Day, Anniversaries of great men, etc.)?

15. Is any record of such activities kept by the school and in what manner?

16. What types of incentives are given by the school to the students for the meritorious performance in:

    (a) Studies.

    (b) Games and Sports.

    (c) Co-curricular activities.

    (d) Other activities.

PART F

Relation of School with Parents and the Community in General

1. Does the school have a Parent-Teacher Association?

    (i) How is it organised?

    (ii) What co-operation and help does the school receive from the parents in various school programmes?

2. How much and what is the involvement of parents in the school activities:

    (i) Academic.

    (ii) Games and Sports.

    (iii) Co-curricular Programmes.

3. How are the Parent-Teacher Association funds utilised and on what purposes?

4. How far does the school participate in various activities of the community (in rendering Social Service or other type of help)?

5. What success has been achieved by the school in enlisting and ensuring support of the community in this programme?

PART G

School Administration

1. How has the Head of school distributed the schoolwork amongst his colleagues?

2. Has the Time Table been drawn?

    (i) In advance of the academic year?

    (ii) Has the work been equally distributed amongst the teachers?

3. Does the Head of the school take class himself and teach as required under rule 59(2)(xxv):

    (i) Subjects and classes taught.

(ii) Number of periods taught.

4. (i) How many subjects can the Head of School effectively supervise?

(ii) What does he do in respect of other subjects, how are they supervised?

5. How have the subject faculties been organised?

6. (i) What type of record does the Head of school keep for supervision of teaching work?

(ii) Inspection of Home Work.

(iii) Class-work of students.

(iv) How does he plan the inspection of this work?

7. How far has his supervision been effective and useful?

8. (i) How are staff meetings organised by the Head of school and how often?

(ii) How and in what manner is the record of such meetings kept?

(iii) How far have these meetings been effective in bringing about cordial relations amongst the staff, students and the Head of school?

9. (i) How are other activities organised by the Head of School?

(ii) Games and sports.

(iii) Co-curricular Activities.

(iv) Other activities involving the community.

(v) National Cadet Corps, Scouting and such other activities.

10. How much co-operation and help does he receive from his staff, parents and the community in the school programmes?

11. (i) How does he manage, control and organise the office work?

(ii) How much time is devoted by him for?

(a) Office work.

(b) Supervision work.

(c) Teaching work.

(d) Other activities.

12. (i) How does he maintain the school record?

(ii) Is proper and up-to-date statistics maintained and if so, in what form?

(iii) Does he furnish statements, returns and other required statistics to various authorities in time?

13. (i) Has the Head of school formulated any "Institutional Plan" for the school?

(ii) If so, with what results?

14. What incentives the Head of school has given to the students for meritorious performance in studies, games and sports, co-curricular and other activities of the school?

15. Are cumulative record cards of the students maintained by the school, if so, in what manner?
16. (i) Does the school publish a magazine? If so, how many times in the year?
    (ii) What is the contribution of the students in it?
    (iii) How much does an issue cost the school?
17. (i) What arrangements the school has made for a regular Medical check-up of the students?
    (ii) Is there a qualified Doctor, Dispensor or Nurse?
    (iii) How many times is the Medical Check-up done in a year?
18. What percentage of school funds is spent on Medical Aid and Check-up of students?
19. What percentage of school funds is spent on purchase of medicine and other appliances every year?
20. Educational and Vocational Guidance:
    (i) What facilities have been provided for Educational and Vocational Guidance of students?
    (ii) How far have they helped the students in the choice of subjects and vocations?
    (iii) Is there a Guidance Counsellor in the school, if so, how much time does he devote in the school for providing guidance to the students?
21. (i) Are there any Career Masters in the school?
    (ii) Do they maintain proper records of the psychological test served and guidance given?
    (iii) Is this work followed up, if so, how?
22. Does the school use prescribed and recommended books duly verified by the Director or the Affiliating Board?
23. (i) How are his relations with the Members of the Managing Committee?
    (ii) How does he maintain records and proceedings of the meetings of the Managing Committee?
24. How does the Head of school maintain the school plant?
25. What efforts have been made by Head of school to raise the academic and other standards of school?
26. What are his main problems and difficulties in running the school smoothly and efficiently?

PART H

Accounts of the School and their Maintenance

(a) What are the sources of income of the school?

(b) Are payments of salaries of staff made by the 7th day of each month?

(c) How are the records pertaining to the fees and funds as specified by the Director maintained by the school?

(d) When was last Audit done?

(i) By A.G.C.R.

(ii) By Internal Auditors.

(iii) By Chartered Accountants.

(e) (i) Have the observations or requirements of the Audit been settled?

(ii) What are the pending Audit objections?

(iii) Reasons for delay, if any, in their settlement.

(f) Have the purchases been made according to rule?

(g) The Test checks of the Vouchers, Cash Book and Stock Registers may be made and remarks about their maintenance are given.

(h) Are the stocks verified annually and if so, what action has been taken on the deficiencies noted, if any?

(i) Is the Cash Book regularly maintained and verified by the Head of school?

(j) Who handles the cash in the school and what are the arrangements of keeping it safe?

(k) How are the accounts of fees and funds maintained in the school (General report may be given)?

PART I

The School Plant and its Maintenance

1. (i) Is the school being run under a *Pukka* Building or prefabricated Building?

(ii) Tents.

(iii) Partly in tents and partly in buildings.

2. Whether proper lighting, ventilation and laboratory facilities exist and if so, are they adequate?

3. Whether the classrooms have enough space for existing enrolments?

4. (i) Whether drinking water facilities have been provided in the school?

(ii) Are the water taps sufficient in number to meet the requirements of school? If not, what other arrangements have been made by the Head of school for this purpose?

5. (i) Whether electric connection exists in the school and if so, are the electric installations kept safe from danger?

(ii) Are they regularly inspected by the Head of School, the C.P.W.D.

6. (i) Whether the minor repairs to the school building and its appurtenances being regularly done by the C.P.W.D.?
   (ii) Does the school also get repairs done, at its own cost, and if so, how much money has been spent during the year?
7. Whether the school building and the school premises are kept neat and tidy?
8. Has any project for beautification of school been taken up by the Head of school, and if so, with what results?

PART J

Attendance and Discipline

1. Does the Head of the school and members of the staff come punctually to the school?
2. If not, what steps have been taken by the Head of the school to ensure punctuality and attendance of the whole teaching and non-teaching staff?
3. What is the average of attendance of students in the school?
4. What steps have been taken by the Head of the school to check amongst the employees and students: Late attendance; Truancy; Absenting without prior leave?
5. Does the Head of the school maintain discipline amongst students and employees of the school?
6. Brief remarks about the behaviour of the students and employees and on the general tone and tenor of the school may be recorded.

PART K

Observance of Rules and Instructions

1. Does the school maintain all the records and registers, etc. and other documents which have been specified by the Director?
2. Does the school have a copy of the Delhi School Education Act, 1973 and the Rules made thereunder?
3. Does the school possess necessary books of rules and regulations on different subjects, *viz.*, Fundamental Rules, General Financial Rules, Treasury Rules, Leave Rules, Latest Pension Rules, Classification, Control & Appeal Rules, and the like?
4. How does the school maintain different orders and instructions issued by the Director or other authorities from time to time?
5. Does the Head of school maintain a table showing the statements, returns and statistics which he has to submit to the Director and other authorities on different dates of the year?
6. Does the school follow the rules and regulations insofar as appointments, leave, General Provident Fund, admissions,

promotions to the next higher class and such other rules or instructions issued by the Director from time to time?

7. Have any lapses been found in carrying out the instructions of the Director? If so, give particulars.

Guidelines for the Supervisors and Education Officers

The Supervision or Inspection shall: —

(i) Aim at providing academic guidance to the teachers and help the institution in promotion of higher standard of education;

(ii) Not be fault-finding of teachers and their work, but concrete suggestions for improvement of teaching, class work, homework and its correction thereon shall be given;

(iii) Help the institution in organisation of co-curricular and extra-curricular programme in a manner conducive to the all-round development of the students, and help in co-curricular development of the school;

(iv) The Supervisor/Inspector shall:

  (a) Formulate a clear definite plan of supervising the subjects and classes of each teacher;

  (b) Focus his attention on the teaching-learning situation and not only upon the teacher as a person;

  (c) Emphasise upon the professional growth of teachers by developing powers of self-direction;

  (d) Give the teachers requisite freedom to try out new experiments, methods and innovations in the process of teaching;

  (e) Help the teachers to understand the role of the school, the objectives to be achieved through the teaching-learning process in this school.

Responsibility of the Supervisory Staff

(i) An objective assessment of the adequacy, efficiency and effectiveness of the work of teachers and also of the total school programme in all its aspects.

(ii) Encourage exchanges between different schools and sharing all experiences in raising the standard of education.

(iii) To provide link between the Education Department and Delhi Administration schools, teachers and management and keep in close touch with the parents and community in general for ensuring their co-operation.

(iv) Ensure that the schools utilise public funds prudently for the purpose for which they were received and that the school properly complies with the rules and departmental instructions.

(v) So organise the administrative work pertaining to his office and conducting of enquiries, sending reports to the schools or

Education Department and Delhi Administration in such a manner that it may not interfere with his supervisory work.

(vi) As provided under sub-section (1) of Section 24 of the Delhi School Education Act, 1973 sub-clause (I), each school shall have to be inspected at least once in each financial year.

(vii) The Education Officer shall specify the months, dates and timing of inspection for the schools during which period the school shall be inspected.

(viii) At the commencement of the year, each Education Officer or Inspector shall prepare a schedule of inspection for the ensuing year, indicating the school within his jurisdiction which will be fully inspected either by a team or panel or by himself individually; and shall also mention the time and month when inspection is proposed to be carried out.

(ix) The Education Officer or Inspector shall submit a copy of his plan to the Deputy Director and to the Director of Education for their approval.

How Inspection should be made

(i) During inspection, the school work should be carried on as usual, so that the Inspecting Officer or a panel of Inspectors may be able to see all the aspects of the school programme and its organisation, No disturbance in the normal functioning of the school need be done, except under very special circumstances if the Inspector so considers necessary.

(ii) In addition to a full-fledged inspection which may last for two to three days, Education Officer/Inspector should also visit without advance notice, the school within his jurisdiction to see the working of the school or any particular aspect of its working or to observe the progress of any significant work or experiment taken by the school or by way of follow-up action on the suggestions given by him earlier.

(iii) After each inspection whether full-fledged or a surprise visit, Education Officer/Inspector shall point out the weakness or deficiencies noticed by him with a purpose to remedy those defects. The points of strength shall also be carefully described to enable other schools to derive benefit out of them. Work of merit shall be given commendations due to it and negligence or dereliction of the responsibility and incompetence shall be clearly marked out.

(iv) Every Inspecting Office shall devote in a school as much time as a just assessment of its programme and nature of difficulty require him to do.

Panel Inspection

(i) In secondary schools that provide instructions in a variety of school subjects, a term or panel of subject experts shall make full inspection.

(ii) The approval of the Director may be taken before the team or panel for inspection work is constituted.

(iii) The Zone Education Officer or Inspector shall be the Chairman of the team that may consist of not less than three members, according to the size and organisation of the school to be inspected.

(iv) The members of the team or panel shall be selected from amongst those persons who have a special knowledge and experience of secondary education and who are considered to be experts in school subjects.

(v) The subject expert/specialist member of the team or panel shall inspect the work of the school relating to their own field of specialisation. In addition, it shall be the responsibility of the whole team or panel to acquaint itself with the school programme in its totality, the academic side, the organisation, corporate life and the quality of education it offers to the students.

Inspection Report

(i) The Zonal Education Officer shall receive the comments of the members of the team or panel and thereafter a Chairman shall prepare, on behalf of the panel and in consultation with them, a detailed report on the inspection or supervision carried out by the team or panel as given in Form V.

(ii) The inspection report shall be prepared in the final form within 15 days of the conclusion of the inspection and shall be sent to the Director of Education and copy to the Deputy Director of Education of the District and the school concerned. Notes on the visits or surprise inspection of the schools shall be sent by the Education Officer separately or may be recorded in the logbook of the school concerned.

(iii) A copy of this note shall also be sent for the persual of the Deputy Director of the district and the Director of Education.

(iv) The Zonal Education Officer shall add a summary of the salient features of its detailed inspection report and shall also indicate in margin the names of the authorities which are expected to take immediate action on the points and observations made in the inspection report.

(v) The Education Officer or Inspector shall see that follow-up action is taken after the inspection is over.

10

Household Based Industry: Is Big Brother Watching?

Introduction

Household Industries are classified as those that employ up to 5 people with machinery drawing 5 kW of electricity (changed from the earlier 1 kW in September 2001) or one that employs upto 9 people with no machinery drawing electricity being used.[1] A person willing to set-up a household unit has to get a valid license from the Factory Licensing Department of the Municipal Corporation of Delhi (MCD). In this chapter we shall look at the regulations and procedures required to establish a household industry and comment on their effectiveness.

Procedure for Starting a Household Industry

Section 416 of the Delhi Municipal Corporation Act, 1957 places an obligation on the person desirous to establish in any premises—or materially alter, enlarge or extend—any factory, workshop or trade premises in which it is intended to employ steam, electricity, water or other mechanical power to obtain previous permission of Commissioner, MCD in writing.

Once the permission is granted under this Section to install some machinery in premises, it is also obligatory to obtain a trade licence as laid down under Section 417(i) before actually starting the trade. The provisions of DMC Act, 1957, are ostensibly implemented in larger public interest to minimise the nuisance, health hazard and pollution for the industrial growth in the NCT of Delhi. In order to achieve this, certain restrictions are imposed in the form of licensing conditions. In this chapter we shall only explore the household category of industries.

---

1. *What will be Delhi in 2001: Delhi Master Plan* 1990. Fifth Revised edition, 1998 Delhi: Akalank Publications.

Conditions for Household Category of Industries

1. The applicant should normally be residing at the premises where the trade is proposed to start.
2. Licence in this category is granted for the trades mentioned in the classification of industries as mentioned in Groups A & A-1 (Provided in Apendix A) in the MPD-2001.
3. Power load is restricted to 5 kW with maximum number of 5 workers or 9 workers with no power load.
4. The covered area for the usage of Household Based Industries should not be more than 300 sq. ft. and not less than 30 sq. ft.

Documents to be Filed with the Application Form to Obtain MCD Licence

1. One copy of site plan with dimensions (blueprint).
2. One copy of key plan earmarking the salient features (blue print) in neighbourhood.
3. Proof of ownership/tenancy/legal occupancy.
4. No Objection Certificate from the landlord/landlady.
5. Copy of the Ration Card.
6. Affidavit under Household Category (See Appendix–C for the Affidavit).

List of Household Industries

Initially, there were 70 industries under the Household Industrial Units list. The Union Urban Development Ministry later increased this to 76 in September 2001 (See Appendix–A for the List).

Fees and Charges

The Corporation has fixed Rs. 1000 as security fees for household category for granting permission under section 416 of the DMC Act which is chargeable only once at the time of giving permission under the said section. The fee for obtaining the licence is Rs. 120 per annum per unit and a charge of Rs. 12 per HP per annum subject to a minimum of Rs. 40 per annum.

Trade Timings

For licensed units located in the areas other than the industrial areas, the working hours are restricted between 8.00 a.m. to 6.00 p.m.

Offences and Penalties by MCD

Violation of Section 416 of the DMC Act

Section 416 of the DMC Act states that factory, etc. are not to be established without the permission of the Commissioner. Whosoever establishes an industrial establishment without prior permission of the Commissioner, MCD, shall be liable for penalty upto Rs. 5000 and in the event of repetition of violation a daily fine of upto Rs. 500 can be imposed.

Changes Permissible in the Municipal Factory Licence

There is no restriction of change of trade within the permissible trades specified in the MPD-2001 subject to submission of consent from Delhi Pollution Control Committee if applicable.

Role of DPCC[2]

Delhi has been declared as an Air Pollution Control Area, under sub-section (1) of Section (19) of the Air (Prevention & Control of Pollution) Act vide notification No. GSR 106(E) dated 20-02-1987. This implies that no industrial plant (any plant used for any industrial or trade purposes) can emit any air pollutant (any solid, liquid or gaseous substance including noise) into the atmosphere without prior consent of the State Pollution Control Board/Committee, as the case may be. It also implies that no person shall, without the previous consent of Delhi Pollution Control Committee, establish or operate an industrial plant in Delhi. Giving effect to this notification, Delhi Pollution Control Committee issues "Consent to Establish" to any industrial plant before its establishment and "Consent to Operate" before the plant starts its operation.

Consent to Establish is the first step for any industry/trade (this includes any activity involving manufacturing process or emitting pollution, by way of water pollution, air and noise pollution.)

---

2. Sourced from Delhi Pollution Control Committee [official website]. Accessed on 10 February 2004 at www.dpcc.delhigovt.nic.in

"Water Pollution" means such contamination of water or such alteration of the physical, chemical or biological properties of water or such discharge of any sewage or trade effluent or of any other liquid, gaseous or solid substance into water (whether directly or indirectly) as may, or is likely to, create a nuisance or render such water harmful or injurious to public health or safety, or to domestic, commercial, industrial, agricultural or other legitimate uses, or to the life and health of animals or plants or of aquatic organisms.

"Air Pollution" means the presence in the atmosphere of any air pollutant (including noise).Any unit defined above should obtain consent to establish before setting up the plant. The duly filled application has to be submitted with the following documents:

1. Application in prescribed format.
2. Project Report giving details of the unit:
   (a) Proposed capital investment (The gross capital investment shall include cost of land, building, plant and machinery without depreciation).
   (b) Activities Process.
   (c) Raw materials (with quantity per day).
   (d) Products with quantity per day, and sources of waste water/emissions and proposed pollution control systems/ measure (details and constitute units).
3. Proof of possession of the plot/allotment letter/Rental Agreement/Lease Deed.
4. An affidavit having declaration in the prescribed format, duly attested by a public notary.
5. Prescribed consent fee under Air Act, 1981 and Water Act, 1974 can be submitted through a single Demand Draft. (Consent fee under Air Act is to be paid based on gross fixed capital investment of the unit without depreciation till the date of application and consent fee under Water Act is based on water consumption by the unit.)

The consent to establish will ostensibly be granted by DPCC within a period of four months after the receipt of the application for consent. The State Board shall, by order in writing, and for reasons to be recorded in the order, grant the consent applied for subject to such conditions and for such period as may be specified in the order, or refuse consent.

Consent to Operate shall be applied before commissioning of the unit in the prescribed application format with the following documents:

1. Application in prescribed format.
2. Proof of possession of the plot/allotment letter/Rental Agreement/Lease Deed.
3. An affidavit having declaration in the prescribed format, mentioning date of Establishment of the unit and duly attested by a public notary.
4. Prescribed consent fee under Air Act, 1981 and Water Act, 1974 can be submitted through a single Demand Draft. (Consent fee under Air Act is to be paid based on gross fixed capital investment of the unit without depreciation till the date of application and Consent fee under Water Act is based on Water Consumption by the unit.)
5. Separate demand draft in favour of Delhi Pollution Control Committee for Rs. 100, if the form is downloaded from the web site.
6. Certificate from Chartered Accountant regarding Capital Investment.
7. List of raw materials used, product manufactured and by-products generated during the process with maximum quantity per day.
8. Manufacturing process in detail.
9. Layout plant of the unit, location map of the unit and proof of possession of the premises.
10. Other documents (if applicable):
    - (a) Proof of CETP Membership *(Attested by a Gazetted Officer)*.
    - (b) Stack/Chimney monitoring report.
    - (c) Effluent analysis report.*
    - (d) Noise monitoring report.*

---

* Reports not more than 3 months old from the date of submission of application

(e) Adequacy report of ETP.

(f) Adequacy report of ECS.

(g) Copy of MCD/Local Body Factory Licence duly attested by a Gazetted officer, as a proof of existence of the unit.

(h) Proof of sanctioned Electricity/power supply.

(i) Proof of sanctioned water supply by DJB.

Consent to Operate is to be granted only after the Delhi Pollution Control Committee is satisfied that the unit has completed all other formalities such as MCD licence, Power-Water connection, CETP Membership (where CETP exists) and has installed the requisite Pollution Control Devices.

In Household Category i.e. A and A–1 type of industries, consent is granted by the Assistant Environmental Engineer of the concerned area. Also any unit that applies for Consent to Operate without first obtaining Consent to Establish is required to pay condonation fee for the entire period of its existence subject to a maximum of seven years.

Case-studies

It must be mentioned that in the course of our studies on household based industries (HBIs) we were frequently met with suspicion and consternation by the owners regarding the potential damage that the publishing of these studies could do to them. Though they accepted the ubiquity of payment of bribes, yet they refused to disclose any details. In one instance, a group of HBI owners got together and had the researchers expunge the negatives which contained shots of HBIs in residential localities.

Tailoring

In one of the Patparganj co-operative societies, an informal interview was conducted with the owner of a tailoring household industry. The tailoring unit has been running for the last 6 years, employing 4 tailors with 2 manual and 2 electric machines and the power drawn is 3 kW. Till date there has been no inspection by any of the government authorities.

Although all other conditions are met by the industry, yet a license has not been obtained. The reasons for not obtaining a licence were fear of being harassed by licensing inspectors, and also because it is an expensive and time consuming activity.

Book–Binding

Subhash Gupta, owner of a book-binding enterprise in East Delhi said, "I opened the industry 8 years ago with 2 persons and obtained a licence henceforth. Now I have 15 persons working in the enterprise. I know that I am violating the rules that sets the limit on number of people but I pay some money to the licensing inspector whenever he comes."

"The amount given to the inspector depends upon an individual's negotiation skills", he added.

Bakery Products

A manufacturer of bakery products in Gautam Nagar, South Delhi revealed that there are 12 persons working in his factory baking biscuits, buns, etc. He supplies to local shops near his area of operation. He does not have a license. In the last seven years of the business, the inspectors have visited his bakery only thrice. He avoided problems by bribing them. He also said that there are a large number of household industries in the above area but verification is next to impossible.

Flour Mill

This flourmill in South Delhi has been in operation for the past 35 years (it started in 1968). The license was secured in the name of *Dulari Devi*. Since then the mill has changed hands and is being operated by Ram Karan for the past 15 years. Despite this, the license (issued by the Factory Licensing Department of the MCD) still hasn't been transferred in the new owners' name. There is also no information available on the policy despite repeated visits to the MCD office by Ram Karan.

The licensing fee was around Rs. 25-30 at that time (1968) and the renewal fee at the time of the last renewal was Rs. 300. Further, checks are made on a regular basis (once a year) by Department of Fire (MCD), Delhi Vidyut Board, Weights and Measures (Govt. of NCT of Delhi) and Sales Tax Department. The Department of Labour, Department for the Prevention of Food Adulteration, Directorate of

Industries, Delhi Jal Board, Delhi Development Authority and DPCC make no checks.

Assembly and Repair of Electrical Gadgets

In an informal chat with the owner of a small enterprise of assembly and repair of electrical gadget in Malviya Nagar, South Delhi, it was found that the enterprise does not have a licence. In the last few years, there have been very few visits by the inspectors. Also whenever they have come, the owner has given bribes to avoid any complaints being written against him.

Reforms

Removal of Licence-permit Raj for HBIs

There is an urgent need to rethink the whole approach of licensing for household based industries. Talks with officials and informal surveys show that it is impossible to inspect each and every household-based industry (HBI) that comes up in the city. Inspections, if any, are primarily complaint based. Unofficial numbers of HBIs are much higher than the stated number of 5,000. So only a fraction of the HBIs fall into the net of the licensed category. Most of the unlicensed HBIs pay the costs of illegality and work under fear of being detected and inspected regularly. Many of them are not even aware of the requirement for a license. A problem that HBIs face is that they may fall in the category of the industries but they don't follow the conditions of the HBI. The conditions stating the HBI owner to be normally residing in the premises, limiting the area between 30-300 sq. ft only and timings between 8 a.m. to 6 p.m. cannot always be followed. A HBI owner may find it inconvenient or unprofitable to conduct the business at his premises and obtain rented premises to conduct his business. That very condition makes it illegal. A prime purpose of the HBI categorisation has been to allow for non-nuisance businesses in residential neighbourhoods. However, making the business illegal because it does not follow particular conditions only serves to perpetuate the costs of illegality for the business and probable nuisance for the neighbours. Not surprisingly, clustered neighbourhoods have formed which are predominantly HBI based. The conditions also limit the scale of the business, an issue that cannot be overlooked by businessmen.

A pertinent question arises regarding the list of allowable HBIs mandated by the government. Technology has made many more categories of industries non-polluting: what about them? How does the government prepare a list of allowable HBIs thus mandating that all others are illegal? Is the loss of opportunity for these other entrepreneurs taken into account? How regularly does the government update this list to reflect the dynamic changes in manufacturing technologies?

Common Law of Nuisance

The common law of nuisance as outlined in the chapter on urban land management would deal with each nuisance issue on a case-by-case basis. Hence the judgement would be dependent on the outcomes and independent of the inputs or the processes. If pollution or disturbance results then the HBI will be judged against, otherwise not. An urban municipal regulation would only impose a blanket ban/ restrain on all HBIs, thus discouraging any "peaceful" economic activity.

Restrictive Covenants

Ward Committees may also set up restrictive covenants in their ward areas and in the process have conditions that are most likely to be followed and monitored better: after all, one cannot undertake or expand an activity when the neighbour knows the existence of rules that prevent it.

Upcoming areas/townships would have restrictive covenants drawn beforehand that would specify what kinds of HBIs may be allowed and to what extents. These are subject to better enforcement and not simply regulated by political machinations. Another advantage is that the conditions can also be easily changed with changes in time and better developments in non-nuisance technology, something that will not happen so easily in case of government regulations.

Appendix – A

The List of Industries under Household Category is of both type of industries i.e. A and A–1 lie in household category.

Category A

1. Agarbati and similar products
2. Assembly and repair of electrical gadgets
3. Assembly and repair of electronic gadgets
4. Assembly and repair of sewing machines
5. Batik works
6. Block making and photo enlarging
7. Biscuit, pappey (what's this), cakes and cookies baking
8. Button making, fixing of button and hooks
9. Calico and Textile Products
10. Cane and bamboo products
11. Clay and modelling
12. Coir and jute products
13. Cardboard boxes
14. Candles
15. Copper and brass wares
16. Cordage, ropes and twine making
17. Carpentry
18. Contact lens
19. Canvas bags and holdalls making
20. Candles, sweets, rasmalai etc. (when not canned)
21. Cotton/silk printing (by hand)
22. Dari and carpet weaving
23. Detergent (without bhatti)
24. Embroidery
25. Framing of pictures and mirrors
26. Fountain pens, ball pens and felt pens
27. Gold and Silver thread, kalabattu
28. Hosiery products (without dyeing and bleaching)
29. Hats, caps, turbans including embroideries
30. Ivory carving
31. Ink making for fountain pens
32. Jewellery items

33. Khadi and handloom
34. Lace products
35. Leather footwear
36. Leather and rexine made ups
37. Production of following items:
    - i. Blanco cakes (what's this?)
    - ii. Brushes
    - iii. Kulfi and confectionery
    - iv. Crayons
    - v. Jam, jellies and fruit preserves
    - vi. Musical instruments (including repairs)
    - vii. Lace work and like
    - viii. Ornamental leather goods like purses, hand bags
38. Name plate making
39. Paper stationery items and book binding
40. Pith had, garlands of flowers and pith
41. P.V.C. products (with one moulding machine)
42. Paper machine
43. Perfumery and cosmetics
44. Photosetting
45. Photostat and cyclostyling
46. Preparation of Vadi, Papad etc.
47. Processing of condiments, spices, groundnuts and dal etc.
48. Pan masala
49. Repair of watches and clocks
50. Rakhee making
51. Stone engraving
52. Sports goods
53. Surgical bandage rolling and cutting
54. Stove pipe, safety pins and aluminium buttons (by hand press)
55. Silver foil making
56. Saree fall making
57. Tailoring
58. Thread balls and cotton fillings
59. Toys and dolls
60. Umbrella assembly

61. Velvet embroidered shoes/shawls
62. Vermicelli and macaroni
63. Wood carving and decorative wood wares
64. Wool balling and lachee making
65. Wooden/cardboard jewellery boxes (subject to no objection certificate from the department)
66. Wool knitting (with machine)
67. Zari Zardozi

Category A–1

1. Black Smith
2. Village pottery industry (without bhatti)
3. Village oil ghani

Appendix – B

Example of the Technical Conditions of a Household Industry
(as per Section 417, DMC Act)

Trade of Manufacturing/Preparing of

Sweets and Confectionery goods

1. The premises shall be structurally sound and kept in good state of repairs at all times.
2. The floor and walls upto a height of one meter shall be made of impervious smooth concrete material and the corners rounded to facilitate thorough washing and cleaning of the premises.
3. The floor area shall not be less than 10 sq. m. and height at least 3 m.
4. The premises shall be drained into a sewer, and where there is no sewer, into a surface drain to the satisfaction of the Health Authorities.
5. The premises shall be well ventilated and adequately lighted.
6. Continuous supply of safe water shall be ensured in the premises. In case of intermittent water supply adequate storage arrangements shall be made available in the premises.
7. The premises shall be completely fly proof. The prepared stuff shall be stored in proper show-cases/cup-boards protected against insects and dust.
8. At least two sinks with draining board, detergent and hot water shall be provided to ensure proper cleaning of utensils.
9. Wash hand basin made of porcelain/stainless steel shall be provided alongwith soap and nail brush for thorough cleansing of hands.
10. The walls and ceiling shall be white/colour washed every six months and the wood work painted every year and more often if so required.
11. Waste-bins of adequate size with pedal operated covers shall be provided in the premises for collection of waste material. The same shall be emptied and washed daily with a disinfectant.
12. All tables, racks, shelves, boards etc. shall have zinc/aluminium/stainless steel/marble, sunmica top to facilitate proper leaning.
13. A sign board shall be prominently displayed at the premises indicating the nature of cooking oil being used.
14. The floor and skirting shall be washed daily with a disinfectant and more often if so required.
15. The premises shall be kept free from rodents/vermins, flies and other insects.
16. The premises shall not be used for residential purposes nor shall it communicate with any residential quarter.

17. No person shall manufacture, store or expose for sale or permit the sale of any article of food in any premises not effectively separate to the satisfaction of Health Authorities from any privy, urinal, sullage drain or dust-bin.
18. All vessels used for storage or manufacture of the articles intended for sale shall have proper covers to avoid contamination. Copper and brass utensils shall be got tinned regularly.
19. All raw and semi prepared stuff shall be stored in proper containers with covers so as to protect them against dust, insects, pets and rodents. The same shall be kept on wooden trestles having a minimum height of 9 inches and with a minimum of 6 inches edge projecting on all sides.
20. No person suffering from contagious or infectious disease shall be employed in the establishment. All person working in the premises shall be medically examined and immunised against Cholera and enteric group of fevers at the time of issue/renewal of license. The certificate of medical fitness and immunisation shall be displayed prominently at the premises alongwith the license.
21. No obnoxious articles or materials considered unfit for human consumption shall be kept for sale in the premises.
22. A high standard of personal hygiene shall be maintained by workers at all times. They shall wear clean aprons and head-gears. No smoking, chewing and use of snuff shall be allowed in the premises.
23. Failure to comply with any of these instructions shall entail legal action against the defaulter and even result in revocation of license.

Appendix C

Affidavit For Household Industry

Affidavit

I, ____ S/o Shri ____ R/o ____

do hereby solemnly affirm and declare and undertake to abide by the statements made as under:-

1. That my/our unit will undertake/continue to undertake the trade of ________________________________ situated at ____ A/A – 1, of the Master Plan of Delhi-2001 and will not do any other trade which neither my unit has applied nor has been permitted.

2. That my/our unit also undertakes that my/our unit will continue subject to the master plan parameters, i.e., (i) ____________ K.W. Load, (ii) 5 No. of workers, (iii) required 30 sq. meters space and non-pollution unit and the factory of trade.

3. That in case my unit is found violating any of the master plan parameters or terms & conditions of the MCD licence, MCD shall cancel/ revoke the licence without any further proceedings or formalities.

4. That my/our unit has no objection if the unit will be inspected by the MCD and Department of Industries time to time.

5. That I/we have not applied for industrial plot in the relocation scheme of NCT declared in 1996.

DEPONENT

Verification

Verified at Delhi on this date that the contents of the above affidavit are true and correct to the best of my knowledge and belief.

DEPONENT